In Praise of *Job Hunting 3.0*

"*Job Hunting 3.0* will seriously enhance your chances of finding and securing the job you want. Having worked in the recruitment industry for a number of years, as both an employee and running my own recruitment business, I found *Job Hunting 3.0* logical, emphatically thorough and very easy to read. Finding a job is a process and this book provides a step-by-step guide to navigating the job market and all its nuances successfully, by giving practical examples and emotional support for what I would call 'best practice'. Whether you are a high flying executive, looking for your first job, or at any point in between, this is the 'bible' for modern day employment success."

Jordan Dudley, Director, Dudley Child Executive Recruitment Ltd

"This immensely readable book is compulsory reading for anyone who is trying to navigate their way through the whole job hunting and recruitment process. It provides a detailed road map, with practical insights, examples and step-by-step directions to ensure success is achieved. It is clear, complete, with easily applicable tools that can make all the difference, and the engaging writing style keeps you hooked. I particularly liked the '*Minute To Win It*', which is a fantastic tool for anyone who may find themselves at a networking event or in an important elevator situation, irrespective of whether the next job move is in sight. Job hunting is difficult and time-consuming, fraught with worry and potential pitfalls, especially in a time of fluctuating market conditions, where competition is high. This book helps to ease some of that tension by providing a practical framework and the opportunity to reflect and review achievements helping an individual to realise their potential and employability."

Pippa Dickson, HR Business Partner, Schroders Investment Management

"As an experienced recruiter, the effect on candidate morale produced by the competitive job market is well known to me. Survival kits for applicants are essential, therefore, and *Job Hunting 3.0*'s useful techniques, which are brought to life with the author's first-hand illustrations, make this book a must for every candidate's toolkit!"

Mel Armstı

"This book demystifies the process of looking for a job and I would recommend it to anyone, but I wouldn't give them my copy; it's a keeper. For a start, it makes clear that job seeking is a process with a series of steps to follow. The author breaks down each step, explains why it is important and what it achieves, and gives lots of tips and hints and examples. I recommend reading straight through to get the big picture and then going back to each step when needed, in detail, to really absorb and practise the advice.

Doing this is really useful because there is nothing so simple as common sense when someone else has taken the trouble to spell it out. This book is full of it, delivered in a tone that is friendly, wise and encouraging.

In addition, this book is not just about getting a job. It's full of things that will help the reader to stand out and get noticed in whatever endeavour they are engaged. Certainly that may include looking for a new job, but there are a myriad of other situations where the advice given in this book will make a real difference."

Geoff Nelder, Director, Fellowship and Enterprise Centre, Cranfield University

"A unique, insightful and warmly humorous look into the world of job hunting. Inside you will find practical advice and examples of essential items, such as clearly laid out CVs, cover letters, answers to difficult interview questions and tips on how to build rapport with people. Buy this book and you will have a great companion on your job hunting journey and be well on your way to success!"

Meg Pringle, Managing Director, Milburn Property Development Ltd

"A compelling read and a great book with valuable content based on what actually works. *Job Hunting 3.0* is an essential part of your toolbox, whatever your age or background is. This is an easy book to understand and apply, in order to help you get your next position, especially when people are faced with more competition and fewer jobs. This book is also about understanding yourself and will help with many other situations that you may find yourself in on a day to day basis. The details are laid out logically and are easy to understand and practise. These days one has to have the edge on the competition and *Job Hunting 3.0* will give you that edge."

Jonathan Farnfield, Operations Director, Firth Rixson Forgings Ltd

JOB HUNTING 3.0

JOB HUNTING 3.0

SECRETS AND SKILLS TO SELL YOURSELF
EFFECTIVELY IN THE MODERN AGE

BY RICHARD MAUN

Marshall Cavendish
Business

This edition published in 2012 by Marshall Cavendish Business
An imprint of Marshall Cavendish International

PO Box 65829
London EC1P 1NY
United Kingdom
info@marshallcavendish.co.uk

and

1 New Industrial Road, Singapore 536196
genrefsales@marshallcavendish.com
www.marshallcavendish.com/genref

Other Marshall Cavendish offices:
Marshall Cavendish Corporation, 99 White Plains Road, Tarrytown, NY 10591 •
Marshall Cavendish International (Thailand) Co Ltd. 253 Asoke, 12th Flr, Sukhumvit 21
Road, Klongtoey Nua, Wattana, Bangkok 10110, Thailand • Marshall Cavendish (Malaysia)
Sdn Bhd, Times Subang, Lot 46, Subang Hi-Tech Industrial Park, Batu Tiga, 40000 Shah
Alam, Selangor Darul Ehsan, Malaysia

Marshall Cavendish is a trademark of Times Publishing Limited

A CIP record for this book is available from the British Library

ISBN 978 981 4361 11 8

Front cover design by Opalworks
Page design by Lock Hong Liang and Benson Tan

Printed and bound by CPI Group (UK) Ltd, Croydon, CR0 4YY

FOR OSCAR AND HARVEY

You are two lovely people.
Enjoy being you and enjoy
what you do.

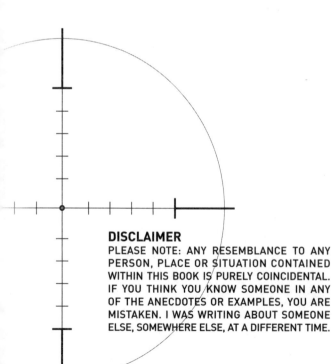

DISCLAIMER
PLEASE NOTE: ANY RESEMBLANCE TO ANY
PERSON, PLACE OR SITUATION CONTAINED
WITHIN THIS BOOK IS PURELY COINCIDENTAL.
IF YOU THINK YOU KNOW SOMEONE IN ANY
OF THE ANECDOTES OR EXAMPLES, YOU ARE
MISTAKEN. I WAS WRITING ABOUT SOMEONE
ELSE, SOMEWHERE ELSE, AT A DIFFERENT TIME.

CONTENTS

PREFACE FOR NEW EDITION

YOU CAN GET A JOB

You may not know exactly what you next role is, where it's located, or for whom you might be working, but that doesn't mean it isn't out there. It is – and it's waiting to be snapped up by you. To get it you need to have the right skills and the right attitude – and this book is here to support you in achieving both.

In the pick and mix world of *Modern Careers*, where role changes and job hunting can be a regular occurrence you need to have more than just technical or vocational skills to get a job. You need to be a skilful, polished job hunter and *Job Hunting 3.0* gives you the tools and techniques to become one. It's based on real-life experience of what works well for people, it walks you through the process of finding a job and shares with you the *three big secrets* of success. In addition, this book will help you to celebrate achievements, identify key skills and practice your answers to tricky interview questions.

THE ODDS OF SUCCESS ARE BETTER THAN YOU THINK

It is possible to find work because if there are 1 million unemployed people, for example, it doesn't mean we're in competition with all of them. Potentially, only 20% of those might have had any worthwhile job hunting training, which means there are now only 200,000 serious competitors. However, not all of them are in our field of expertise, so maybe we're now competing with 5,000 people. Of these, it's probable that half had the training and forgot most of it, leaving 2,500 people who remembered it. When it comes to good practice, such as including numbers on our CV to add value, or rehearsing interview answers before the big day, about 50% of people tend to trust to luck and don't put in enough hard work to make them successful. That means we're now competing with 1,250 people to get a job, which when spread around the entire landmass of a country means that we're up against maybe 20 to 50 people in our area. By honing our skills and being diligent with our planning and execution, we can increase the odds of success even more, so perhaps we end up with only 2 or 3 serious competitors.

In some cases, such as graduate first jobs, there may be intense competition for a few prized places and people will have more direct competitors. However, the logic still applies and simply by becoming a skilful and polished candidate you will considerably increase your chances of success.*

SOCIAL MEDIA REALLY COUNTS

It's importance to use social media websites and networking groups to find our next role, because they are a great route to market for us. Pause for a moment and ask yourself: Who knows I'm looking for work? How many people am I connected to in the world? We need to aim for a target of at least 2,000 – because the more people we know, the wider our network is and the greater the chance that one of our contacts will know someone who is looking for a person with our skills and abilities. It's a numbers game and we can all play it effectively.

Job hunting can be a lonely, time consuming task and social media is a great source of new friends and business contacts. Spend as much time building your network and talking to people as you do filling in forms and posting off job applications, because it takes effort to turn new contacts into friends, who might then be able to help you. Also, make sure you use all the major platforms, such as Twitter, Facebook, Google+ and LinkedIn. If you decide to avoid one you're limiting your potential network, because not everyone uses them all and you don't know where that key contact is hiding.

OUR JOB IN OUR WAY

We all have our own ways of working and have our own preferences and likes, and it's the same when we're job hunting.

---

* In my experience I've rarely worked with a group where more than 10% have any significant job hunting skills.

There is no one 'best way' of going about things, although there are some *better* ways, so at all times you remain responsible for your actions and inactions and decisions that you may make as a result of reading this book. This is an important point because there is nothing more irritating to me than someone who says; "Oh you simply *must* do it like this." There are no 'musts', 'oughts' and 'shoulds' here and at all times you're free to make up your own mind and choose the path that you feel works best for you, in your country, in your situation.

BACKGROUND

This book is based on the real life experiences of myself and my colleagues, of what works really well and what gets in the way of success. I've used the tools and techniques myself, have lead workshops, coached people and delivered job hunting lectures at a leading UK university. I've taken people from knowing almost nothing about CV writing, rapport building skills, networking and campaign management to being successful at stressful interviews. In addition, I have also run formal assessment centres, hired people, worked with recruitment agencies and had to sell to people as a senior manager and then as a consultant. I've also spent many years working with Transactional Analysis and have used Lean thinking extensively. I love what I do and I know that we all have the potential to succeed.

ACKNOWLEDGEMENTS

The first thank you goes to all the Fellows on the Fellowship in Manufacturing Management programme, and to all the staff and to the late and much missed Richard Clayton. Also, I need to say thank you to Chris Smith and Tristan Lomax for allowing me to adapt their material, to Rachael Lear for her distraction antidotes and to Jackie and Bill Shannon for their love and encouragement.

My trusty writing support team of Steve Tracey, Julie Holmes and Frances Donnelly also need to stand up and take a bow, or maybe for Julie and Frances; bob a curtsey. Writing, like job hunting, needs people to power it along and you three have been helpful, kind, thoughtful and generous with your time. Thank you. Four special people get a mention here, because they make me smile after a hard day of typing: Lucy, Theo, Oscar and Harvey; you are lovely people and you can be great at job hunting when you're older. A fifth special person is Beck: Thank you too, without your love and patience this book would not have been possible.

Simon Hall and Paul O'Malley from Halls PR get a special mention for letting me invade their office, to become their self-appointed 'writer in residence' in order to produce the manuscript. Thank you both! My final thank you goes to the team at Marshall Cavendish for their hard work and in particular to Martin Liu for his support and advice, for his marketing genius and for publishing this book; thank you Martin.

Richard Maun
England

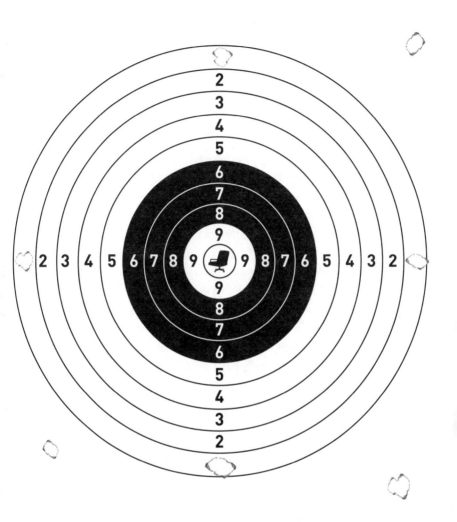

Section 1
GETTING STARTED

NOTHING TO FEAR

I'll start here with a confession; I used to be terrified of job hunting. I knew that it was all about selling, which was the one thing that I never wanted to do. If I had to telephone somebody to follow up on an application, I just wouldn't do it. If I had to tell people what I did well, I would feel embarrassed and waffle. If I was invited to an interview I would drive to the business the day beforehand in order to practise navigating there and to find out where the nearest car park was; worried that on the day something terrible would happen and I would get lost, end up in a ditch, or be eaten by monsters.

That was in the beginning and now, after having had some training and a lot of practice, I've *learned* how to sell myself successfully and that I can do it well.

I know what to say, how to answer questions and how to build rapport with people. I can write a great CV and a value-adding cover letter, have learned to enjoy networking and now feel confident during an interview. I know that if someone sees me and says 'no thanks' they're not suggesting that I'm a worthless person; they're simply saying that I don't have what it is *they* want for the role. I might have some of 'it', but I don't have enough, which seems reasonable to me.

I used to be terrified and I'm not any more, because I know *how* to sell myself effectively in order to get a job. I've realised that there is nothing to be scared of; it's all about learning the practical tools, skills and secrets in this book and applying them. It really can be that easy.

I've also realised that I'm *okay*. This means that I'm a decent, lovable human being and that if I'm rejected for a job these core qualities are not dented. They remain 100% intact and it's the same for you. We are all *okay* and we remain so whatever rubbish is thrown at us. Sometimes in the hunt for a job we may trip and scuff our knees, or get bruised by some thoughtless feedback, but that's just part of life. It doesn't mean that we have become diminished in any way. We're *okay* and we remain so at all times.

You are *okay*. You have value and are loved. You have friends and family. You have skills and talents. Looking for a job does expose you to the possibility of rejection and the thing to remember is that job hunting is a process for you and it's a process for the person looking to fill a role. If you don't fit into their process it's likely that you'll be bounced out at some point and that's just how life goes sometimes. There will be other opportunities and new people to meet.

There was a time when you didn't have the friends or the partner that you have now. You found each other and now enjoy each other's company. Along the way you will have met hundreds of people who didn't fit into the role of 'your friend'. When you think about it, life itself is a constant series of little interviews where people are accepted or rejected and we don't even think about that on a day-to-day basis. Job hunting is a heightened version of that and because the consequences of success or failure can be more severe, people tend to become more sensitive to the possibility of rejection.

I mention these things because not only have I learned them for myself, I've come to realise that they are basic truths that we need to accept in order to be really successful at job hunting. There's a job out there for everyone. It might not be our first choice, or in the best location, but it is there and this book has been written to help people learn the skills, tools and secrets they need in order to be successful. There's no magic to job hunting and it doesn't matter how old you are, or what qualifications you have; by reading this book and applying the contents you will get ahead of the competition, who are often more ignorant and trusting to luck than people realise.

IT'S OKAY TO BE FED UP

If you've been made redundant, you might feel thoroughly fed up with the world of work. If you're looking for your first job you might feel that it's impossible to get started on your career. If you're trying to change careers you might feel it's an uphill task. All of these are perfectly normal reactions and it really is okay to feel feelings and to share them with someone you trust, because dealing with our feelings removes the negative energy that holds us back and drains our motivation. Like pulling a splinter out of our foot, we can stand up straight again and walk forwards with confidence.

If you are looking for work and are fed up, frustrated and feeling tired, don't despair; it just means that you haven't found a job *yet*. Keep going and you'll get somewhere in the end.

IT'S OKAY TO ADMIT IGNORANCE

A surprising thing I've noticed about job hunting is that some of the people who tend to be the *best* at it are the ones who, at the start, hold up their hands and say:

"I don't know what I'm doing. I'm 35 years old and have to face the fact that I really don't know how to write a CV or how to do well at an interview."

By admitting their ignorance they open themselves up to new ideas, find it easier to ask for help and to practise key skills. Conversely, I've also noticed that people who think that they *should* know what to do because they were 'once somebody important' often seem to do badly, because their ego gets in the way of good honest learning. Pause for a moment and ask yourself if you need to admit that you have gaps in your job hunting knowledge? It's *okay* to do so.

DON'T COMPARE YOURSELF

A human trait is to rationalise our position by comparing ourselves to others and we might find ourselves saying things like:

"Oh it's easy for her, she has an MBA." or

"I wish I was the Captain of the First XI like him. No wonder he found it easy to get a job." or

"I'm too old! I wish I was young, like her."

These kinds of statements imply the other person is better than us and that we are 'worse'. We say these things to make us feel better when we are struggling to get ourselves sorted out, but they tend to overlook the other person's deficiencies and our own strengths and talents. A colleague of mine, who knows how people tick, has a great phrase that really challenges us to wake up to our own possibilities. He likes to look people in the eye and with absolute and genuine conviction say to them:

"Be careful! You're *in danger* of finding out that you're *really talented*."

You are too.

WE CAN ALL BE SUCCESSFUL

What I've seen is that *all* people can be successful, no matter how young or old they are or what qualifications they have. There is no blueprint for the successful job hunter, there is just good process. There is no one set of skills or talents that *makes* you employable and an alternative set that means you're not, and I've come to realise that you can't line people up and pick out the ones who are likely to be successful just by looking. You don't know what demons they have inside them, what concerns they have, how good they are at interviews and how much they're looking at you and saying to themselves:

"It's alright for you. You have skill and talent. If only I could be more like *you*!"

Looking confident doesn't mean that they are feeling confident on the inside. Sounding nervous doesn't make you a poor candidate. It could mean that you really want the job and that this shows you up in a better light at interview than somebody who is ice cool and comes across as a bit detached and uninterested. You can never tell what the other person is really thinking or feeling, so the only thing you can do is to focus on yourself, remind yourself that you're *okay* and to go for it.

USEFUL AFFIRMATIONS

One way to stay in an *okay* place, instead of going to a *not-okay* place and feeling worthless and victimised, is to accept one or more Affirmations[1] for ourselves. These are true statements that fill a gap or overturn an old instruction in order for us to develop. For example, the first thing I do when running an assessment centre is to say to people:

"You can have gaps in your knowledge and still be successful here today."

Candidates assume we are looking for experts. We aren't. We're looking for talented people and when I've offered them this Affirmation I can see them visibly relax as the pressure generated by a false underlying assumption is bled off. In order to remain in an *okay* place, it can be helpful to use Affirmations to keep our footing, because they tend to do the same job for us that a tight-rope walker's balance pole does. Here are some for you to consider and feel free to adjust the words, if you need to, in order to make them sit more comfortably in your head:

✓ You have a right to be here.

✓ You can still be talented and not know things at the same time.

✓ You can know that you have value.

✓ You can enjoy finding a new job.

✓ You can get help if you need to.

---

[1] An 'Affirmation' is a term from the world of Transactional Analysis. Commonly used to support learning and development, they can make a real difference to the way people go about their lives.

✓ You can practise and find ways to increase your confidence.

✓ You can be successful.

✓ You can choose what you do and how you do it.

✓ You can state your case and ask for what you need.

✓ You can be you.

It doesn't matter who you are or what job you are looking to secure. Everyone can feel feelings and everyone can remind themselves of the skill and talents which they have and which can be harnessed to make them employable.

There is nothing to be scared of. There are no monsters under the bed. If you have a bad experience, then file it in your head under 'bad experiences'. That's all it is. Your next experience can be a better one and what has gone before might just be telling you to practise more thoroughly or to sit down with someone you trust and talk through your job hunting activity.

I've noticed that, in general, what all people want is to go to work and do a good job. Sometimes people get a bit carried away by their impressive-sounding job title and sometimes they don't realise that they're under so much pressure that they're not communicating effectively. The interviewer can often be more nervous than the interviewee because when they accept a candidate and offer them a job they become responsible for that candidate's future performance. Therefore, it's highly likely that the next time you go to an interview you will be one of many people in the room who are nervous!

✳ SUMMARY It's *okay* to feel nervous, or to be fed up; they're normal human emotions and we can share them with people we trust and have our grievances heard. It's not helpful to compare ourselves unfavourably to other people, because that just gives us an excuse to put ourselves down, when we need to get up and feel great. Instead we can remind ourselves of our skills and talents and choose an Affirmation or two, to keep ourselves balanced and to prevent ourselves from falling off our job hunting process. There is a job out there for everyone. What, where and when is up to us and if we apply the tools, skills and secrets in this book, then we can sell ourselves effectively and get ahead of the competition.

SETTING THE SCENE

This book is called *Job Hunting 3.0* to make the point that the world of work has really moved on in the last few years, in the same way that man learned how to make fire, how to make bricks and then how to use social media websites to connect with tribes from all around the valley. The job market has developed in roughly the same way.

Go back 50 years and all you needed to get a job then was a parent willing to put in a good word with the boss. Family connections counted.[2] Go back 30 years and all you needed was a Curriculum Vitae (CV), or résumé, or personal biography, very wide lapels and a cheeky grin. At that point I might have written *Job Hunting 1.0* to make the point that a smile and a suit were the essential tools to get a job. In this first great age, we had the approach of the 'fashionable job hunter', which detoured slightly in the 1980's with floppy hair and mascara for men. Go back 15 years and things had changed again. The rise of the psychometric profile meant that people were being effectively screened into and out of jobs. So now you needed to know something about yourself and in this second great age of job hunting we had the rise of the 'behavioural job hunter'. I might have written *Job Hunting 2.0* to get people thinking about themselves at a deeper level in order to be able to answer searching questions about personal preferences.

THE NEW AGE

Now we have the age of the 'applied job hunter'. Increasingly, people are hiring 'application', where they want to know what we can actually *do*. I've seen this at first hand when people with MBAs have struggled to differentiate themselves in a crowded market and have joined our university programme to get a boost of practical, *applied* skills. Vocational qualifications are becoming a 'must have' accessory because they tell potential

---

[2] They still do in banking, which is why the world has a financial meltdown about once every 20 years. It's not so much a case of 'who you know' as 'who's got the same chin as you?'

employers that you really can do the job. Don't worry though if you don't have any right now; there are still plenty of things you can do to get ahead of the competition.

This focus on application does raise the prospect of having to work for free as an intern, or on work experience, in order to get a practical foundation that you can add to your CV. These are worth considering. Annoying perhaps, in the short term, if you want some money today, but helpful in the medium and long term if they open the door to a job for you.

The daughter of a colleague of mine recently applied for a job in advertising. She was one of over 1,500 applicants and earned a place at an assessment centre after a couple of preliminary rounds of sorting and sifting. There were 20 people in the room on that day for five jobs. Although she did well, she was unsuccessful and the advice she was given was to go and work in advertising for a year (for free) and then reapply. The implication was that with some experience she would have been much more likely to have been hired.

> As competition increases, people want to know what we can do. This isn't a bar to changing jobs or moving career; it just means that we all have to work a bit harder in order to do so. This isn't necessarily a bad thing either because it means that if we really want something, then we will do what it takes to get there and this will get us ahead of the competition, who otherwise might have been gifted our job by an unthinking recruiter.

Ultimately, all organisations have to balance their budgets and activity counts more than qualifications. I've worked with many people who were using Lean process improvement techniques to add value to their organisation. I've known some of them get *fired* for lacklustre performance, poor communications skills or for spending too much time planning and not enough time doing. I've never seen anybody fired for not knowing anything about Lean. You can read about that in a book. What counts is application, or as I like to say sometimes: **Putting the pedal to the metal.** (If you don't, your car won't go anywhere.)

What we now have is an age where employers are less fussy about how old you are (helped by the law on this issue) and more fussy about you actually being able to *do* the job. So now we need to marshall all our skills and experience into a package that allows us to go out and sell ourselves in terms of practical application and tangible achievements rather than relying on qualifications and time served.

I've seen the trend in recent years for people to hire 'grey hair', which is a term to mean more mature and more experienced people. The stereotype of companies wanting to hire only people under 30 because of their long-term career prospects and their 'party all night, work all day' energy levels is a myth. On our programme, we extended the age range and accepted a number of people in their late 50s who went on to secure tough consultancy jobs, working alongside much younger people. They were hired because they had the *skills* and the *attitude* that the company was looking for.

This shift towards applied skills was confirmed to me recently when I learned that in the top year at a local secondary school, 50% of the students were in the *vocational* stream and 50% in the academic stream. When I was enjoying my school days the figures were 95% in the academic stream and 5% pushing burgers at our local fast food restaurant. (I use the term 'restaurant' very loosely here.) Businesses need people who can help their organisation to become more successful, and they've realised that being able to quote Chaucer is great for posh parties and less useful when asked to deal with a grumpy customer.

THREE NEW PARTS OF THE LANDSCAPE

The world has changed. It has moved on. People looking for work need to adapt to this and in the third great age of job hunting, we have several forces that have all come together to change the landscape forever. These are:

Jobs don't tend to last as long. The average job tenure now lasts between two and five years, depending on which source you quote. This means you need to have great job hunting skills, because you're going to be using them much more often.

The rise of the Internet. I mention this because it's undeniable that while being a cumbersome know-it-all, the World Wide Web has increased the speed of communications and the opportunities for people to link up, chat and work together. It also means people can find you more easily and you can find them. This is not always a good thing if your next employer finds the photographs of *that* party, where you dressed up as a chicken and did something outrageous with a melon and bottle of tequila. Be careful; it's *okay* to have fun, but keeping an eye to the future doesn't hurt.

The death of the career. When I was a young boy, with long socks and short trousers, I was often asked: "What would you like to do for a career?" This is one of the stupidest questions ever invented, because it forces us to think in terms of 'career' and 'one choice'. It's never *careers* or asked as "What would you like to do for your *first* career?"

I always found this a difficult question to answer because I hadn't tried any jobs yet, I didn't know what work was like and in fact one of the jobs I now have (as a business coach) hadn't really been invented in its modern form. Answering the question with:

"I would like to do something not yet invented, using technology that hasn't been devised yet and requiring skills which I'm not going to be taught at school,"

… would have been a prescient and pretentious answer. Some people train as teachers, pilots, or barristers and spend their whole career teaching, piloting or barristering. Many others adapt and develop their 'career' as opportunities wax and wane and changes in technology, manufacturing infrastructure, social circumstances and climate affect their local economy and the choices available to them. This means we all need to be *agile*. We need to have a flexible skill set so that we can respond to changes, shift our viewpoint, learn new skills, discard the bits we don't need any more and generally stay on top of things to stay in the employment game. *The career ladder has gone*: chewed up by the industrial shredder of progress. It's been replaced with a pile of planks, a hammer and a bag of nails and it's up to us to build something that works well.

THREE GUIDING PRINCIPLES

When we think about the world of work, there are three words that sum up the world today and what is needed from us in order to survive and thrive. They are:

1. Agility
2. Application
3. Assertiveness

1. Agility because the world changes fast and we need to have robust and responsive job hunting processes, built on a foundation of core skills. With good basic skills and a level of competency *in all of them*, we can jump from opportunity to opportunity as the need arises.

2. Application because the emphasis of the new age of job hunting is on practical application: What have you actually achieved in the past? How did you add value in your previous role? What did you actually do when leading the team? We need to know what we have done and writing everything off as simply being a 'natural part of the job' isn't helpful. We need to account for the good things that we have achieved and recognise that although we were paid to do them we still made a real difference to our host organisation.

3. Assertiveness because we are surrounded on all sides by competition. I'm not talking here about brashness either; just simply being able to speak up and be proud of what we've done. Answering searching interview questions successfully requires a knowledge of useful answering techniques and an ability to say "*I* did this" instead of "*We* did this." Many of the people I've worked with have struggled to turn 'we' into 'I', but it's a key feature of success and one that ripples through this book. We can all overcome our natural modesty and shyness and speak up for ourselves.

✳ SUMMARY The world of work is now about *application*. The two key questions people want answers to are: What have you done and tell me how you did it? Simply having qualifications isn't enough and although they can help, they do need to be balanced with tangible success in the field. We need to be agile and have a complete set of core job hunting skills. We need to focus on application and to celebrate our success, and we need to be assertive and tell people confidently how we can add value to their organisation.

A QUICK GUIDE

I'm used to doing something called 'helicopter thinking' which is when we get into our mental helicopter and go for a buzz round the problem.[3] We can hover high up in the air and look down at the scene below us, take in the view and really see the world at a glance. This chapter is the job hunting equivalent of helicopter thinking because we can see all the constituent parts of the job hunting process. We can zoom in and check out the rest of the details in each of the specific chapters, but for now this is a good place for us to start.

We can notice too that job hunting activity tends to be iterative. This means that we do something, then go back and refine a previous step, then go forwards again and so on. We can bounce around as new information sparks off new thoughts. When considering CVs, for example, I've known people update them each week, so that their CV becomes a responsive living document instead of a dusty old dead thing tossed casually onto the high shelf and left to rot until needed, when it will be out of date.

CVs can take time to hone and polish, so it's worth updating ours every time something significant happens at work. If all we do is to write a note, or type in a new bullet point, at least we can smarten it up later and edit out the weaker points.

SKILLS, SECRETS, TOOLS AND TECHNIQUES

There are specific things which we can learn to help us in our job hunting activities and these will be explained in more detail throughout the book. Here is a selection for you, to whet your appetite and to encourage you to ask yourself: Which items in the table on page 14 do I know about, or use already?

---

[3] Unlike most aeroplanes, helicopters have bubble canopies for a great view out, round and down.

The 90/90 Rule p. 151	The Three-Horse Race p. 49	Minimum Walkaway p. 236	Minute To Win It! p. 110	The Five-Slide Formula p. 199
Aces High p. 85	Using Numbers p. 90	The STAR Technique p. 191	How CVs Are Really Sorted p. 33	The Three-Feet Rule p. 134
The Demons Model p. 142	Performance Ratios p. 56	The Value of Stories p. 114	Killer Questions p. 196	Pause Button p. 224

THE JOB HUNTING PROCESS

There are eight component parts to our job hunting process and below is an overview of each one, together with top tips that can help to keep us on track. Keep the secret ones in sight, as they are called 'secret' for a good reason: People seem to ignore them on such a regular basis that they might as well be locked in a box and buried in a secret location in the middle of the Antarctic.

Two points about learning: Although all of these items below are repeated throughout the book, expanded on and explained in more detail, *quick learning* can be great learning. Also, to get into the habit of *reflective learning*, read them all, circle the ones that you like most and then take a break and let them sink in. Reflective learning means to have a go at something and then to review the experience and make new decisions and choose what we will do differently next time.

Some people can be panicked into over-work, but the problem is that quality tends to drop as we get fatigued. We need to only ever plan a maximum of 80% of our day for job hunting activities and leave the remaining 20% for interruptions, coffee breaks and general work-avoidance. We all like to play a bit, so if we plan realistically then we are more likely to reach our targets, feel good about what we're doing and actually *achieve more* overall than if we're constantly beating ourselves up to keep jumping over a bar that is set too high. I can always remember at school dreading the high jump event during sports day. I wanted the bar to be set low so that I could hop over it with ease, rather than be fixed at a height carefully calculated by my P.E. teacher to smack me on the forehead.[4] What counts are results, *not* time spent. Go easy on yourself. You can work hard at job hunting and still take time off and enjoy yourself. Here is the process:

1. GETTING STARTED

It's always worth taking a moment to put our job hunting spectacles on and view the world as it is and not how we would like it to be. We also need to start our process by reminding ourselves that we're *okay* and can get support. I've worked in isolation before and regretted it (I don't make that mistake now), and it's always better to check in with a job hunting buddy once a week. In addition it can help us to be reminded of these points:

- ✓ **Start by stopping.** If you've recently left a job, give yourself at least a one-week holiday (even if you spend it at home) to get some clear water between you and your old job. That will help you to think more clearly about the future.

- ✓ **Line up your supporters.** Identify four or five people whom you trust and ask them to be in your job hunting supporters club. Treat them to a telephone call or coffee and biscuits once a week and chat through your plans and your progress with them.

- ✓ **Clear a space.** Find a space to work in that will allow you to be productive. This might mean borrowing a spare desk in an office or somebody's study. It's worth finding a good work space for yourself as the environment we work in does tend to affect our output.

---

[4] P.E. stands for physical education. The name was a misnomer: My body learned nothing.

✓ **Getting angry is good.** The chances are that at some point in your job hunting process you will feel angry. Angry at losing your job, or at the level of competition, or at the slowness of a company's decision-making progress. That's *okay*. Check in with your supporters and have a good grumble; it will clear away the weeds on your job hunting path and speed things up for you.

2. SECRET NO. 1 – PASSION

Being interested is great. Being *really* interested is better. Being *very enthusiastic* is best of all. Here are four points to think about:

✓ **If you like something, say so.** People cannot read our minds.

✓ **Smile.** People like it.

✓ **Follow your energy.** Our energy is finite, so we need to let our own flow guide our direction.

✓ **If we're not 100% interested, then don't go to the interview.** Our heel-dragging lack of enthusiasm will show up on our faces and in our voices, so we may as well use the time for other, more constructive activities.

3. CAMPAIGN

A campaign gives our job hunting an overall structure and a process to follow. We need to know where we are heading, keep track of progress and celebrate our successes. Some key points for a successful campaign include:

✓ **Make our campaign visible.** We can turn it into a chart and put it on a wall or on the desk in front of us. Hiding it away increases the chances of forgetting all about it.

✓ **Invite comments from our supporters.** Giving our campaign a health check by sharing it with them can be a wise move. They will see us differently to how we see ourselves and we might be underplaying our skills and opportunities.

✓ **Update progress on a daily basis.** A campaign has to be a living thing and it's always satisfying to tick off work done or targets reached.

✓ **Spot opportunities for change.** After a while our campaign chart will show us where we've spent our energy and what results we are getting. This is useful information as it tells us what to do more of and what to change. Looking at trends is a useful way to get objective information about how well we're doing.

4. TOOLKIT

Having a CV is a good start and there are some other things that we need to have in order to be successful. For example, I've met people, introduced myself, handed over a business card and then watched as they patted in pockets or rifled through a handbag, looking for a scrap of paper or a crumpled card to give me in return. Given that first impressions count, it's good to be prepared for these situations and to assemble a useful job hunting kit. Think about the following:

✓ **Get the set.** Make sure you have: A business card (or calling card), a CV, a good cover letter and a *Minute To Win It*. It pays to have the set because they all do a different job for us.

✓ **Always carry a pen and a small notepad with you.** You never know when you will need to make notes. You can also use the pad to swap contact details.

✓ **Borrow from the best.** When writing our CV and cover letter, it's *okay* to copy from examples that we like. There's no need to reinvent the wheel if it already exists.

✓ **Looks count**. Pay attention to both the content and the look of your CV and cover letter. Layout and clarity are as important as accurate spelling and useful detail.

5. SECRET NO. 2 – NETWORKING

This is so obvious that it's often overlooked. There are some skills to successful networking, although in my experience fear is the biggest thing that holds people back. These points can help us:

✓ **Who knows we are job hunting?** We need to tell our family and friends. There's no shame in it and if people know what we're looking for, they can help us to find it.

✓ **Update our Internet presence**. LinkedIn, for example, is great for business-to-business connections. Update your profile and invite people to connect to you.[5]

✓ **Join a real-life networking group**. Networking groups are a great way to meet people and build confidence.

✓ **Always ask in the third party**. *Never* ask people directly if they might need you. Instead always ask: "Who do you know who might be interested in my skills?" If the answer is them, they will still tell you.

6. SELF-AWARENESS

We need to get a feel for how we are appearing in the world around us. This is because if we know what we do well, we can celebrate it, and if we know what we do badly, then we can improve it or do something different. We can help ourselves by remembering the following key points:

✓ **Ask for feedback**. Then add the number of times we get the same piece of feedback from different people. Any piece that we get more than twice needs to be acted upon.

---

[5] LinkedIn is gathering a reputation as a sensible place to be listed and there are plenty of other good networking sites to choose from.

✓ **Look at the person we're with.** How is he responding to us? Is he smiling, or is his brow furrowed with concern? What is this telling us?

✓ **Follow our own energy and intuition.** If something feels right (or wrong), then it probably *is*.

✓ **Stop and think about what our body is doing.** Are we slumped? Are we twirling our hair? Are we staring out of the window? We can shift our position in the chair in order to 'break state' and settle back into a more assertive posture when at an interview.

7. INTERVIEW SKILLS

We need to sell ourselves effectively because we want someone to lease our skills for a day, a month, a year or more. We may go to several interviews and meet a range of people. We might also go to networking events, talk to business contacts, be introduced to people and make presentations. Therefore, we need to be mindful of the following:

✓ **An interview is a conversation, not an interrogation.** If we get asked a long, multi-part question, we can ask the interviewer to rephrase his question.

✓ **Be scrupulously polite to everyone we meet.** We don't know who they are yet.[6]

✓ **Beware of the 'silence'.** If an interviewer falls silent, that is an invitation for us to keep talking, which invariably results in us saying something stupid. We can be silent too; let them speak first, or ask them what they want to know.

✓ **Make notes and take notes with us.** We can forget things when we're stressed. To help us remember, it can help to write down the name of the person we're talking to. Using people's names is a good way to build rapport. Much better than the vague 'mate'.

---

[6] In one company, I was walking to the exit and chatting amiably to the Operations Director who had interviewed me, when we bumped into the gardener. "Who was that scruffy old bloke?" I asked with disdain. "The MD's father," came the terse reply. I said nothing and went a dark shade of red.

8. SECRET NO. 3 – PRACTICE

I've learned from my own experience that knowing all the right things is not as useful as being able to talk about them. Practice helps us to 'get it into our muscle' in the way that athletes train hard in order to hone their bodies. Muscle memory allows us to perform better on the interview day. Consider these points:

- ✓ **Get ahead by practising.** Most people don't bother. If we bother, we will do well.

- ✓ **Interviews only happen once.** There's no second chance so knowing what we will say and how we will say it means that we are more likely to have a better time.

- ✓ **Practice creates flexibility and develops confidence.** This is because it increases our repertoire of things to say, so that we can cope with unusual situations. It's just like when we learned to ride a bicycle; once we stopped thinking about how to balance, we could ride anywhere.

- ✓ **Make our mistakes in private.** Practising with a friend means that we can make all of our mistakes in a safe environment, instead of a live environment where the stakes are higher.

✱ SUMMARY Job hunting is a process and by working through all stages of the process, we can have better outcomes. If we miss a whole section, then we're missing important knowledge, tools and equipment. It's the same when we go camping. We need to take all the items on our checklist, because once we're stuck in a field with nothing but grass under our feet and stars overhead, we have to rely on ourselves. There's no popping out to the shops for an emergency pint of milk, and job hunting is the same. We can take what we need from each part of the process and enjoy feeling more competent and more confident than we did before.

SILLY THINGS THAT PEOPLE DO

I can still remember my first interview. I was about 17 years old and keen to take on a Saturday job stacking shelves in our local supermarket. Actually, the truth is that my *parents* were keen. I would have preferred to stay at home and read a book, but it wasn't to be, so I answered an advertisement in the local paper, caught the bus into town and was interviewed by a supervisor in the shop. We were surrounded by boxes, bits of plastic packaging, and all the smells of food and dirt that tend to waft round the back door of a large retailer.

"How keen are you on this job?" he asked me directly.

I stroked my chin thoughtfully, tried to sound sincere and said: "Very."

He didn't seem convinced. "Yes, but we've had lots of applicants, so how keen are you really?"

Really? I thought I had made myself clear. Apparently not. I gave him my most sincere thank-you-for-this-award grin and looked him straight in the eye.

"Very *very* interested," I replied slowly and with heavy emphasis on the second 'very'. There was no doubt now; he knew I was interested. He thanked me politely and said that he would be in touch. I assumed the job was mine, but it wasn't.

It was only on reflection, after the bus had meandered its way home like a happy drunk, that I realised he had wanted me to *sell myself*, by telling him what I could do for him, by extolling my love of cardboard and by highlighting my willingness to push around trolleys piled high with potatoes and carrots, whilst whistling a merry tune to the shoppers. Why didn't he say so directly? Perhaps he thought he had. Either way, I didn't exactly sizzle.

We all make honest mistakes, largely through ignorance, fatigue, haste or inattention to detail. Job hunting is no different, and I've realised that the trick is to learn from other people so that when our turn comes, we can be even more polished and poised. I would acknowledge that since my shaky start, I've improved my interview skills and general job hunting performance *considerably*.[7] Some people maintain that there's no substitute for experience and that may be the case. However, if you've never had an interview before, then what experience do you have to draw on? The answer is put simply in this quote:

"A clever person learns from his mistakes, whereas a *wise* person learns from someone else's mistakes."[8]

This is where our rogues gallery of mistakes comes in. These are all real things that I've experienced for myself, normally when I've been interviewing on a one-to-one basis, or sitting at the back of the room as part of an assessment panel, and all of them could easily have been avoided. Read and learn.

1. THE 'DETAIL' STORY

Imagine you're about to interview a candidate for a job. You're handed his information pack, which contains the results of his psychometric profile, a cheesy shot of him trying not to look nervous, a few pages of standard correspondence prior to the interview, and his CV. You scan the contents, smile at the photo, pull out the CV and begin to read. This is what you see:

---

[7] I've had training. I've practised hard. I've learned it all from the ground up. We can all be great.
[8] I'm not sure who said this. It could have been Confucius. He said a lot of wise things, so I wonder that he spent all his time watching other people fall over, fluff their words or spill their egg fried noodles.

CV

Arthur Pendragon

Mobile: 077716 5995123

Email: arthurp@roundtableknights.com

Introduction

I am good leder with lots of experience of managing people. I work for many companies and have the following skills that I can Demonstrate in n office:

- Fantastic timekeping

- Greet attentaiotn to detail

- Good woth words and able to wrte reports to a hi standrad

- Know typing and email wel

- Led a team of for juniors in the planning depratment

- Did wel at school and workd hard

How many mistakes are there in the above example? (The actual one really was as bad as this.) What would you make of this candidate? What might you like to ask him?

In the CV in question there were more than 100 (yes, one hundred) spelling and grammatical errors over two wretched pages and in fact I stopped counting after I had reached a hundred because I was so fed up. There was clearly the question of how the candidate had even made it to the interview, and those questions were asked afterwards.

---

[9] Remember the old adage: If it looks too good to be true, it probably is.

Be careful if you're typing things out in a hurry, like a pianist nearing the end of a particularly lively concerto, and you send off your CV without bothering to check it for spelling, meaning or grammar. It could come back to haunt you.

In this example, what makes things even worse is the use of rusty old clichés, which do nothing other than sound too good to be true.[9] Superlatives are always dangerous ground: Eagles have eagle eyes and for good reason. Bats have ears like a bat, although they prefer to use sonar most of the time. They could put these facts on their CVs and you would believe them. However, I'm always suspicious of overblown abilities and I'll use the interview to see if a candidate really does match up to his CV. Having so many errors in one CV contrasted with the candidate's stated strength of attention to detail, so it was natural to want to find out more:

"Welcome, Arthur," I began, "Could you tell me something about yourself?"

"Oh yes, thank you, Richard, I'm hard working, enjoy leading people and have a real eye for detail."

This was interesting, given that his CV suggested he didn't, so I showed him what I had found and asked if he could explain what had gone wrong. It turned out that he had quickly typed it late one night and in his fatigue (and hampered by an old keyboard) had sent it without reading it through. Even though he seemed honest with his answers, it still left a yawning credibility gap, because if he really did have a detailed approach, the chances are he would have read it through at least once, or run it through a spell checker (which is useful, but not to be relied on in my experience).

Filling a CV with exaggerated claims and then not making those claims consistent with our actions are classic job hunting traps to fall into. There is nothing wrong in being honest and there's nothing wrong in highlighting what we do really well. However, in practice, many adjectives such as 'superb' or 'fantastic' or 'excellent' are easy to say, but hard to substantiate in any meaningful way. Interviewers are becoming wary of unnecessary superlatives, so I would urge caution with their usage.

It's also worth highlighting that many applications are made via the Internet, where keystrokes can be lost on the long journey from our keyboard to the website. This problem can be exaggerated if we're typing fast and it's much easier than people realise to end up with what they think is a great introduction to themselves, but which in reality is splattered with errors and misspelt words. We need to be vigilant and double check anything which is going to be sent out with our name on it, because the process of recruiting people is like going shopping: You are faced with two tins of baked beans on the shelf in front of you. One has a dent in it and the other doesn't. Which one do you instinctively reach for?

> Remember this is a story about a CV, a piece of paper which we have *complete control* over and which has our name at the top as a seal of quality. Therefore, it is always worth making the time to thoroughly check our work.

2. THE 'TELEPHONE' STORY

This is one of my all-time favourite stories about mistakes, if only because when I tell it to people, they don't believe it happened. The interview was part of an all-day assessment for a post-graduate programme, and it was progressing reasonably well, although I was finding it hard to get any warmth from the candidate, who was professional, if a little detached. This is what happened, and we pick up the conversation about 20 minutes into the interview:

"Thank you for answering that question and it's good to hear about your experience, Sarah. What I would like to ask next is about your commitment to a programme that lasts for a minimum of 15 months. How do you feel about the possibility of ending up working away from home?"

"I'm okay with that because I worked as a consultant for five years and am used to travelling. I don't see that as an issue."

"Okay, fair answer. So how interested are you in joining us?

"Very. It would make a big difference to my career and…" Ring-ring-ring-RING.

Sarah's mobile phone rings loudly and she fishes it out of her handbag. I think she's going to turn it off and apologise, but no, she pushes her chair back, stands up and walks over to the corner of the room, as if a two-metre space renders me deaf to her conversation.

"Excuse me," she mumbles as she completes the manoeuvre.

"No, don't worry," I mutter to myself. "This is only an interview after all."

"Er hello? Sarah speaking. Oh hi! Nice to hear from you, how are you? Uhuh… uhuh… really? Yes, I'm well too, thank you. Uhuh… uhuh… oh that would be great! Oh, I can't do next Thursday. Could you do Friday the week after? No, okay then, which day works for you? Tuesday… umm [thinks for a moment] Yes, I could come to an interview on Tuesday that week. What time? Uhuh… two o'clock would be fine. That's great, thank you for calling and I'm really looking forward to seeing you. I'm sorry to have to rush off now, but I'm actually in an interview, can you believe it! Sorry about that, okay, bye-bye!"

She switched off the phone, dropped it casually into her bag and sat down again, while I stared at her in amazement.

"Well, I think that concludes the interview," I said brightly and watched her smile fade as the realisation of what she had done sank in.

"Oh, sorry," she apologised unconvincingly, "I didn't mean to interrupt your interview."

Actually it was *our* interview and if she hadn't meant to cause a problem, she shouldn't have answered her phone.

"That's okay," I said. "You're lucky, because if that had been a regular job interview, then I would have been wondering why you were here. For this programme, though, we expect people to have some rough edges and therefore, if you're going to do such a thoughtless thing as answer your phone during an interview, this is about the best place to do it."

As a postscript to the story, she turned out to be great at interviews, once she had polished up her interview technique. She went on to secure a great job and has never looked back.

> Switch off your phone, or at least have the decency to send a call through to your voicemail. If you think you might be telephoned for an emergency, disclose this fact to your interviewer *before* he begins, to let him know what's going on.

3. THE 'PHD' STORY

Sometimes, and thankfully not too often, individual candidates can overlook the importance of what I know as "*congruence*" in their CV. Congruence is a term from Transactional Analysis and means that things fit together. For example, I used to work with a director of a large multinational, whose idea of a smile was to turn up the corners of his mouth and leave his eyes alone, which reminded me more of a ruthless assassin about to strike than a big-hearted individual attempting to impart love and good humour to a fellow human being.

Smiles are there to convey positive, warm emotions, and to be successful, the look on your face needs to match up with the feeling it's trying to convey; the look and the emotion need to be *congruent*. A lack of congruence meant that on the rare occasions when this particular director was intending to be seen as a sincere, friendly chap, he failed. Miserably.

At the same assessment centre described in the previous example, although in a different year, I was faced with a candidate who, on paper at least, seemed well qualified. His CV proudly stated in his opening profile that he was writing a doctoral thesis for a PhD. He listed it as one of his achievements and it also turned up again as a qualification in his section on qualifications, a section which seemed a little light on other high-level degree awards which, I've noticed, tend to be precursors to doctoral studies. There was no escaping it; this person wanted us to know he was studying for a PhD. The actual feeling I was left with was that he wanted me to be impressed that he was *studying* for it as opposed to me being impressed that he had *achieved* it. Given that we were at a university, which per square foot contains more PhDs than a tin contains sardines, he was not in a place where anyone was going to be much impressed with merely starting such a project. My experience of PhDs is that people tend to be quite modest about them.[10] I read through the CV one more time and was left with a feeling of unease. There was something that didn't feel *congruent* about it; this candidate was appearing to make a lot of mileage over something that he did not have yet, so what do you think my first question was at the interview?

"Hi Gavin, I'm really interested in your thesis. How is your research going?"

"Oh that? Well I did the first six months and then stopped."

"Oh," I paused at this unexpected answer. "How long ago was that?"

"A year."

---

[10] We will look at the issue of misplaced modesty when considering CV construction in more detail.

"And when are you planning on restarting?"

"I'm not sure that I will as it was turning out to be much harder than I thought."

"So why is your PhD mentioned so prominently throughout your CV?"

There was a long and uncomfortable silence as he contemplated this obvious, but sadly not prepared for, question. It turned out that he had genuinely started a PhD, but in reality it was because he was more in love with the idea of having 'Doctor' instead of 'Mister' on his letterhead, than he was in contributing serious research to the world at large. Now he was being scrutinised, the lack of congruence made him look like a low-flyer who had drawn a jet engine on the side of his fuselage in the hope that that would make him at least look like a high-flyer. It didn't and the more he talked, the more I realised he was living in a little fantasy world of his own. That's fine for him, but not for me, as I had to manage and mitigate our risk during the interview process.

> When you're hiring a person, for whatever position, you want them to be truthful. If you're interviewing them and you trip over a large untruth, or a hole in their CV, or the varnish vanishes, how would you feel about them?

4. THE 'ATTITUDE' STORY

When I was working in industry, working hard to launch a new factory, I needed to hire a sales manager. After working closely with a recruitment company, we ended up with a shortlist of two persons, to be invited to our factory to meet the managing director. Both candidates were well qualified and had relevant prior experience. One of them had a slightly sharper edge to his manner, had asked more business-focused questions and had generally impressed me more. That's not to say he was the better candidate, he just *came across* better at his first interview.[11]

The first candidate was the slightly quieter one during the initial interview round and she did well enough on the day. She didn't sparkle, but she was friendly and polite and smiled at all the right times. People seemed to like her and although she didn't have direct experience in selling the same products as our factory produced, she was a reasonable candidate.

At the end of her day, people commented that she was 'nice'.

We then repeated the exercise on a different day with the other candidate, who made useful observations about what he saw, asked intelligent questions and was clearly interested in the detail and the market place appeal of the products. He did have direct experience of selling a similar range of items and gave me the distinct impression that he knew what would sell and how to sell it. The day was going well and I was sure I had found the right person for the job. All I needed to do now was introduce him to the MD and then make him a formal offer. Unfortunately for him, the MD's wife had already popped in for a chat and she asked: "Can I stay in the room?"

"Of course!" beamed the MD, "That would be great."

The four of us drank tea and talked and the MD asked questions and probed the candidate's knowledge, whilst his wife said nothing. Suddenly she looked at him and said:

"What do you think about women at work?"

"I think they're fine," he replied, and with a wink added, "as long as they stick to tea making or the typing pool."

Eyebrows shot up. Eyes opened wide. Mouths dropped. The MD caught my eye. The eyes, eyebrows and mouths in question belonged to us. His wife narrowed her own eyes and hissed her next question:

"So you do think women are better off at home?"

Ignoring her stiletto stare, he answered confidently:

---

[11] I will keep repeating this theme throughout the book: The 'best candidate' does not always get the job. The one who gets the job is the one who impresses when face to face. Being successful means generating positive feelings about yourself in other people. Facts can come a poor second to this. It's a bit like the journalists' motto: Never let the facts get in the way of a good story.

"Absolutely. Work is for men, home is for women. That's what I say."

The MD's wife turned a nasty shade of purple and the faintest trickle of steam vented out through her ears, just curling gently through her hair and hardly noticeable, if you lacked a trained eye.

Replying to the MD's wife in this way was a crass move and although the candidate was probably only intending to be humorous, his comments were sexist and wholly inappropriate. In a flash he had needlessly derailed his chances of success because the company would, quite rightly, not tolerate this kind of behaviour. In addition, given the fact that he would have been a sales manager travelling around the country to generate new orders, it raised the question of what else he might say that could damage the business. He might have been the better candidate on paper and he had performed well at previous interviews, but that counted for nothing in the face of his responses at this final interview.

Interviews are stressful situations and that stress loading tends to bring out genuine responses from people. However, that is never an excuse for sexist, racist or other discriminatory behaviour.

To say that you need to show good manners at all times when dealing with an organisation sounds so obvious that I can hardly bring myself to write it, but you only have to work in a shop for five minutes to realise that many people can be very unpleasant to deal with. If you want to avoid a knock-out blow to your chances, even though you might think you're the best candidate, check every email and re-read every letter before you send it. Be super-polite every time you telephone the organisation and always smile when you meet someone. People can be easily offended and if you think you might say something foolish, then don't say anything at all or nod and ask them to explain their question. Asking a question buys thinking time, which reduces the risk of making a snap comment that you may instantly regret.

5. THE 'INSTRUCTION LETTER' STORIES

It's a basic tenet of good examination technique that the first thing you do is to read the exam paper *thoroughly* before you attempt to write any answers. There's an exercise that teachers sometimes use to make this point to their students. Each person is given a double-sided exam paper, full of complex math questions to answer, and the students are told that they have ten minutes to complete the exam, starting *now*. This time pressure creates a level of stress in the room, which is done deliberately, because when we are stressed we often move to a default behavioural position of 'fight or flight' that, in exam terms, translates into 'get on with something, or freeze into inaction'. The first line of the exam paper says:

'Please read both sides of this exam paper before you attempt to answer any questions.'

In the case of this exercise, most of the students get flustered at the tight timescale, put their heads down and start to write furiously, anxious that they may fail the test. Then something strange happens. They begin to notice that one or two of their colleagues are sitting quite still and clearly not rushing to answer as many questions as they can before 'time's up' is called. Stranger still, the silent students are smirking and winking at their friends, who get a creeping feeling that all is not as it seems. Then the teacher calls time, holds up her hand and asks everybody to put their pens down. She walks around pointing at the people who have written answers to the questions:

"You, you and you," she says smiling, "have all failed."

She looks at one person who has not written a single word: "You have passed, well done."

The 'failed' students are baffled. What could be going on here?

The answer is simple and when the teacher reveals it to them, they sigh, smile and feel foolish. At the very bottom of the second side of the exam paper it says:

'Do not answer any questions. Attempting to answer a question will mean that you automatically fail this exam.'

It's a trick. It catches people out every time.[12] Stress causes people to scan the pages in their haste to get started, instead of calmly following the clear instructions. In addition, to compound the problem, people make an *assumption* that because they have seen something like this before, this particular piece of paper will conform to a pattern and therefore they know what to do without needing to read it.

It's just the same when we're job hunting. Information, advertisements, interim contracts and job specifications are there to be read *thoroughly*.[13] People often don't do this and the results can be embarrassment at best and failure at worst.

When being invited to an interview, or an assessment centre, we will often be sent a written letter explaining who will be meeting us, what will be required and so forth. This is the same for many sales pitches, where the client explains the rules to potential suppliers. A colleague of mine runs these events in the building industry where suppliers have 15 minutes to make their business case and sell their products. They don't have 16 minutes. They have 15 and this is clearly laid out in the letter which invites them to pitch for the work. The client wants to be fair to everyone and also to manage the time taken to see all the relevant people who might be interested in supplying them.

The same is the case for job hunting.

If you are asked for something specific, then the first thing

---

[12] Including me.
[13] More than once and with key words underlined or highlighted. Paying attention to the detail at this point means that our application will be more relevant and can stand a greater chance of success.

to do is to make the assumption that the clients *do know* what they are talking about. They will not have written the letter on a whim or made it up to annoy you. The clients *will* know what they want and *will* want you to deliver. It's one of the hidden tests in job hunting – can you follow instructions carefully? This goes back to the 'excellent at detail' story we had at the start of this chapter. If you really are good with the details, you will be able to read their letter and put it into practice. In the case of my colleague, when a possible supplier is still talking as the clock ticks past the 15-minute mark, they are cut short and asked to leave.

"But… but…," they protest, "I haven't finished yet!"

"Yes, you have," says the chair of the client's panel. "You were asked to talk for 15 minutes, you've had 15 minutes and you're now out of time. Goodbye."

"But… but… but…" The suppliers can be heard muttering as they are wheeled out.

People seem to think that they have been asked purely as a joke, or that 'you have 15 minutes' really means: 'You have about 15 minutes, but if you want to take longer then you can chatter on if you wish. Although it's our business, our letter and our time plan, just help yourself.'

I did one of these pitches myself and made sure that not only did I have a 15-minute presentation, but that I had a secret weapon in my pocket – a stopwatch. I delivered the presentation and stopped dead on time at 14 minutes 45 seconds, to a big smile from the members of the panel.

> It might sound bafflingly easy, but a great way to win points in a cover letter, at an assessment centre, or at an interview, is to stick to *what the client wants.*

In my experience of seeing hundreds of candidates deliver 10-minute presentations, I would say that less than 30% finished on time, with the others being asked to stop and click through any remaining slides in silence. Some even had to be reminded that 'in silence' meant keeping their mouths closed.

Under this collective heading of 'Instruction Letter Stories' we have:

✗ The man who didn't bother to prepare a 10-minute presentation. He thought it was optional and went a sickly white colour when, while chatting to the other delegates, he realised he was the only one to have made that mistake. We said he could still have 10 minutes to talk about his work and he filled it with an entertainingly useless ramble about his dog and his childhood and his hobbies. This suggested that not only did he not pay attention when reading, he didn't listen too well either.

✗ The man who prepared a hugely detailed presentation. He was still on slide one out of 21 after 10 minutes and had to be very firmly invited to stop, because he just kept on talking. He looked shocked and clearly couldn't believe that we could be so heartless as to keep to a strict time plan (in order to be fair to all the candidates).

✗ The lady who saved her PowerPoint presentation to Microsoft Vista software. She couldn't use it because our system ran on Windows 97 software. The two are compatible if your programme is saved in the *right format*[14] and this was helpfully explained in our letter, which the lady had ignored. After she suffered the agony of her presentation not loading up, we shuffled the order of the candidates, gave her an opportunity to go away and re-save it so she could have another turn later on. She did, although the experience had clearly drained her energy and knocked her confidence.

---

[14] This is often PowerPoint 97-2003 presentation, or Word 97-2003 document for CVs.

✗ The man who turned up in his old jeans and very scruffy t-shirt. The letter asked for formal business dress. His cheeks burned bright red when he walked through the door and realised his mistake. He then had to spend the rest of the day not fitting in.

✗ The lady who never turned up. She didn't telephone us to say she wasn't coming, and then when we tracked her down, she said that she hadn't been able to contact us because our telephones *and* email had been engaged (which they hadn't). She explained that her car had needed to go in for a service and that she had *only* remembered on the morning of the interview. Would you have believed her? We didn't.

✗ The lady who arrived late and then argued. Clearly embarrassed at her slip up, she decided to compensate by shouting at the office manager that the start times were not in her letter. She was wrong. There is no point in arguing. If you're wrong then you're wrong and the only thing to do is to be gracious and apologise.

All of these things were completely avoidable and in each case they made the candidate look inept. People will form an opinion about us at each point of contact and we need to strive to tick all the boxes, complete all the tasks and manage ourselves through the interview and assessment process. Remember that the skills we need to do this are exactly the same skills that we need for the job, in most cases, so one mirrors the other. People assume that if we're good at doing the job hunting bit, then we must be good at doing the job. So, let's finish this section by asking a question:

> When was the last time you read a job advertisement or a letter inviting you to an interview or an assessment centre and you *underlined* keywords with a highlighter pen *and* ticked them off when you had actioned them or included them in your cover letter or CV?

MYTH-BASED MISTAKES

Sometimes we make the mistake of overestimating our chances of success, because we assume the job market is more friendly and welcoming than it actually is. Rarely do people stoke the fire, settle themselves comfortably into a snug armchair and read our letters and CVs through at leisure. This is a myth. People might have a thousand or more job applications to deal with and so might use random sorting techniques to cut down the numbers to a manageable level. They just want one good person to fill the role and if they lose 200 good candidates simply through chance, then never mind, there's plenty more left to read through. Here are some *true* stories from the world of job hunting to remind us that life can be full of surprises:

1. Interview candidates selected by throwing a box of CVs down a flight of stairs and collecting the first six that were on the top of the resulting pile.

2. Job applications sorted into two piles at random, called 'lucky' and 'unlucky'. The unlucky pile was thrown away without even reading or opening the letters.

3. Emailed CVs sorted electronically by keywords to produce a 'scan-sort' system.

4. CVs given to assistants, colleagues or receptionists and letting them choose whom to invite to interview.

5. Shortlisted candidates invited to afternoon tea where they were interviewed in a relaxed manner by the whole staff, over coffee and cream cakes. The successful candidate was the one people liked the most, not the most qualified.

6. Interviewers making a decision after the first 10 minutes of an interview, but continuing for another 50 minutes in order to appear 'fair' to people.[15]

---

[15] It was reported in the UK press in 2009 that a survey revealed senior executives tended to make up their minds about a candidate in the first 10 minutes of the interview.
[16] She was a radio producer who had seen a lifetime of letters.

FINAL COMMENT

The world is a conservative one and although we might like to joke and laugh, we need to remember that humour, or opinion, tends not to travel too well. For example, a colleague of mine said recently how much she used to dislike people who wrote letters in green ink. She always equated that with the writer being slightly unhinged and this robust opinion had been formed over many years of noticing how people who wrote with green ink tended to have strong views and express themselves forcibly.[16] On principle she would always throw the letters away, if they had the 'green-ink curse'. In passing, she also mentioned (and this did make me laugh out loud) that an advertising agency had commented on how fed up they were with students sending in genuine CVs which contained the line:

"Speaks three languages: English, Elvish and Klingon."

> **✴ SUMMARY** We all make mistakes and that's *okay*. It's part of life. The key thing is to make as few as possible, or to make them in a safe environment when they don't count as heavily against us. A safe environment, for example, would be a practice interview with a friend, or when networking with people we know. If we do make a mistake at some point in the job hunting process the only thing to do is to apologise, smile and carry on. In fact, how well we recover from a mistake can be a piece of 'live-action' experience that demonstrates our presence of mind and coolness under fire. I wouldn't recommend making mistakes just so you can recover from them, but a good recovery is worth striving for, as it can paint us in the warm glow of professionalism.

---

[16] She was a radio producer who had seen a lifetime of letters.

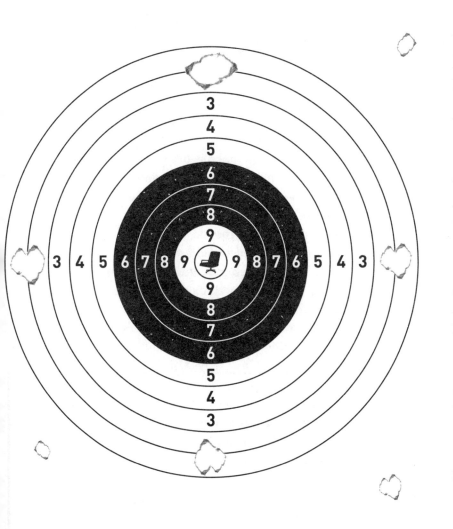

Section 2
SECRET NO. 1
PASSION

2.1 THE IMPORTANCE OF EMOTION

FEELINGS MAKE A DIFFERENCE

Being able to feel feelings and project passion is an important asset in our job hunting activities. However, it's something that in my experience is rarely taught and is often missed from lists of things you need to get a job, which is why I think of it as a secret. Passion is placed at this point in our process because tapping into our feelings can shape how we put together our campaign, how we edit our CV, where we network and what happens to us at interview.

When I talk about 'passion' I'm using the word as shorthand for *deep-seated enthusiasm* and even *love* for the subject area. It's about being *energetic*, being *really interested*, being *excited*. It's what runs through my own interview story at the beginning of the previous chapter. The person hiring me wanted me to be really enthusiastic. I didn't know that; I was just answering his question truthfully and to the best of my abilities. I didn't realise he had seen lots of people for the job and even though it was 'only a Saturday job in a shop' he wanted someone who had a bit more 'go' about them than me, because the job was important to him. No job is ever 'just a job'. They all involve a level of responsibility, cost real money and have a knock-on effect on colleagues, customers and organisational performance.

BEWARE OF FAKE PASSION

There are two kinds of passion: Genuine and plastic.[17] Plastic passion is the kind of fake sincerity we sometimes see on TV shows, where people are so enthusiastic about *everything* we begin to suspect they are actors hired to be professionally gushing:

"Oh my, your lovely house is so lovely! I just love the way you've arranged your wheelie bins, and that cat flap is just so lovely...."

---

[17] The term 'plastic' is also used in Transactional Analysis to describe a fake unit of recognition, which means when you appear to say something positive, but do so in an insincere way.

This kind of plastic passion is the same as a fake fried egg you can buy from a joke shop. It looks genuine, but when you get up closer and sniff, it smells of rubber and your heart sinks as you realise that for a moment you *were* fooled. In a job hunting situation, the giveaway is when the people claiming 'passion' have no depth of evidence to back up their claims. Here's a genuine example to make the point:

"What motivates you Simon?"

"Well Richard, I'm *passionate* about learning."

I like learning too and would claim to be passionate about it, having spent a considerable amount of my own time and money on gaining qualifications. I'm also suspicious of anyone who readily *tells* me that they're passionate. The best thing to do is to *convey* passion and to let *me* decide that you're passionate. I decided to find out if Simon was being truthful:

"Really? Perhaps you could tell me what books you've read, or what courses you've done recently. What's your top three?"

"Er, ah, I, er, um. Hmmm. I read a book about leadership last year…"

> If we don't have the detail, then it's likely that we're not passionate. Think about how people get passionate about their favourite football team. They go to all the home games, collect programmes and will spend hours debating with their friends as to who the best player is, or whether that goal was really offside. That's passion. I often ask for a 'top three' because people can easily have read one book. If you're really passionate, you will tend to have read widely, been on training courses, invested time and money and be knowledgeable about your subject.

Another classic trap is to be passionate about something we think the employer is looking for, such as *change*. The need to continuously improve, or to keep changing, is what is driving many organisations these days. I interviewed a lady once who confidently told me that she was 'passionate about change'. Given that this is a very vague word and therefore difficult to be genuinely passionate about, I was curious and asked her what she had changed about herself in the last two years. She couldn't answer that. Her mouth worked, but no sound came out. She had clearly been exaggerating.

THE VALUE OF PASSION TO AN EMPLOYER

Deep-seated enthusiasm is great. Doing something we love, or at least have real affection for, makes our working days seem short and fun filled. Work no longer becomes a chore and we don't have to drag ourselves out of bed in order to struggle into the office. Instead, we bounce in and have a great time. In a job hunting situation, such as when we're networking or being interviewed, passion is *essential* to have because it performs several important tasks for us. These include:

- ✓ **Differentiation.** In marketing circles people talk about the difference between products, services and competitors. Job hunting is the same and we need to meet the criteria for the job and make ourselves appear different to our competitors. Being enthusiastic is one way to achieve this. Who would you want to hire – the dull guy or the effervescent lady?

- ✓ **Risk reduction.** If someone hires me and I'm not too interested in the job, but decided to take it anyway, then there's a chance that I will get bored and will leave. However, if I'm passionate about the role, or a significant portion of it, then I will want to stay and make a success of it. That means the risk of hiring someone who is interested is lower than hiring someone who is less interested. Passion reduces risk and that makes us a *much* better proposition.

✓ **Being liked.** We are all emotional beings and we want to like others and be liked ourselves. Given that we have to make a good impression quickly when we go to an interview, it helps to be passionate because that's a likeable quality. People tend to like people who are passionate.

✓ **Stamina.** All jobs are tough in some way and there is always an element of stamina required, whether physical or mental. If you are passionate about something, then the chances are that you will stick with it and continue to work hard even when you're fatigued and others are beginning to fade away. It also means that you will tend to keep going over the longer term and not get tired after a couple of months and want to go and do a different job.

✓ **Gap-filling.** Showing our passion is a powerful way of reassuring an interviewer that we are prepared to learn and to make good any deficiencies in our skills or experience. I've heard several colleagues comment after an interview with a passionate person: "I know that he's not qualified and that he lacks experience, but I *loved* his passion and I want to hire him, because I can teach him the rest."

✓ **Displaying potential.** Many employers want to hire someone who can do the job today and who can develop in the future. This means that if they see us as an enthusiastic and energetic person, then we are more likely to have the energy to develop, which makes us more of a potential asset over the longer term. Even if they don't have a clear idea of what the 'longer term' could look like, the fact that we are perceived as having potential is what counts today.

* **SUMMARY** Passion is essential. The energy and enthusiasm we bring to our job hunting activities, particularly networking events and interviews, can make a crucial difference to our chances of success. Being able to display genuine warmth and affection for a subject, or a craft or an activity, helps people to buy into us and our potential. Passion can't be bought or trained in, or stuck on, which means that if we don't have it on day one, we're unlikely to ever have it in that environment. If we do have it, though, and can display it, then we can come across as being just the kind of person they are looking for. Employees might even overlook some of the gaps and shortfalls that we may have, because when we strip the job hunting process down to its most basic level, people buy people and people prefer to buy from *passionate* people.

HOW TO MAKE AN IMPACT

Knowing that passion is useful is one thing, but being able to display it when it counts is something else. We often learn that feelings are good to have, but not good to show. Think about when we were little and at school. We might have been teased for crying and we decided that it wasn't safe to show our emotions. This can be reinforced in a working environment where sometimes showing emotion is seen as a sign of weakness. For example, when did you last see a salesperson cry because he just lost an account? Or witness a personnel manager shaking with nerves when he had to make someone redundant? Probably never, and if I had a wish it would be that people at work could show their emotions more often. Not because it would make things different, but because it would be more honest.

Fortunately, the bullish old style of command and control management is being replaced by a more empathetic coaching style. People don't want to be told what to do all the time. They want to have their opinions canvassed, their ideas listened to and their fears and concerns taken into account. This is good news for all of us and means that we can relax a bit and start to remind ourselves that whatever happened to us at school, or elsewhere, it is *okay* to show emotions in a job hunting situation, because we're all *okay* and we can all harness our enthusiasm to make an impact in order to sell ourselves effectively.

HOW TO SHOW PASSION

Showing passion is *okay* and there are four stages to consider when we want to convince someone else that we're really excited about a particular opportunity:

1. **Follow our energy.** If we're heading in a direction that we don't want to go, then it will be hard work to keep going. I started my working life as a trainee accountant because I wanted a company car. The thought that I didn't really like working in accounts never crossed my mind. I wasn't a success and I've learned since that cars are less important than doing a job you actually like. If you're having to choose between two options, a good suggestion is to go for the one you feel more drawn to. When you stop and think for a minute, it's highly likely that you will have put more energy into it, done more research, talked about it more often, spent longer applying for roles and so on. Follow your energy and then when you are in an interview situation you're already heading in the right direction. It will be much easier to talk about your passion from this position.

2. **Remind ourselves that it's *okay* to talk about passion.** It really is. Nothing bad is going to happen. We might have a voice in our head telling us to be quiet, not to blow our own trumpet, or that this kind of selling is 'a bit pushy'. It doesn't matter. The choice we have is to do the best we can in order for us to be successful at our job hunting activities and being enthusiastic, excited or passionate is one very important thing that we can do to achieve this. If we don't talk about it then people won't know about it.

3. **In the moment recall a happy memory and smile.** If we can think of a memory associated with something that we like very much, it will make us smile and our demeanour will change. We will then be perceived as more enthusiastic and more engaging and that can increase our chances of being hired.

4. **Use keywords to convey enthusiasm.** Now that we know it's okay to be passionate and to talk about what interests us, here is a list of suggested words and phrases for us to copy and adapt as we need to:

✓ I really like…

✓ It's great fun to be involved in this kind of work because…

✓ I love working in this kind of business because…

✓ I find it *really* rewarding to do this job because…

✓ I would enjoy this work because…

✓ I love it when I'm working with…

✓ I'm *really* interested in…because…

✓ That would be *really* great…

✓ Yes please, I love doing that kind of work…

Notice how in many cases you need to say why you like it so much, to convince people that you're serious. Also there's a point of caution here; be careful with the word 'love'. People rarely love stacking boxes or cleaning windows, per se. However they might love the variety of working in a shop, or the freedom of working outdoors, or of being on their own, or of working in a team. The skill is to think about what it is *precisely* that you love so much and work that detail into your reasoning. Then you will be telling the truth, will sound utterly believable and will impress whoever is listening to you.

THE WAY TO REALLY CONVINCE PEOPLE

When you're talking to people in your job hunting activities a good tip is to use the word 'really', because that adds emphasis. If you compare "I like it" with "I really like it" you can see the difference. Typical examples that we might encounter are: "What I'd really like for my birthday is…", or "This year I'd really like to go on holiday to…" In the way that gravy makes a roast dinner taste even more juicy, the word *really* can jazz up our sentences and *really* enable us to come across as a passionate person.

* SUMMARY Passion is a package, because demonstrating it requires us to blend words, knowledge and smiles. If we follow our energy, remind ourselves that it *is* okay to show feelings (because nothing is going to hurt us), and then use some carefully chosen words, such as 'really like' and 'great' then we will come across as someone with a bit of sparkle about them. When advertising sausages, people cannot give us a taste directly through our television, but they can give us a lingering shot of a plump sausage sizzling in a pan. The same occurs when we're job hunting; we need to sizzle so that we hook people's enthusiasm for us. Remember that the *really* smart move is not to use the word 'passion' itself. Let the other person use it to describe us and that way they will have a stronger memory of us.

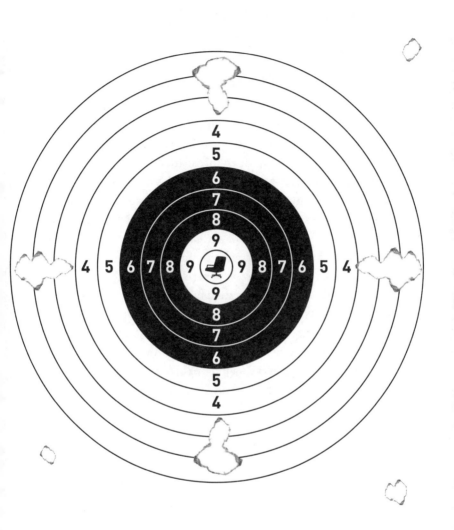

Section 3
CAMPAIGN

3.1 THE VALUE OF CAMPAIGNS

PROCESS THINKING ADDS VALUE

Job hunting is hard work. There's no pretending that it isn't. It can be fun, it can be a great way to meet new people and it can lead to new and interesting opportunities. However, it does require effort, a degree of patience and the ability to keep going when you just want to throw it all in and go and play. Some playtime is a good idea because as with all hard work (and job hunting is a job in itself), the law of diminishing returns applies: The more you put in, the more fatigued you will get and the less you will get back.

This is where a campaign is useful.

A campaign is a *process*; a series of managed activities, in the way that an advertising campaign is a series of advertisements, press articles and public relations activities. Process thinking means making sure we follow the stages through from beginning to end, so that our campaign flows successfully and delivers us job opportunities. This approach can make us more successful than looking for a job in a random or haphazard manner and trusting to luck to sort things out for us.

FAMILY BENEFITS

The point of a campaign is to bring structure to our job hunting activities and to provide us with useful information. We can also share it with our family, in order to keep them informed and to keep them supporting our activities. People tend to get anxious if they have no information, so it's always better to share our progress with our loved ones, rather than keeping it to ourselves, perhaps hoping for some surprise good news. Life only goes like that in films, where at the last minute the hero bursts through his front door and sweeps the love of his life off her feet and reveals how his secret plan has brought them everlasting happiness.

DISCOUNTING

We can also share our campaign progress with our supporters and invite their comments and analysis, because it's very easy for us to *discount* what is going on in order to keep our sense of reality intact. 'Discount' is a word from Transactional Analysis and it means to ignore or distort. We all do this all the time in order to keep the world as we like it. For example, have you ever gone for a walk and not taken a coat, even though there are black clouds scudding over the horizon? I've certainly looked up, noticed that the sky is blue and ignored the obvious rain showers that are heading my way. We do this because accepting the information means changing something. In the case of my walk, if I accept that it's going to rain, I either have to go into the house and ferret around for a coat or do something different, like take the car. When I'm standing outside the house, with my shoes laced up and my walking trousers set to 'march' do I really want to go through the fiddle of unlocking the house, going inside, removing shoes, finding a coat and getting sorted out again? No, I just want to get going, so I ignore the clouds and head off.

This is human nature and it's useful to know about *discounting*. We can discount ourselves and what we do, our feelings, other people and the severity of the situation. We can also ignore problems, our ability to think through new options and even our ability to take action.

DISCOUNTING EXERCISES

It's worth pausing for a moment and really getting the word 'discount' to lodge firmly in our brains, because the tricky thing is that we do it out of awareness. We don't even realise that we're ignoring the obvious, which is what makes the need for a campaign so great. Here's an exercise to get you thinking:

✓ If you are reading this in a room, have a look around and see if you can see any cobwebs, any piles of rubbish, any cracks in the wall and any marks on the floor. These are things that we routinely screen out because acknowledging them generally means we have to do something about them.

✓ If you're reading this outside, put the book down, close your eyes and listen for both natural and man-made sounds. What do you hear? Often we filter out sounds so that we can maintain the dialogue in our heads in order to keep ourselves concentrating when reading.

✓ Wherever you are, notice the temperature, the time, the position of your body, whether you are hungry or thirsty, and what you might be discounting in other aspects of your life.

ACCOUNTING

A campaign is a useful tool to keep us *accounting* for our activities, because accounting is the opposite of discounting. When we *account* for something we recognise it, deal with it and respond appropriately to the reality of the situation. This is an essential skill for successful job hunting because it's amazing how much we filter out. We do it to avoid making awkward decisions and to avoid coming to terms with unpleasant truths. If we are going to be successful with our job hunting, we need to be able to drop, change or let go of cherished plans and ideas, if they're unrealistic. At the same time we need to account for our skills and experience, and our ability to learn things and to realise that our intuition can help to guide us.

REALITY CHECKING

This book has been written to help people find a job. This doesn't mean that we can't be ambitious and want to stretch ourselves, change careers or try and get promoted. However, we do have to factor in a dose of reality. I can remember applying for production director roles when my current job title was production planner and I didn't have any line management experience. I used to say to myself that 'it was worth a try'. It wasn't because I was *hopelessly* under-qualified and lacking in experience. I was just wasting my time.

If you send out 100 CVs and 40 go to jobs that you don't have a chance of getting, how many opportunities do you have in your sales pipeline? The answer is of course 60, but I've worked with many people who insist that the answer is 100. We really need to be firm with ourselves and not inflate the numbers just to make ourselves feel better.

A current example of this is Twitter. This can be a useful way to meet new people, find out information and tell the world what you're up to. However, is it better to have 35 followers or 1,350 followers? The instinctive answer is that bigger is better, but if we drilled down into the detail and found that of the 1,350 there were 1,340 multi-level marketing machines which had used crawlers and bots and other Internet insects to track us down and link-up, we might be less impressed. Quality counts, not pure naked volume, and a campaign can help us to maintain the quality of our job hunting activity.

* SUMMARY A campaign formalises our job hunting activities and gives them structure. This enables us to manage the process, to take a step back and see what we're doing well and to see what we need to change. We can more easily notice what we're *discounting* and take appropriate action, and we can *account* for all of our strengths and talents. When we consider that job hunting involves our family, having a campaign is a great way to demonstrate to them that we're being methodical and conscientious in our approach, because they can see what we're doing and how hard we're working.

3.2 CAMPAIGN MANAGEMENT

EASY STEPS TO FOLLOW

A job hunting campaign builds a pipeline for us, which starts with basic research activity, moves on to meeting people and sending out job applications and ends up with interviews and job offers. A good campaign avoids the mistake of choking the pipeline with hundreds of Internet applications, which can make people feel good, but ignores other ways there are to find a job. Instead, our pipeline-building activity needs to account for *all* of the things that we can do.

Creating a campaign is very simple, and all it requires is a handy chunk of thinking time and something to write on. We don't need to use computer spreadsheets if we prefer paper, and I've seen some good ones scribbled onto flipchart pads. Doing it is what counts, and if you're making it look very smart with little flower pictures and zigzag doodles then you're probably going a bit too far. Ease off the artwork, keep it simple and keep it functional.

When we're thinking about our campaign, we need to take account of our *budget* because although business cards can be purchased for free on the Internet and we can borrow books and ask friends to give us practice time at no cost, if we're going networking or want to meet people then we may incur travel costs, have to buy a few drinks and perhaps even treat ourselves to a smart new suit. Given that we're looking to get a job, which means that someone will pay us thousands of pounds, we need to acknowledge that we may have to invest some money in our campaign and set a budget, rather than ignore it and get a surprise when our next credit card statement turns up.

Once we've thought about the cost of investing in our campaign, the work of planning and executing it can follow a simple process structured around:

✓ Deciding what to look for and where to look.

✓ Setting up targets and measures.

✓ Sending out letters and CVs.

✓ Going to interviews.

✓ Reviewing progress.

✓ Celebrating success.

Sometimes people might be asked to attend several second interviews in different parts of the same organisation, to meet relevant stakeholders, and this tends to happen for more senior people, working at director level or above. Clearly these appointments can have a huge impact on a business, so they need to be properly scrutinised. There might also be several hurdles to jump for graduates entering a management programme where thousands of applicants need to be whittled down to five lucky trainees.

Be prepared to do whatever you're asked to and only stop the process if you've really honestly lost interest in the job or in the people making you jump through hoops. Sometimes, though, this steeplechase approach is all part of the weeding out process; cutting out the half-hearted and the unrealistically ambitious.

A job hunting campaign supports our activities, gives them structure and provides us with direction and a way of measuring our progress. Our supporters are a key resource for us to use and if you haven't already done so, stop reading and write down the names of *five people who can help you* during your job hunting campaign.

A campaign is comprised of a sequence of steps and because we're effectively building a *sales pipeline,* it pays to consider each one in turn. Like all pipelines, if it springs a leak then we'll only get a trickle out of the other end, rather than a steady flow of opportunities. The steps are:

STEP 1: CHOOSE THREE HORSES

This is what I call the 'three-horse race'. Finding a job is like riding a horse and if we could ride three at once then we have trebled our chances of winning. This approach also gives us the option to experiment with more ambitious jobs or to try something different. The three horses are:

Horse #1 'The Thoroughbred'. This is a job that we really *really* want to do but which only around 20% of our CV is relevant to, in terms of the experience we've had or the transferable skills we can draw on. This is a job we *could* do and we might need a lucky break to get it, or need to generate an interview via networking activities. It's worth racing this horse a bit, because it keeps our optimism up.

Horse #2 'The Jumper'. This is a job that we are keen on doing and which around 50% of our CV is relevant to. These jobs are ones that keep us really motivated as we can probably make good some of the missing 50% with a sparkling cover letter and great interview technique. They tend to provide the most realistic opportunities for being ambitious and applying for things which are more aspirational in nature.

Horse #3 'The Hack'. This is a job which we can already do and which slots into 80% of our CV. (I'm making the assumption that things are rarely a 100% fit. Some people write job specifications that Superman would struggle to fill.) Although it's great to have some ambition, if your aim is to get a job then it pays to consider the roles which you already have expertise and experience in. I've worked with people who, in their rush to do something new, have overlooked their past working life and so this horse is a good one to race. It's also worth considering that working for one poor company, or one bad boss, doesn't make the role a dull one. In another company with better leadership, it could be great fun.[18]

---

[18] I've experienced this firsthand and a great boss can make all the difference. In your search, it's also worth considering applying to people and companies you like.

STEP 2: WORK OUT A SEARCH AREA

People tend to overlook the fact that the number of opportunities decreases significantly as you reduce the area you're looking in. For example, an area two miles by two miles contains four square miles. If each one of those had a business in it you might have four opportunities to look for work. However, if you reduced each side of your search box by half you reduce the *total* area by three-quarters. In our example, a box of one mile by one mile only contains *one square mile* and would only have one business in it. Therefore, it pays to look at a map and think realistically about how far you can travel to work, because greater distances mean many more opportunities. I once coached a business manager who complained that he couldn't find work and I asked him how far afield he was looking:

"About one hour of driving time from my house," he replied firmly and continued, "I refuse to go any further than that."

"No further?"

"No."

"How long was your drive to work before?" I asked curiously.

"Ninety minutes."

There was a long pause whilst the words '90 minutes' rattled around inside his head. Then he pursed his lips thoughtfully and said:

"Hmmm, I suppose I *could* look for work that's 90 minutes from my house."

He had a job within a month, because 90 minutes' travel time meant that he could apply for one particular job at a company where his CV was ideal. He was successful purely because he lifted his gaze and extended his search horizon a few extra miles.

A suggestion is to show your support group your search area and ask them for comments. I didn't apply for a job once because I thought it was too far away and it was only when my wife saw the advertisement by chance and gave me a stern look did I realise my error. I applied and of course, I got the job, much to my wife's amusement. Extending our search area may raise the issue of relocation which, given the short-term nature of many roles, is always worth considering, even if only on a temporary basis. After my own success at extending my local search area, the next time I needed to find work I increased my range so far that we ended up moving across the country.

STEP 3: SET TARGETS

We need measures to help us reflect on how well we have done so far and what we might change. Measurement gives us useful information which can help to steer us in the right direction, and when looking for work we need to pursue all these activities on a regular basis:

- ✓ Formally applying for jobs.
- ✓ Sending in cold-call letters to people.
- ✓ Telephoning contacts to make appointments.
- ✓ Meeting contacts to network and to look for hidden opportunities.[19]

You can choose the weekly targets for creating *live* job opportunities that makes most sense to you, given your circumstances. Choose a number that reflects quality and not just pure volume (the section about ratios might help to give you a guide). By 'live' I mean those which are current and could happen within about six months. Any longer than this and the chances of them disappearing are increased as there is a greater risk of the organisation changing its needs.

---

[19] I've mentioned the 'n' word here, but it's a secret. Shhh… don't tell anyone. It is a hugely important part of our campaign, so much so that there's a whole section on it later on.

A tip here is to leave your home at least twice a week to meet people. A target of meeting two people a week sounds quite low, but actually requires diligence and effort to maintain. If you can achieve this, then in my experience you are out-performing the majority of people who are trusting to their typing skills to find them a job.

STEP 4: GET TOOLED UP

We all need the right kit to put up a shelf, change a car battery, or cook dinner for our friends. Trying to make an omelette without having any eggs to break is naturally an uphill task, and as eggs are difficult to substitute, we would need to rethink our menu if that was the case. It's the same with job hunting, so rather than go into detail here, the whole of the next section is all about the kit we need.

STEP 5: GO LOOKING FOR OPPORTUNITIES

How many places can you think of looking for information, or contacts, that could lead to a job? Have a guess and write down your answer. I've found that people don't tend to think clearly about exactly which stones to turn over in order to find work. Instead, they often follow the safest path that they know, which might be to buy a newspaper or upload their CV to an Internet job hunting site. Whilst these can be useful, a job hunting campaign needs to consider *all* possible options, so here is a list of places where we might consider looking directly for a job, or for contacts who can point us to further opportunities:

1. **Local newspapers:** These often contain jobs or stories about local businesses who may be expanding and need people.

2. **Local newspapers for a neighbouring district:** Visit the *next* town and buy their local newspaper.

3. **Trade magazines:** These often carry job advertisements in them, or have interesting articles that could prompt a speculative letter. Similarly, if you belong to a professional organisation, it's worth making sure you receive any magazines or newsletters that they may produce.

4. **Local business advice centres:** A visit to our nearest Citizens Advice Bureau, or similar, will yield a list of local organisations that help businesses. We can then contact them or pay them a visit.

5. **Local libraries:** These are a gold mine of free information. They also contain helpful librarians who can point us to the right section.

6. **Central libraries:** Some places have bigger libraries that service the smaller local ones. They will tend to contain information that covers a much wider geographic area.

7. **Local business directories:** These are often found in our local library.

8. **Local networking clubs:** Organisations like Business Networking International (BNI) or The Best of… hold regular meetings or networking events and are always on the look-out for new people. Often we can have a couple of trial visits for free before we commit to joining and these organisations are worth getting to know because networking meetings, or exhibitions often contain business owners and you can take their cards and write to them directly afterwards. In addition, many people work as a freelance consultant, or skilled tradesman, whilst looking for a full-time job and it's no harm considering this as an option, if only to meet people.[20]

9. **National newspaper job pages:** Everyone looks here, but they can be useful for specific types of jobs. Buy a newspaper each day so that you can find out what kind of jobs are advertised when, or look online to see what is listed. However, see the section later on about networking to find out why this is a long shot.

---

[20] If you're thinking of setting up in business you're welcome to read my earlier book, called *Leave The B@$T@*DS Behind*, which covers this subject in detail. You can find it via: www.richardmaun.com.

10. **National newspaper *news* or *business* pages**: Unlike the job pages, nobody looks here. When we read a newspaper there are lots of stories about companies who are expanding, merging or looking to develop in some way. We can cut out the articles and write directly to the people mentioned in them, using the article for reference and making our cover letter relevant to it. This is a great way to find work, because we will tend to be the *only* person writing to them.

11. **Internet job search sites**: There are millions of people already listed, but there's no harm in joining them. Be careful to update your CV regularly, or even remove it and put it back after a couple of weeks, as the search engines can pick it up again and treat it as a new listing. New CVs posted often get sent to people, whereas existing ones can languish like dead fish at the bottom of a pond.

12. **Internet networking sites**: This year I boosted my contacts on the site *LinkedIn* from 50 to 240, simply by diligently visiting it each day and sending out a couple of invites to people. LinkedIn is a good place to be if you're a job hunter and its search functions are increasingly being used by recruitment agencies to target specific people. Facebook can also work for you if you expand the number of friends you're connected to and if you let them know about your job hunting activities. Given that these websites are free to join, it makes sense to use them in order to increase your Internet footprint. Amongst a group of job hunters I worked with, about 60% had no Internet presence at all, which they hastily corrected. The Internet can be a force for good, although it still pays to be cautious of whom you link up to and what information you put in the public domain.

13. **College or university notice boards**: These often promote *career fairs* which can be a good place to meet people and to find out more information about working for different organisations.

14. **Trade shows:** These typically host lots of companies from one sector, are a good place to do research and can be stuffed full of senior managers, who are meeting people and helping to run stands. Although they probably won't have the time to talk to us about jobs, we can show an interest in their business, take a card and write to them later on.

15. **Job centres:** These have jobs in them and when we next visit we can take a few minutes to scan the job boards.

16. **Recruitment agencies:** These can be a good place to find a job. Please read the next chapter for more information.

17. **Social clubs:** Sometimes these have notice boards with advertisements, or if you're chatting with people during a regular meeting let them know you're looking for work.

18. **Our family:** It might sound obvious, but our family might be able to help. I worked in a factory once where several people had secured jobs for relatives, so there's never any harm in asking.

19. **Friends:** The same as family applies to our friends. However, never ask them directly if they can hire you as that could cause embarrassment. Always ask if they *know* someone who might hire you. If the answer is 'them', then they will tell you anyway.

20. **Neighbours:** If you're chatting, tell them what you're up to, unless they're nosey curtain-twitchers who just like gossip.

21. **Competitors of businesses you used to work with:** If you want to work in the same industry these people are worth writing to. They may already know you and like you.

22. **People whom you know, who are already doing the job you would like to do:** This is something that I've used myself. These people often have an interesting story to tell and I always ask them: "How did you get to be doing this kind of work?" This has helped me

to find out what I needed to do to join them in that occupational niche.

23. **As an intern, or a consultant, working for free:** This can be a good way to be hired and is particularly useful for people who have less experience and therefore carry more risk. The 'no-cost option' makes it more attractive for people to see you in action and get to know you. Write to an organisation you like and offer your services to them for a set period of time, such as a couple of weeks or a month. As a tip, it's worth asking for travel expenses because some people can take advantage of an offer which is totally free. Paying a very small amount still means that they're getting a good deal and you won't tend to feel taken for granted.[21] I predict that the concept of 'internship' will be taken up more widely by all sorts of organisations as it's a seductive offer: *Come and work for free and we can see you in action.* Who can resist this idea as a way to recruit people for their business?

24. **Your supporters group:** Obvious, really. Ask them for contacts whom they would be happy to introduce you to.

25. **Your address book or email contacts list:** You might have contacts you've not talked to or emailed in a long time. Dig them out and say hello. We all know more people than we think: old school friends, distant relatives and ex-colleagues. If you're a recent graduate, or a school leaver, it might be worth a trip to visit your old Head of Department, because he or she might be well placed in the local community and be able to put you in touch with useful contacts.

How did you do with your guess? Did you have more than 15 options written down? If you did then you're a star, because when I've done this exercise with other people, they often tend to get fewer than 10. This is why a campaign is important; it's a systematic process that means we can keep all of our options in view.

---

[21] A colleague of mine set up a seminar and charged people £2 on the door. I was surprised at this and asked why he didn't make it free. "Because it cuts out the time wasters who have only turned up to drink my coffee," was his answer. I think it's reasonable to ask for a notional donation towards travel costs as a test of mutual commitment.

STEP 6: USE RATIOS TO MANAGE PERFORMANCE

Ratios are a great way of checking that we have enough activity at the front end of our sales pipeline to make sure a job trickles out at the other end. For example, a ratio of 100:4:2:1 means that for every *100* applications we send out we might expect to be invited to *four* first interviews, which might result in *two* second interviews and from these we might receive *one* job offer. This means that if we have only sent out 50 good quality job applications then we are unlikely to get a job, because there isn't enough activity going in at the head of our pipeline. Like panning for gold, the more grit we start with, the more likely it is that we will find some glinting nuggets at the end of the washing process.

In good times, when many people are being hired, or if you have a special skill which is in particular demand, such as engineering or mathematics, a ratio of 25 *applications to 4 first interviews to 2 second interviews to 1 offer (25:4:2:1)* can be realistic. However, in tough times the ratio can be as high as 800:4:2:1 or even higher. A colleague of mine sent out over 400 cold-call letters before he was invited to a single interview. His persistence did pay off, though, and he managed to secure a job, after he spent an entire Christmas holiday writing up a speculative marketing plan to launch a new product. His efforts, which were on his own initiative, so impressed the managing director of the firm who had interviewed him, that he was offered a full-time role.

We need to set targets that work for us and take into account that the three 'horses' we're racing will perform differently. It will generally take more effort to get a job where only 20% of our CV is applicable than for roles where 80% of our CV is applicable to it. As a *guide* we can use the following ratios to give a starting point for our campaign.[22]

---

[22] Please note: These numbers represent a broad average of my experience of working with people at a managerial level. They may be very different for you. Please use them as a way of stimulating thinking and of finding out whether you are doing enough to make your own campaign a success.

HORSE	APPLICATIONS	1ST INTERVIEWS	2ND INTERVIEWS	JOB OFFER
#1 Thoroughbred (20% of CV)	400 to get	8 (2%) to get	4 to get	1
#2 Jumper (50% of CV)	100 to get	6 (6%) to get	3 to get	1
#3 Hack (80% of CV)	50 to get	4 (8%) to get	2 to get	1

The numbers illustrate how it becomes more difficult to get a job as we apply for things that have less obvious relevance to our CV. This is to be expected because it considerably increases the risk for the employer. Also notice how I've kept the conversion rate between first and second interviews the same for each category. My experience is that with some good interview training, we can do well when face to face with a client and I've seen this in action. The hard part is getting to the interview in the first place, although obviously, the higher risk we are, the more likely we are to be pipped at the post by a more suitably qualified candidate. Being invited back to a second interview is a great achievement in its own right, but we might be the 'outside candidate' and may need to work harder to get the job.

STEP 7: MAKE IT VISIBLE

I used to have a habit of creating spreadsheets and then forgetting to look at them, and one of the things I've learned is that visual management makes a big difference. This means that our campaign information needs to be stuck up on a wall where we can see it. However you choose to capture the information, pin it up where it can be seen. A simple table of activity gives us something to fill in each day and we can see if we're meeting our own targets for our work and if we're on target in terms of the ratios. The example below shows activity. I've left out zeros for clarity. Note how the activity has generated interviews for one of the 'horses' (I've used a real life example of job titles):

JOB HUNTING DAILY ACTIVITY CHART

Activity		Mon	Tue	Wed	Thu	Fri	Total for this week	Total for all other weeks	Grand total
Thoroughbred 400:8:4:1	New Job Applications	1	2	1			4	5	9
Title: Operations Manager	Follow up Telephone Calls & Emails	1	2	3			6	3	9
	Meetings & Networking Activity								
	Interviews Attended								
TOTAL		2	4	4			10	8	18
Jumper 100:6:3:1	New Job Applications	1		5			6	50	56
Title: Shift Supervisor	Follow up Telephone Calls & Emails		2				2	56	58
	Meetings & Networking Activity				1		1	4	5
	Interviews Attended								
TOTAL		1	2	5	1		9	110	119

Hack 50:4:2:1	New Job Applications	4	2	2			8	56	64
Title: Team Leader	Follow up Telephone Calls & Emails	3	4	2			9	30	39
	Meetings & Networking Activity							15	15
	Interviews Attended				1	1	1	1	2
TOTAL		7	6	4		1	18	102	120
CAMPAIGN TOTALS		10	12	13	1	1	37	220	257
Campaign Targets		10	9	9	1	1	30	210	250

The above summary shows that the productivity has generated two interviews and that two days a week are kept aside for meeting people (hence the low target for activities on those days). As well as a summary activity chart, it can be helpful to see our top 'live' opportunities, so that we can keep them in sight and make sure we send out follow up emails and/or make telephone calls to show our enthusiasm for the role. An example for the team leader role is shown on the following page and it makes sense to have one for each of the job titles you are applying.

JOB HUNTING LIVE OPPORTUNITIES SUMMARY

LIVE OPPORTUNITIES FOR THE ROLE OF TEAM LEADER

Company	Closing date	Application posted	Acknowledgement letter received	Follow up call or email	1st interview	2nd interview	Offer
Pets & Co	21st March	5th March	Yes	Yes			
Cheese Mixers Ltd	10th March	2nd March	No	No			
Widget & Gadget Bros	25th Feb	20th Feb	Yes	Yes	Due 1st April		
The Bread Partnership	6th Feb	25th Jan	No	Yes			
Jones the Cake Ltd	15th Jan	10th Jan	Yes	Yes	20th Jan	15th March	Waiting

The table shows that this person is waiting for a job offer and has another first interview to go to. Once the closing date for an application has passed, it makes sense to remove the opportunity after four weeks have elapsed and we haven't heard anything about it. Some jobs give specific dates when people will have been contacted by and these can be included in our table. The 'follow up call or email' is there for us to be proactive; sending a confirmation letter or email never hurts and if we've sent in a CV cold (on a speculative basis, as opposed to a 'warm' one from a networking lead) then following up is essential to avoid our letter going into the bin.

STEP 8: UPDATE WEEKLY

Having charts and a tally of performance is great and it all needs to be updated once a week, on whichever day suits you best. Personally I find a Friday-tidy is a good way to end the week with up-to-date information and a clear desk, ready to begin again on Monday. If you've spent the whole week booking appointments, going to meetings and sending out job applications, it's okay to have the weekend off to relax and recharge your batteries.

Once you've updated your information, look at it. What is it telling you? What patterns and trends are there? Are you on track to meet your targets? If not, what will you do differently next week?

'Do differently' is always a good way to make changes and simply saying to yourself "I must try harder" isn't going to make a substantial difference over the longer term. Instead, be realistic and make *structural* changes. This means actually changing a routine, a working pattern or our environment. For example, I know people who have walked to their library each day in order to do some quiet reading in the morning, or who have turned the spare bedroom into an office to make their job hunting activities more professional, instead of camping out on a crowded kitchen table.

STEP 9: FOLLOW UP

The point of following up an opportunity is to maintain a dialogue, however small, in order to keep our name in front of the other person. If we have been to a meeting, we can send an email to say 'thank you' and to book a second one for a few weeks' time. People often need a couple of meetings to begin trusting each other and it makes sense to have a first shorter meeting followed by a second longer one.

If we have sent a letter to someone and ended it by saying we will contact them, then we need to make sure we do so.

Letters can be a good way to get past a receptionist or a personal assistant (who can be ruthlessly efficient gatekeepers). A letter might seem a bit old fashioned, but *paper has presence* and letters tend to be forwarded on. They also take more time to write and post and so make it look like we're putting in some effort. Anyone can punch out a quick email, but who takes the time to post a letter?

Many people don't make telephone calls because they don't know what to say and are scared of being rejected. There's a pro-forma in the toolkit section to help people who haven't done this kind of thing before, and the tips that I recommend to boost people's confidence are:

1. **Block all calls together.** This gets you into a 'flow' and you can quickly make one after another.

2. **Make a couple of easy calls first.** Perhaps to a colleague you are on good terms with, or to one of your supporters, to get into the habit of using the telephone.

3. **Write down your opening sentence.** I often do this to avoid 'drying up' through nerves as I don't believe life needs to be a test of memory.

4. **Use a headset.** Having a headset frees up our body posture and we can talk and write at the same time, or walk about, or relax in our chair. It makes the conversation seem more natural, and in doing so can increase our confidence.

STEP 10: CELEBRATE MILESTONES

Job hunting can be hard work and so it pays to celebrate when we have reached a key milestone, perhaps when we post our 100th job application, or complete our 10th face-to-face meeting, or have made 20 cold calls. We all need an incentive and each time you pass a target, find a way to say 'well done'. Perhaps you might have a chocolate bar, or an afternoon off, or go out with a friend for a drink. Go and have some fun to recognise your hard work, or the whole process of job hunting can become a thankless drudge.

✳ SUMMARY Job hunting is a process and a campaign gives order to our process. If we put enough good quality opportunities into the front of our pipeline, we can expect some interviews to flow out at the other end. It might take time and hard work, but with a sensible campaign we can keep ourselves focused and on track. Miss a bit and we might be building a flawed process, so it pays to make sure we have ticked off each one of the following steps:

1. Choose three horses.
2. Work out a search area.
3. Set targets.
4. Get tooled up.
5. Go looking for opportunities.
6. Use ratios to manage performance.
7. Make it visible.
8. Update weekly.
9. Follow up.
10. Celebrate milestones.

3.3 RECRUITMENT AGENTS

ANGELS OR DEVILS?

If you're looking for a job then it's a fair bet that you will at some point bump into a recruitment agency and the key thing to remember when dealing with them is that they're staffed by *people*, not robots. This means that recruitment agents are people, like us, wanting to do a good job, earn their money and generally get on in life. They don't go to work to find new ways of wasting people's time, and whatever your view of them is, they need to be treated with respect, because they may just be holding our next job in their hands.

THE NUMBERS GAME

Many recruitment agencies manage their staff by setting them volume-related targets. For example, a recruitment consultant may have to make *so* many calls per day, find *so* many new candidates and arrange *so* many interviews. This can mean that to them you're just a number and part of a quota to be filled. Don't take this personally; if you were to meet them socially they would be friendly, warm-hearted people, but when they're in the office they are under time pressure and have a job to do.

People tend to work in a way that ensures they meet performance targets, so if this means all telephone calls have to be a maximum of five minutes (in order to meet a quota) then don't be surprised if they don't want to talk to you at length. The same goes for face-to-face meetings. You might have travelled a long distance and had a quick ten-minute interview with an agency, but don't worry; the ten minutes ensures you are known to them and that makes you a step closer to a job than you were before.

We need to recognise that recruitment agents tend to have a heavy workload and don't really know us, so therefore our mindset when dealing with them has to be:

✓ How can *I* help *you* to help *me*?

HIGH STREET OR SPECIALIST?

Think about the kind of jobs you are applying for and compile a list of agencies to visit. Some of them are found on the 'high street' and offer general services to local businesses. Others focus on specific industries or types of jobs and these tend to be found via local business advice centres, through networking or via the Internet. Some agencies have a 'stock' of people and try to place them in jobs, whilst others take contracts from a company and then go out and research possible candidates. This is one reason to have an Internet presence; you don't know who might be looking for you.

Be prepared to travel to meet suitable recruitment consultants and to work to their timescales. It can pay to end a first meeting by agreeing a date to catch up again, even if it's only for a quick 20 minutes. This is because recruitment is about *people* and people tend to be cautious and naturally reserved towards people they don't know. Meeting someone for a second time helps to build confidence and allows you both to find out more about each other.

BE HONEST

People can easily get defensive about revealing personal details and can embellish them to feel better. They might feel that a higher salary makes them seem more successful than a lower salary, that managing more staff is more impressive than managing fewer, or that more qualifications makes them more desirable. This is not necessarily the case. When dealing with a recruitment agency always, always, always tell the truth, because it makes it easier for them to match you to a job.

A colleague of mine who specialises in senior management posts gets exasperated when people inflate their salary, because it means their CV doesn't match their aspirations and so are harder to place. Alternatively, they could be put forward for an interview that under closer scrutiny they're not suitable for and this could cause embarrassment all round.

> Some people seem to think that dealing with recruitment agencies is a game and that you can shade the facts to get ahead. You could try that tactic, but once you get found out do you think they will want to give you time and attention ahead of someone who is honest, reliable and easy to deal with?

BE RESPECTFUL

You never know who an agent knows, what opportunities may arise tomorrow or which organisations they are negotiating with. This means at all times when we're dealing with them, or going to job interviews, we need to be:

✓ Polite

✓ Punctual

✓ Presentable

This might sound glaringly obvious, but all recruiters have stories of people who didn't show up to an interview and then complained that the agency wasn't doing enough to help them find work. We can help ourselves by being a friendly professional at all times because we do want them to *recommend* us to a potential employer. If we have some grumbles we can always complain later to our supporters and decide to use a different agency if we feel that's right for us.

ASK QUESTIONS

It can be intimidating when meeting a recruitment agent because they're a link in the chain between us and our next job. However, we can help ourselves by finding out about their business and what *they need* from us. It's okay to ask them questions, to find out about them and to decide whether we want to be part of their world. Useful questions to ask include:

✓ What is your business model? For example, do you research candidates for jobs or jobs for candidates?

✓ Do you need to have my CV in a particular format?

✓ What can I do to help you find a job that is suitable for me?

✓ How do you keep in touch with candidates?

✓ When and how is the best time to contact you?

✓ When do you pay travel expenses for interviews?[23]

✓ What is the market like at the moment for the kind of role I'm looking for?

✓ What advice do you have for me?

Asking questions will give us the information we need to be successful with them and allows us to check out our assumptions about what they do and how they do it.

---

[23] It's always worth asking for travel expenses to interviews, particularly if you have to go a long way, or stay overnight somewhere. Asking doesn't offend people and if you never ask then the answer is always 'no'.

✱ SUMMARY Recruitment agents are not angels or devils. They're just people. They might be frustrating, they might not contact us, they might not make us feel special, but they are a gateway to a job. Remember that they tend to be busy people and whilst time can drag for us as we look for work, they will be rushing to meetings and to hit deadlines and targets.

Our job is to make their lives easy, to be friendly and to answer their questions truthfully, and we can help ourselves by finding out how they work and what we can do to help them. This might be counter-intuitive, when they are there to help us, but if you were a recruitment consultant whom would you rather recommend to an employer – someone who causes you nuisance or someone who is easy to work with? And remember; it's always worth building up a good relationship with them because we may need to use their services more than once.

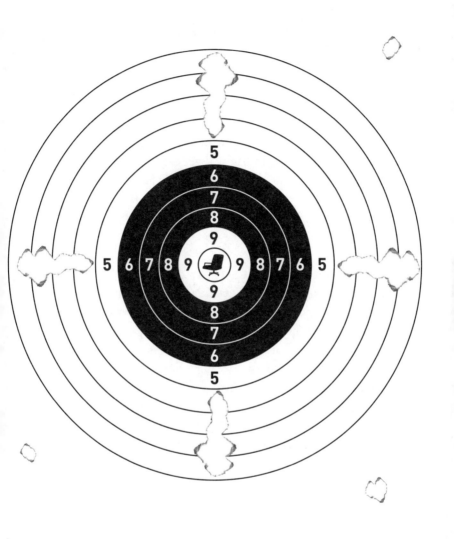

Section 4
TOOLKIT

GETTING EQUIPPED

We not only need to have the right tools for our job hunting activities, but it makes good sense to have *all* of them. I'm always amazed to find that people go off looking for a job without the necessary equipment to hand, because taking the time to assemble our kitbag will get us another step ahead of the competition. The things that we need fall into two groups:

✓ Small items
✓ The Big 5

The small items are the everyday things that people can overlook, simply because they are so ordinary. We will deal with them in this chapter and then the 'Big 5' get a chapter each, because they are the chunky sweaters in our job hunting drawer of warm clothing. The Big 5 items are: Achievements, CV, Cover Letter, Minute To Win It and Telephone Call Pro-Forma. I've rarely seen a CV or a cover letter that wouldn't benefit from a few tweaks, so I would encourage you to read all the chapters in this section and use them to benchmark your work against.

SMALL ITEMS

Many of the successful people with whom I've worked have tended to carry about with them a useful toolkit, and my view is the more tools we have the better we can craft our opportunities, because job hunting is a bit like being sent on a survival course. It's you and the contents of your pockets against the natural elements. You have to look for food, build a shelter, navigate around obstacles and keep yourself alive. Job hunting is the same, except you don't have to eat weird berries for dinner and sleep under a heather duvet. So what do you put in your pockets? For most job hunting activities you will need some or all of the following small items:

1. A business card or a calling card.
2. A calendar or diary.
3. A pen.
4. A suit or something smart to wear for interviews.
5. A bag to carry your kit.
6. A decent handshake.
7. A smile[24].

A business card, or a calling card, is for giving to people in a meeting when there isn't time to scribble details on a scrap of paper. Also, cards look professional and mean that we don't have to rack our brains to remember our own telephone numbers, which invariably is a tricky thing to recall in a stressful moment. They can be printed for free on the Internet and under our contact details we can include a line about us, such as 'An experienced Operations Manager'.

A calendar or diary is for taking note of dates, and I've met people who have missed appointments because they didn't have a diary. I even had a delegate on a time-management course once who proudly told me that he never ever wore a watch and used public clocks to tell the time. He was late for the start of the workshop, but failed to see the irony.

If we have a pen with us at the interview, we look organised. It's a small point perhaps, but people do notice details like this. Just make sure the pen works, or better still, take two.

A suit, shirt and tie isn't always necessary for interviews, although as a fallback it's worth assuming that formal dress is required, on the premise that we can never be over-dressed

---

[24] I'm not being funny here. A warm smile goes a long way. Few people carry one all the time and yet they're so light and easy to store.

for an interview.[25] We can always take off a jacket, and it's better to do that than regret that we had not brought it with us.

I'm used to carrying a briefcase, but if you're used to carrying a plastic bag, or an eco-friendly, hessian-woven, climate-saving bag, then ask yourself if it matches your smart interview attire? Sometimes all we need is a neat-looking folder to keep our interview kit in, and these can be cheaply purchased and will still look business-like.

Handshakes are an easy thing to master and are an essential part of our job hunting equipment. It's worth practising yours with a friend to make sure it's not too soft or too tight and there's more information about handshakes in the chapter about rapport building.

A smile is an essential piece of kit if we want to sell ourselves effectively. If you want to come across as a warm and friendly person, then make sure your eyes and mouth work in harmony to project genuine enthusiasm and to welcome people into your world, because if you smile with your eyes looking off to one side, that shows a lack of confidence and people will pick it up. Practise on yourself in the mirror; look away then look at yourself and smile and say hello. Keep going until you can switch on your smile at will. It will serve you well. There's more information about smiling in the chapter about rapport building and the word *smile* crops up repeatedly in this book, because a friendly smile can help to build relationships.

---

[25] This assumes we're not going in a dinner suit, or a ball gown and tiara. That would make an impression certainly, but probably not a good one.

* SUMMARY We can help ourselves by paying attention to the small things that could otherwise trip us up. If we're telling someone how organised we are whilst they watch us fumble for a pen, what does that really say about us? If we write a cover letter talking about our super-confidence, but can't shake hands and smile effectively, how confident will the other person think we are really? The first thing people will notice when they meet us is our bag, clothes, smile and greeting. Get them right and we're off to a great start, whatever the situation.

VALUING OUR PAST

When we meet people on our job hunting campaign we have to sell ourselves effectively and this means making a good impression, talking and smiling with confidence *and* making reference to the things that we've done with our life so far. We will tend to focus on our working life and if we're a bit lacking in that area then it's okay to make reference to our leisure time, or academic studies, or vocational training. However, people often *discount* the content of their working days and find it hard to talk about their achievements. If you are frowning at the word 'discount', skip back to the first chapter in the Campaign section, where all is explained.

One reason why we overlook things is that, because there is so much going on in our lives, it can be hard to pick out the details. For example, can you remember the date when you first met your partner, what you had for dinner a week last Thursday and the exact stopping distance of a car at 70mph in the wet? I can't and I'm sure that's the same for most people.

WHERE ARE ACHIEVEMENTS USED?

This chapter could have been tucked into the next one as part of CV writing, but that would be to overlook a fundamental truth about our achievements; they are used in all sorts of places. We might put them in our CV, or pick out a choice one for a cover letter, perhaps pepper our conversation with them when meeting a recruitment consultant, or have two or three printed on our calling card. If we have a website presence on a networking site, we might write a couple of sentences to highlight our talents, and if we're making a telephone call to an agency then it can help to have them at hand, ready to drop into the conversation to make ourselves stand out.

WHAT IS AN ACHIEVEMENT?

In essence achievements are little stories, or vignettes, which contain information about *targets* we have reached, *goals* that we have achieved or organisational *benefits* which have resulted from our hard work. However, bigger is better here. Turning up to work every day might feel like an achievement if you hate your boss, but it's not likely to impress anybody much. Instead, tell people about the *significant* things which you have completed: The times when you showed strength of character, worked really hard, solved a complex problem, were flexible in the moment, overcame obstacles, or pushed yourself to the limits of patience and endurance. All of these things shout loudly and clearly that you are special and talented, and if you were writing a sales brochure about yourself, you'd put them on the front cover to grab attention.

Here's a real example of an achievement from an application form, which helped the person in question to beat 1,250 other graduates to a job interview:

QUESTION: Tell us about something you're proud of?

ANSWER: I was at university and wanted to play in the women's football team, but I broke my back when I slipped over on a patch of ice. The doctor told me my football-playing days were over. What did he know? After four months in a brace, I devised my own programme and practised my skills every day. Six weeks later I joined the team on a trial basis. At the end of the year I was the team Captain and we had won the local league.

My guess is that the other candidates made the mistake of talking about the biggest wave they surfed during their gap year, whereas this person told a story that showed her potential employer what determination she had and made it clear she was prepared to work hard. In this case, recovering from a broken back was an achievement worth mentioning, because even though it's not work-related it effectively *showcased* her skills and abilities.

> **TIPS:** Achievements need to be relevant to the employer and tell them something about us which can be *translated* into their work place. We can also use them to *differentiate* ourselves from our competitors by highlighting the added value in our own unique set of stories.

WHY ARE ACHIEVEMENTS SO IMPORTANT?

Achievements feature most prominently on our CV and for good reason. A CV is not a list of all the jobs we have held, or the qualifications we have gained, or the clubs we've been a member of. A CV is there to showcase what we can *offer* an employer by making reference to what we've *done* in the past.

There's a good psychological reason for this, which is that if you've done it *before* you can do it *again*. This is why I have described the third age of job hunting as the 'applied' age. It's the same for CVs as it is for interviews; people want to know what we have done because hiring people is a *risk*.

It costs money and time to hire someone.[26] Advertisements are expensive. People need to attend interviews and spend time discussing our application. Once we've been successful, our salary will have business-related taxes added to it and we will want paid holidays and will need a desk and a chair and a mug for coffee. The costs just stack up and, given that it often takes between two and six months to settle down and

---

[26] It always costs more than you think it will. A recent estimate put the average figure between £5,000 and £10,000 for a managerial position. That's just to get you into the building. Once you add on the cost of a salary, not to mention wasted time if you can't do the job, the true cost can easily be in excess of £50,000 to £250,000.

get the hang of things, our host organisation is committed to spending money before it sees any return from us. Anything we can do to mitigate the risk of wasting that money is going to count in our favour. In addition, because organisations increasingly need to save money and get more productivity out of fewer resources, the focus on added value is going to become ever more important. There is no room for passengers any more. The second-and-third class carriages have been decommissioned; it's now value-adding-class only, or don't bother to get on the train.

> **TIPS:** Solid relevant achievements are risk-reducing factors. They make it easy for someone to get a clear mental picture of what you have done in the past. People can then make the leap to the future and feel reassured that you *can* do the job.

WHAT MAKES AN ACHIEVEMENT GREAT?

Our great achievements can be honed and polished from raw experience, a bit like watching a flint knapper create a razor-sharp arrow head: They start off with a nodule of flint and gradually hammer off flakes to leave a perfectly designed cutting tool. We can do the same with this checklist to ensure our achievements are of the highest quality:

1. They need to have a number in them to give them a sense of size and scale and to make them more memorable.

2. They need to state the methods or tools used for success, as people want to know how we did it.

3. They need to relate to something we have done and not be about us simply being in the room when it happened, or we could look like a fraud under searching interview questions.

4. They need to be significant in some way, because saving £1 is not as interesting to an employer as saving £1,000,000. Bigger is better.

5. Ideally they need to cover a maximum of two lines, when written on A4-sized paper. This makes it easier to insert them into our CV and easier to remember when in conversation. If we write down pages of detail then we run the risk of smudging the essential element. If people are interested in what we're talking about and want more information, we can trust them to ask us for it.

All of our achievements ideally need to pass *all* five tests in order to earn a place in our CV, and if they don't, then we need to consider swapping them for ones that do. If you're stuck for achievements then read more of this chapter because examples of good achievements and how to remember them are coming up. Also, the questions listed in the interview skills section and at the end of this book may help to jog your memory and get you thinking about what you've done really well.

ACHIEVEMENTS FOR FIRST JOBBERS

This can be a classic Catch 22; you've never had a job, so you don't have any work-related achievements, and here I am saying that you need to have achievements to get a job. This is the dilemma faced by young people, freshly-minted graduates and by people who have come into the job market for the first time. In this case there are two golden rules:

1. **Pitch for your level.** You are extremely unlikely to be hired as a senior manager for your first job and aiming too high for your background means you'll be in competition with vastly more experienced people. Apply for jobs that match your abilities and your experience and not your ego. I've seen many people get demoralised because they're not being invited for interviews and when I compare their CV with the type of jobs they're applying for, there is a yawning gap.[27]

---

[27] I'm not anti-ambition, quite the reverse, really. If you do want to take a chance then go for it, but remember that it's a risk. In my experience people tend to overestimate their own abilities and underestimate the strength of the competition. Be careful!

2. **Make good use of all the non-work activities which you have taken part in.** All of them will have elements that can be related back to a job and all of them can have some value for you. Taking part in sporting activities, outdoor adventure days, voluntary work or specific projects will tend to contain elements of leadership, time keeping, team work, planning, communication skills, decision making, risk taking and being responsible for money. These things are just the same as the skills you need to be successful at work and it's okay to use them to form your list of achievements.

TIPS: The skill is to attach work-related qualities to non-work-related activities and by doing this well you can accelerate past the competition, who will tend to have less added-value content in their CVs.

We can have a look at how non-work-related things can be turned into respectable achievements by comparing these two sets of achievements and thinking about which ones we would rather have in our CV:

CV

Miss Bland

Mobile: 054545 54545454

Email: bland@dullandboring.com

Achievements

- I was a member of the hockey team.
- I spent three months hiking in France.
- I worked in a supermarket to pay for my trip.
- I was a Venture Scout.

These are not really achievements, they are a list of activities and they add nothing to Miss Bland's CV. There's no *added-value* element in their content and simply stating what you did is a lazy way of compiling a CV. Let's have a look at Miss Bland's friend, Miss Bright:

CV

Miss Bright

Mobile: 023123 23232323

Email: bright@interestingandbusy.com

Achievements

- Played 45 hockey matches at club level and scored 80% of the goals for the team.
- Planned a hiking trip to France, which involved organising the route and accommodation for 60 nights. The trip was successful.
- Worked in the Asco supermarket for 3 months to pay for my trip. This involved unpacking deliveries and working on the till, which meant handling £25,000 of cash every day.
- Completed the 24-hour '5 Peaks' hike, which involved navigating across the North Moors at night and walking a total of 40 miles in a team of 6 Venture Scouts.

These are achievements. They tell us something about the positive qualities that Miss Bright has: She can plan, she is responsible, she has stamina and she can work in a team. The numbers used make a big difference too, because they show the scale of the achievements and are easy to remember. Miss Bright starts to become the 'Person who hiked 40 miles' and people often use this kind of shorthand to describe candidates.

Being able to walk 40 miles and navigate at night is a tough thing to do and this tells us that Miss Bright is prepared to push herself in order to achieve a difficult target. We naturally start to assume that she will bring these qualities to work and that in comparison with Miss Bland she shines brighter.

The truth may be that she simply likes to go hiking. We won't know until she starts work, so all we can do is make reasonable assumptions based on the evidence at hand.

HOW TO RECALL YOUR ACHIEVEMENTS

If you had learned seven different languages do you think you would remember them? If you had worked in China or Russia, do you think you would remember the experience? If you had been to Japan on a study trip, do you think you would remember what you saw? If you turned a loss-making organisation into a profitable one, do you think you would remember the achievement?

These are all examples of real achievements, or other useful details that people forgot to add to their CV. They forgot them because they hadn't considered them to be worth mentioning; to them they were merely part of their everyday experience and had faded into the background. In all cases they added value to their CV and gave an interviewer something interesting to ask questions about. In all cases they had needed some help from me, or from their colleagues, to bring them back into their conscious mind.

People are generally modest and there is a natural preference towards being self-effacing. That's great if you're attempting to win a Miss Modest Pageant, where candidates win prizes by eschewing glitz and glamour and saying nothing about their lives or their qualities. Go right ahead and win big. The trouble is that if you're reading this book, it's because you're looking for a job and job hunting requires you to *sell yourself* by telling people what you have done and what skills, qualities and experience you have.

TIPS: There is no mileage in hiding behind *the team*. An achievement that talks about what the team did and how the team performed well is a waste of time. People want to see what *you* did. If you led the team, then fair enough; say *how* you led the team and what the *result* of your leadership was. Don't write about 'we'. Instead, write about 'I'.

If you asked someone to do something and he did and did it well you can still claim credit for the end result because if you hadn't asked him, and hadn't monitored him, then the thing would not have happened in the same way. In these situations, it's okay to be the *catalyst*. If you scan the Internet you'll find it's full of stories about corporate big cheeses who have helped their organisation to increase its share value by 10 points. All of them are proud to be leaders and all of them are happy to claim success, which undoubtedly is down to the hard work and diligence of the myriad of people populating the rest of the pyramid below them.

The reason for raising it here is that, in order to remember what your achievements *were,* you have to think about how *you added value* in your previous roles. You have to see *yourself* and not hide behind the bulky shadow of the team.

This is the time for 'I' and not for 'we'. Many people I've worked with have struggled to remember any of their achievements because they have become so used to talking about the team. They've had to unlearn this and instead start to talk about themselves. It's okay to do this; you're not being a sinner. You can blow your own trumpet. You can be proud of what you have achieved. You can celebrate your successes. After all, you've probably worked hard, given up evenings and weekends and been stressed by it.[28]

We can harvest achievements by thinking systematically

---

[28] Selling is fine. There is a difference between being a thoughtful and articulate professional, who can talk up his good points, and a shiny suited salesman with slick hair and a wide grin. Go for the former and avoid the latter, unless you have a suitcase full of brushes and dusters to sell.

about the high points of our working life, going back over the last 10 to 15 years. Anything before that is generally a bit out of date, unless you feel strongly that it has to be included on your list. Do not write anything at this point, just let the thoughts coalesce in your mind. If you get stuck, go for a walk, or lounge in your favourite armchair, or bask in a hot bubble bath, or find your best friend and talk to him/her (ask them to listen in silence). Any kind of displacement activity will do as it encourages your brain to free-wheel for a bit, which is a good way to let things float up from the filing cabinet of your subconscious mind and drift into the part that is concerned with short-term memory.

In order to help the free-wheeling, here is a list of questions for you to ponder. Similar ones will surface again at interviews, so we might as well start to think about them and generate answers for them in advance. Think of them as the cranial equivalent of 10 laps round a cinder track, or 50 press ups, or a couple of minutes on a heavy punch bag:

1. **When were your best days?** I call these your *diamond days*; the days when you came home and wanted to dance all night to celebrate the greatness of your day. It doesn't matter what the work was: When did you really enjoy yourself?[29]

2. **When did you feel drained?** Sometimes the best work sucks out the most juice and you might recall the feeling of tiredness as a precursor to recalling the reason for the fatigue.

3. **When were you the most anxious?** Same as feeling fatigued, if you've been worried about something the chances are that in that particular period you have worked hard to resolve the situation. Even if things didn't go well, people have often achieved something. For example, closing down your own business can

---

[29] Diamond because if you could have captured the essence of your day it would look like a fat sparkling diamond that you could mount on a ring and flash about to people.

be heartbreaking, but to do it in a measured and orderly fashion is well worth celebrating. There are many people whose business just went *pop* and they pretended they hadn't seen it coming. If you kept your eyes open and did something proactive to cushion the fall, then well done to you. That's an achievement.

4. **When did you show real determination?** Not just to avoid eating until lunchtime, but when you really kept going when others around you faltered?

5. **When did you show flexibility?**[30] Instead of sticking to your safe and well-worn train tracks *you* wrenched *yourself* out of your comforting groove and headed off in a different direction. You might have chosen to let go of your own idea in favour of someone else's. You might have chosen to write off the cost of work done so far and started again. You might have deliberately changed jobs, or industry, or chosen to undertake a tricky new project with a minimum of training and guidance.

6. **When did you overcome resistance and successfully sell your idea?** You might have used clever political arguments to convince people, or you might have presented a winning business case. You might have simply listened to people's concerns and won them over by explaining the facts and the benefits to them personally and to the organisation at large. You might have done all of these at different times, but the key factor in this is that your efforts chipped away at a stubborn 'no' and turned it into a thoughtful 'yes'.

If you recall your feelings and allow yourself to have a sense of pride and a growing recognition that you have done well, that you *did* make a difference and that you *do* have some great things to talk about, then you can collect a hatful of achievements. Once you have collected them, you can stop crying 'but it was only the day job' and start realising that

---

[30] This is about you choosing for yourself. If your boss sent you somewhere and you hated it, but went anyway, that's not an example of being flexible. It just says that you will follow orders.

these things make you *special* and *worthwhile* and, most importantly, *employable*.

HOW TO VALUE YOUR ACHIEVEMENTS

Everything can be measured and measuring your achievements is a great way to make them memorable. If you go into your local supermarket, stand still and look around you, it is an odds-on certainty that the special offers will boast of how much money they can save you. The special offers don't tend to have fancy names; they just scream the numbers at you and let you decide for yourself. It's the same with your achievements. You can value:

- ✓ Time taken.
- ✓ Time saved.
- ✓ Money earned.
- ✓ Money saved.
- ✓ The rate of change.
- ✓ Profits generated.
- ✓ The amount of miles travelled.
- ✓ The number of bricks used.
- ✓ The number of people involved.
- ✓ The number of calls made… the list is endless.

With a small investment in both time and thoughtfulness, it is possible to put a number to each and every achievement. The clever bit is then to think about what the impact was for the organisation, which generally means *valuing* our achievements in monetary terms rather than simply measuring them.

TIPS: There is a little gold-plated question to use here which unlocks the value in our achievements. The best way to use it is to keep asking it, however irritating that might seem, until we have drilled down to the bedrock and found the useful number that needs to be embedded in our achievement. The question is: *So what?*

Many people have said to me that it's impossible for them to value their work because they don't work in sales. I disagree. Organisations are complex and many processes are interlinked. You just have to recognise your part in a key process and follow it through to a logical conclusion, which will end up with you being able to value the impact of your work, in terms of money saved or money earned.

By way of example, what follows is a useful chunk of a real conversation. You can swap the details around to suit your own situation, as the key thing to notice here is the *process* of enquiry. In this example my colleague had made the assumption that because he worked in a supporting function he wouldn't be able to value his achievements and his assumption had locked him into a pattern of thinking that was not helping him to follow a logical process. I decided to help him out by using my gold-plated question to go mining. This is what happened:

"You worked on a new computer programme, Steve. So what?"

"Well Richard, it was designed to improve the quality of our product testing."

"So what was the point of doing that?"

"Um, er, it helped more products to pass through the testing station first time, whereas before they would have been delayed by a day if they failed."

"So what were the 'before and after' numbers?"

"Before the upgrade, 2% of all products failed at the first test and after the upgrade that was down to 1.5%."

"So what is the value of the change?"

"It's only 0.5%… which isn't much."

"That's the overall improvement, but if you look at the change, then the figure is much higher because the failure rate has been reduced by 25%. The question to ask yourself now is: So what was the impact on the business?"

"I don't know, I don't think there is one. I only work in the computer department."

"You're doing yourself a disservice, Steve. Everything has an impact when you follow through the results of the change. So what is the gross profit for each product?"[31]

"About £100 each, I think, and we used to test 400 every day."

"So what you're saying is that every day 2% of 400, which is eight products, would fail, which equates to £800 worth of gross profit. Because you fixed the software the number of failures was reduced to six per day, which means that an extra two passed, worth £200 of gross profit each day?"

"Er… yes."

And now for the big finish:

"So what is so great about £200 a day? I'll tell you. The business was able to sell two more products every day because demand was greater than supply. You have successfully increased output and therefore increased gross profits, by upgrading the computer software, by £50,000 per year. If you wanted to put it in your CV the achievement could look like this: *£50,000 per year of gross profit generated for the iHatstand product, by designing and implementing a software upgrade, which reduced test failures by 25%.*"[32]

"Hmmm, I suppose when you put it like that we did have that impact."

---

[31] Gross profit is income less the cost of production. Net profit is what you're left with after overheads have been removed from gross profit. Overheads tend to include heat and light and rent and salaries of support staff.

[32] Make numbers more impressive by working them out over a year. I generally take five working days x 50 working weeks (lots of organisations have a two-week shut down or holiday period) x unit cost savings or income earned. It's often preferable to talk about profit earned as that is cash you can spend.

"Not *we*. *I* had the impact."

"You're right; I did the work. I designed the software. I made it happen."

"That sounds more assertive and I did put it like that, because *you* did have that impact. The work you did had a knock-on effect and all we're doing here is following the consequences of that work until we reach a business measure."

"I see what you mean. Thank you. I will add that to my CV."

Remember that there is a difference between measuring your achievements and valuing them. The former tells us how big or small they were, whereas the latter tells us what the *impact* was on the organisation. In all organisations there will be budgets that match income, or revenue, with expenditure. Your salary is part of a budget and increasingly, people are being asked to justify their salary. Putting a value to the work you have done effectively says to your next employer that:

"If you pay me a salary I can have a similar impact on your organisation and save you money too."

Don't fret if your salary band is a bit higher than your total achievements, although lower would be preferable, because you're still reducing the cost of hiring you. The thing to remember, which has already been stated, is that many people do not do this, or if they do they tend not to do it very well.

TIPS: Valuing achievements gets you ahead of the competition. If you need any more convincing, there is a great phrase to keep in mind when applying for jobs and meeting people: *Managing directors are only interested in one thing – money.*

SAMPLE ACHIEVEMENTS

In order to help you write your own achievements, here are some samples that you can use to give you a basic framework. Some people like to start each one with a number, others prefer a verb, depending on the context. For CVs you decide which style suits you. These examples have been taken from real CVs:

- ✓ Project-managed the setting up of a new factory, on time and on budget, which involved designing the layout, hiring 20 people and managing a £500,000 budget.

- ✓ Saved £1m per year in helicopter spare parts by organising an improved stocking system, which increased the usable life of each item.

- ✓ Turned a business from loss to profit, by winning 12 new clients, who delivered annual sales worth £750,000.

- ✓ £4.8m contract secured by exceeding customer expectations at launch, by making sure our prototype was 100% defect free.

- ✓ £192,000 of cost savings identified by the use of Lean thinking and then led the Improvement Team to realise the savings.

- ✓ Managed a team of 95 people through a process of office closure and maintained output and quality levels to existing customers.

- ✓ Designed and set up a new clean floor area which reduced product contamination by 78% over a three-month period.

- ✓ Passed a quality audit first time, which involved writing a 200-page manual and training 35 staff.

- ✓ Coached an engineer and helped him to identify £36,000 of raw material savings by multiplying a small daily saving over a whole year.

I've included this last example because coaching is becoming ever more popular and so is finding its way into CVs. The better examples of achievements which mention coaching, mentoring, leading or managing contain a number related to the output of that work. Coaching is great, but difficult to quantify, so it makes sense to put down what happened as a result of your skilful intervention. Also, if we look at the one above about the quality audit, the real achievement there is in *passing it first time*. The writing and training is significant because it was a means to an end, but passing first time is more interesting.

ACES HIGH

Our *aces* are our *very best achievements* which, when we serve them towards an interviewer, slam down just inside the baseline and whizz out of bounds for a clear point to us.

Take a look through your list of achievements and ask yourself if it includes your own *aces* – your best, proudest, most cherished things you have achieved at work, or if relevant to your CV, in leisure and in life.

These aces often become the core of our job hunting activities because they pop up in our CV, when we meet people and when we're being interviewed. However, it's tempting to become bored with them, particularly after you've heard yourself repeating them many times. If you do become afflicted with 'ace repetition syndrome', remember that the person you are talking to hasn't heard them before and is hearing them for the first time. The same thing applies to our CV, cover letters and so on; just because we've become bored with them doesn't mean they are suddenly no good and need to be ripped apart and re-worked.

TIPS: Keep serving your aces. Does a Wimbledon winner grumble when she's photographed holding up her trophy?

* SUMMARY Achievements are essential tools for job hunting. They make us more interesting, more relevant and more employable. They are the essential bedrock of a decent CV, a valuable cover letter and an interesting networking conversation. They are worth taking time and effort to remember, to write out and to polish because they will crop up again and again in our job hunting activities. Whether we are an experienced manager, a fresh graduate, an office worker, a shop assistant or a teacher, we will have reached targets, worked hard, made a difference and improved things around us. I have never met anyone who does not have at least two achievements that he can talk about with confidence, but I have met many people who lack the confidence to be proud of what they have done in their work or in their leisure time.

We can all be proud of what we have achieved and we can value the significant outputs of our lives. We're good people, we have a right to be here and we are as good as the next person, no matter what his job title is or the size of his car or the number of holidays he takes each year. Value your life, be proud and be successful. And keep serving your aces.

4.3 THE BIG 5: CV

READABLE, MEMORABLE, RELEVANT

In this chapter we will look at CV tips, building blocks and sample CVs. However, because we are concerned with the job hunting *process*, a CV is also relevant to future interviews because what you say in it is going to have an impact on the questions which you might be asked and the interesting stories which you are going to tell.

Please remember that it is *your* CV. The comments and points of guidance given below are based on my first-hand experience of supporting people to find work, change careers and get ahead in the job hunting game in the UK. If you wish to disagree, or test out your own style, or adapt things to suit your needs then please do so. It will be you at the interview, not me, so you need to be comfortable that your CV reflects you and your work. Good CVs are always a work in progress and they are always being updated as you think of new things to add, or take out, as you refine and polish it for each different job that you apply.

CV is an abbreviation of *curriculum vitae*, which is cumbersome to keep writing so we'll continue to use CV. If you want to impress people then you might be interested to know that *curriculum vitae* is Latin for 'course of life'.[33]

THE IMPORTANCE OF A CV

I have heard some people say that in today's modern, trusting world you don't need a CV because that's an old-fashioned way to communicate information. They're wrong. You do. A CV is a must-have because it:

1. Provides you with a summary of your work-based activity over the last few years.

2. Provides you with a summary of your work-based activity over the last few years, that you can *give* to someone else.

---

[33] Thank you Wikipedia.

A CV is in essence a job hunting version of a marketing flyer. People often carry a one or two-page leaflet in their briefcases about their products, or services and when job hunting it pays to carry your CV, so that you can hand it over when you meet someone who expresses an interest. As an exercise in dredging things out from our memory banks and dumping them into our current awareness, where they are much more useful in a job hunting context, writing a CV is a practical and useful thing to do as part of our job hunting activities.

> Despite the world of email and the Internet and iEverything, people do still value a piece of paper. If you have a hard copy of your CV on a person's desk in front of him, it demands attention and is much harder to ignore than an email, which can be deleted with one click. *Paper has presence.*

CV TIPS

In order to get a sense of what makes for a good CV, here are my favourite tips, culled from my experience of reading hundreds of CVs. Think of this as a checklist and tick off each item after you have compiled your CV. You would be surprised at how many people make silly mistakes, which can spoil their chances of being invited to interviews, so it's worth being methodical here.

1. **Two pages maximum length.** You can say all that you need to say in two pages. If your CV runs onto three pages you need to get it down to two; people often don't read to the end of the second page anyway, so that third page is a complete waste of paper. One way of maximising the space available is to look for what's known as *widows* and *orphans* which are single words at the end of a sentence that take up a whole line. If you have any, you can remove them by rephrasing your sentence, so that space isn't used up unnecessarily.

2. **Tell the truth.** This is a painfully simple point. If you tell a lie, however much you justify it to yourself, you run the risk of achieving what's known as a *technical knockout*, a TKO. This means that you can face summary dismissal in the future, if you have signed an employment contract containing a clause which makes it clear that falsehoods and fabrications in your original application count as gross misconduct. Even if your employer has not given you a written contract to sign, you will tend to be bound by their general employment handbook, or by the answers you gave at the interview. (The exceptions to this are covered by legislation preventing discrimination on the grounds of age, gender, race and so on.) I once had a 15-minute argument with a course delegate who wanted to lie on her CV and wanted me to agree to it. It was only after 12 of her fellow delegates politely shouted her down that she realised what a fool she had nearly become. Either tell the truth or say nothing.

3. **Leave out interview-specific information.** The job of your CV is to get you to an interview and because it can't speak and answer questions it has to be a model of precision and clarity. This means it makes sense to leave out information that is best handled verbally and which you can talk about at interview. This includes the reason for leaving your last employment, your salary expectations[34] and any health issues that you may have. These are all best handled when you're face to face with an interviewer.

4. **Clear summary of yourself.** Clarity and relevance are essential. If you're applying for a job as a marketing assistant, for example, it helps to have the word 'marketing' in the first line of your profile. It links you to the job, which is a selling point. There's no point in having an opening line that talks about you being a 'successful Quality Manager' if you're applying for a Marketing Manager's role. People do send in these CVs and then get demoralised when they've posted 1,000 and wondered why they've not had any feedback. If I

---

[34] If you're applying to a job advertised by a recruitment agency and they have quoted a salary range then it's worth putting your salary expectations (or previous salary) in your cover letter to establish that you are a suitably experienced person for that role.

go fishing and spend all day with a hook in the water with the wrong bait on it, should I be surprised if I don't catch any fish?

5. **Put your name on both pages in the footer, in case the pages become separated.** This is common sense as CVs might be printed out or the staple removed for your CV to be photocopied. An odd un-named second page is like a pair of pants left behind in the changing rooms at the end of Saturday afternoon football. Unloved and unclaimed, it will soon be thrown away.

6. **Avoid clichés.** Don't use them because they look bland and unimaginative. Classic clichés to avoid include: *blue-sky thinking, thinking out of the box, strategic thinking, entrepreneur, pushing the envelope and base-lining.*[35]

7. **Don't have a section on key skills.** Giving people the opportunity to *infer* our key skills from our achievements is a stronger selling style than *telling* them our key skills by listing them out. Once you've read 200 CVs that *all* talk about excellent communication skills, good time management, great problem solving skills and wonderful leadership, it's easy to see how quickly these statements lose their currency and soak up valuable space, without adding any value. We can let our key achievements do the talking for us instead.

8. **Include achievements and state how you did them.**[36] Increasingly, people want to hire people who can actually demonstrate some practical application, which means that your CV needs to be dripping in cut-glass achievements. In order to make them stand out it is useful to state the methods or tools used to get results. This makes them tiny little stories of success and you can build on them at interview. If you're wondering what to say about your achievements then go back to the previous chapter, which is all about the little devils.

9. **Use numbers.** Eight out of 10 cats who expressed a preference preferred a CV with numbers in it. Numbers are easy to remember and make your case for you.

---

[35] Many people claim to be an entrepreneur, without much evidence to back it up, so it's losing its value as a differentiator.
[36] We will talk about achievements in a lot more detail in a moment.

Saying that you 'improved the business' that you 'saved some money' that you 'have good experience' is bland and pointless. Saying that 'you increased sales by 20%' that you 'saved £10,000 a year' or that you 'have 15 years' experience' suddenly becomes much more interesting and memorable and I would want to know the story behind how you saved that money.

10. **Include a *range* of achievements.** A colleague of mine is a personnel director at a large food-processing company and she sees lots of CVs for people applying for management jobs. Many of them talk about their technical achievements and few of them mention people-related achievements and yet almost all of them mention somewhere that they think 'people are the best resource in the business' or that 'they are great with people'. These are two tired clichés that should be chopped out of any CV. They are meaningless. If you are a manager then you need to have a range of achievements that *show* how you've *added value* in your job, *improved business*, *developed people* and so on. Talking about people without having any related achievements is a classic lack of congruence and an easy trap to fall into. A good tip is this: If you have the word 'manager' anywhere in the first line of your opening profile, then make sure the last two achievements are people-related. That way you will gain some points and can talk with confidence about your 'people approach' at interview.

11. **Avoid spelling mistakes at all costs.** A useful tip here, as used by copy checkers from the days of hand-set metal characters and sticky, black printer's ink, is to read your CV *backwards*. The eye then focuses on each individual word and you see it as it is. When you read something forwards, you will often assume what the next word is based on the expected sentence construction and will automatically edit out any spelling mistakes as your brain auto-corrects. Going backwards switches off that mechanism.

12. **Tear the first page in half.** Do this, throw the rest away and keep the tatty torn half page. That is as much as most people read, like scanning the headlines in a

newspaper before deciding to read an article in more depth. Look at your torn half page and ask yourself how much useful information does it contain? As a guide it needs to have at least your profile and your first two achievements on it.

13. **Avoid silly fonts and crazy colour.** Your CV should look crisp, clear and business-like. Using an odd font, a crazy headline style, multi-coloured layouts or printing onto coloured paper is a minefield of bad taste and reasons not to be liked. You might think you're standing out, being different and celebrating your individuality, but the probability is that the first person to see your CV will be a personnel assistant with a cautious outlook and you could unwittingly harm your chances by being 'creative'. People tend to lean towards being more conservative and you need to respect this. Even if you're applying for a job in the graphics, media or advertising industries they have already seen all the crazy versions of CVs that you could ever think of. One more crazy CV looks much like the rest. Simple is best, it always has been. If you want to do the job well use thicker paper; 100gsm paper feels much more substantial than 80gsm, or less, and gives an air of quality that will make your CV look and feel different to one that has been printed on cheap and nasty tissue paper.

14. **Use a clear, readable font.** Your CV has to be *read* and using a smaller font to make it all fit onto the page is a very lazy way of presenting it. The size of the actual type varies with different fonts so simply saying 'stick with 12 point type' doesn't necessarily make sense. In my experience a font size of 11 is about the smallest you want to go for. If you do need to use a 10 point font then I would be suspicious that you're not being ruthless enough at editing your CV to keep it free from extra clutter. People also seem to prefer fonts called *sans serif*, which means without little curly bits at the end of individual letters. Compare Arial with Times New Roman and you'll see that the former is more stick like and less fussy, whereas the latter is softer and curlier. In a business setting, people tend to use fonts that are similar to Arial.

15. **Use white space to make your CV easier to read.** A tip is to stick your CV to a wall or a fridge door and then take a couple of steps back so that you can see what it looks like from a distance. Does it look like a blurred mess of black type or is there enough white space between sections so that they stand out? People are drawn to elegant, spacious houses in the same way they're drawn to unfussy, properly laid out CVs. Often, less is more.

16. **Be selective about your interests.** I've read plenty of CVs where the last line on the second page says: *Interests – reading.* Reading what? How often? At interview you can guess what I'm going to ask: "Tell me about the last three books you've read?" I also go for *three* because anyone can read one book, but if you've read three then reading is probably a genuine interest. Think about how your interests add lustre to your CV, by showing off your skills, or talents, or commitment. If you have an interest that adds to your employability then use it, but if in doubt, leave it out.

17. **Ask three friends to read your CV.** What impression do they get when they read it? If their response is lukewarm, that probably means they're trying to be polite and not hurt your feelings. Always ask more than one person because asking three people gives you a broader range of possible likes and dislikes, opinions and concerns.

You might notice that several of these tips relate to the *style* of the CV and not the content. This is because people always see the document first before reading the detail. In that tiny gap of time between first sight and first read they will start to form an opinion about how much they like or dislike it and by extension how much they like or dislike *you*.

It's just the same as looking at books in a bookshop, where your eye is drawn to a shape, or a colour, or a picture and you have a sense of something before you look at the detail.

People *do* judge books by their covers (or they would all have plain brown ones) and people *do* judge a CV by how it looks. The next time you pick up a book, stop and ask yourself what it was that caught your eye.

HOW TO WRITE A RELEVANT OPENING PROFILE

The first bit of your CV is the most important one. It gets read first and can be the decider as to whether you go into the 'keep' or 'bin' piles. Now that you have a long list of achievements and have thought more deeply about the work you have done, you're better equipped to write a usefully *relevant* profile and do something that most people fail miserably to do: Be interesting.

Being interesting involves catching the eye of the reader with some juicy detail that makes them remember you. Classic examples include:

✓ Countries that you've worked in.

✓ Languages which you speak.

✓ Blue chip companies that you've worked for.

✓ Industry specific techniques you've used.

✓ Words that appear in job advertisements.

Compare these two examples, both applying for the role of an operations manager:

CV

Steve Dribble

Mobile: 078787 321654

Email: steve@isabitdullreally.com

Profile

An Operations Manager with a large firm of box manufacturers, who has led a team and worked hard to make improvements. Excellent communication skills, hard worker and committed to making improvements every day.

33 words in the profile

CV

Brian Sizzle

Mobile: 067891 654789

Email: brian@isonfire.com

Profile

A successful Operations Manager with 15 years of carton production experience, used to supplying Ford and BMW. Successfully used Lean techniques to improve quality by 35% and maintain 100% on-time delivery performance.

33 words in the profile

The first example contains nothing but bland words and tired old clichés. I've never read a CV that said 'rubbish at communication and never arrives on time', so saying you have good skills makes you just the same as every other person. We can do much better than that, with a bit of jazz and by dropping in some keywords.

Both profiles have the same number of words in them to make the point that it's not about writing more words, it's about being specific with little details. We can assume that the job advertisement was looking for someone who had Lean experience and was used to managing business performance because these things are mentioned in the profile. If you were reading the two profiles, without seeing the rest of the CV, who at this stage do you think is the more impressive candidate?

People reading CVs often go on to find supporting information to confirm their initial predictions,[37] and because an interesting and catchy opening paragraph can be what our next role rests on, it's worth writing a few versions until you're happy with it.

Our profile needs to be *relevant* to the job we are applying for. If not, we are probably wasting our time, unless we've been asked to apply by the person who is recruiting, or are in the habit of calling the personnel department 'Mummy'. If the company is looking for a blonde-haired, battle-scarred viking, then make sure the first line of your CV mentions some or all of the words blonde-haired, battle-scarred or viking.

Likewise, if you can't be interesting, then don't be surprised if people whom you have never met aren't interested in you. The energy that people give out is absorbed by others and helps them to be energetic in turn. I've worked with people who have earned a reputation for draining the life out of you with their tedious banality and morose attitude. You could see people edging away from them when they started to speak,

---

[37] This effect is called 'halo or horns' and crops up again in the interview section. We tend to make snap decisions about 'like or dislike' and then go and find details to support our initial view.

and unsurprisingly, they really struggled to come across well when they met potential employers.

Everyone has unique combinations of skills, experience and achievements and everyone has the potential to write a great opening paragraph. Your biography sketch, or summary profile, is a tasty digest of who you are, what talents you have and answers the question: *Why should I bother to spend 10 seconds of my life scanning the rest of your CV?* Be interesting here and put something special, or a combination of things, that differentiate you from the other possible candidates.

Your opening profile must be short, pin you to the job you are applying for and contain some juicy snippets of information that make you stand out. Think about three things that define you and make you different. Include industry-specific keywords, brand names you've worked with and countries you've worked in. Never use 'I' and always write in the third person, because that makes your profile easier to read.

PUTTING IT ALL TOGETHER

Now that we have a list of achievements, a great opening profile and a bunch of useful tips to use as a checklist, it's time to write up our CV. On the following pages are two samples taken from real life, which I have tweaked to disguise their origin.

The first example is one of the clearest, easiest to read CVs I've come across for a manager and makes the point that we can fit all of our experience onto two pages and can use a 'less is more approach'. It did take the person who wrote it several attempts to get it just as he wanted and I would point out that this CV *did* get him to a job interview, in a new industry, where he was able to talk about his transferable skills.

As you read it, don't worry about the technical language that appears, just notice that there is a good mix of technical words, useful numbers and 'how I did it' information, which combines to give a sense of the person, his capabilities and his experience.

The second CV is from a younger person who needed to make the best of her limited experience and education and is a good example of how, with some thought, we can all present ourselves in a clear and informative way. Although she doesn't use numbers in the same way as in the first example, she still manages to include interesting detail that is relevant to the people who are looking for that kind of role to be filled.

Read the CVs through once and then consider these questions, putting yourself in the mind of a potential recruiter:

✓ How easy was it to read them, on a scale of 1 to 10 (1 being hard, 10 being easy)?

✓ How much information was there in the first half page?

✓ Which details stood out?

✓ What would you like to find out more about?

✓ What did you like about the layout?

✓ What did the personal interests say about the candidate?

Christopher Mass

27 Uppingham Close, Wells, Suffolk, U2 B52
E: chriscareer@hotdogmail.com T: 079876 512356

PROFILE

An experienced Senior Executive and Lean Process improver, who creates value by managing change. Saved a business from closure. Supplied specialist parts to Ford and Renault.

MAJOR ACHIEVEMENTS

- Turned around heat treatment services business. Restructured processing facility, which increased turnover fourfold and net profits from 5% to 14%, then sold company.

- Implemented ISO9002:1994, ISO9001:2000, Lloyd's Register and Investors In People.

- Negotiated business merger with a larger group to raise capital of £250k.

- Successfully defended automotive product liability claim. Awarded £60k costs.

- CHTA Management Committee negotiation of CCL rebate scheme with HM Revenue & Customs.

- Trained a team of 8 'Lean Champions' and led them as they delivered £120k of improvements over a 12-month period.

EXPERIENCE

Fellowship in Lean Management (FLM) Corndale University 2006

Intensive postgraduate vocational programme designed to develop leadership skills and a working knowledge of improvement tools including: Lean and Six Sigma. Major course achievements:

- Identified available capacity increases of 82% at Stroud Coffee Ltd – OEE/TPM/MRP

- Identified cost savings of £192k pa at Wessex Engineering – 5S/TPM/SMED

- Assessed patient movements through A&E and MAU at Blakeney NHS Trust. Facilitated subsequent Trust meeting which accepted proposals to improve performance of acute medicine.

- Six Sigma Green Belt certificate awarded.

Operations Director Hot Forming (West) Ltd 2005-2006

120 people employed across two shifts, producing specialist components for the automotive industry. Clients included: Renault and Ford.

- Responsible for financial performance and Kaizan continuous improvement.

- Reduced process variation by 4% by introducing Lean thinking, which cut scrap by £20k pa.

- Reduced capital investment by 40% by retrofitting new control systems to existing machinery.

- Cumulative effect of all improvements was net profit up by 75% within 8 months.

Managing Director Bowsprit Metals Ltd 2001-2006

65 people employed across two shifts, producing specialist components for the automotive industry. Clients included: Ford and a range of European tier-two suppliers.

- Invested in £150k vacuum processing equipment.

- De-commissioned acid-dip processing line and refurbished premises.

- Re-positioned business in small batch hot dip and specialist treatment market.

- Reduced customer base by 35%, which increased margins and grew sales by £220k pa.

- Successfully sold business to Hot Forming (West) Ltd) in 2006.

Production Director Bowsprit Metals Ltd 1996-2001

- Managed the shop floor and had full responsibility for customer services and quality.

- Increased output by £115k pa by installing a new automated degreasing line.

- Built a new QC laboratory and retrofitted enhanced process flow control systems.

- Reduced a bottleneck in the warehouse by changing the shift patterns, which led to 15% more output and reduced the backlog in 4 weeks.

EDUCATION

2006	Corndale University	Fellowship in Lean Management
2005	University of Cawston	PGCert in Process Leadership
1994	Lanchester University	BA (Hons) 2:1 Geography

TRAINING AND AWARDS

2005	Lloyds Register Quality Assurance	Advanced Audit Techniques
2005	Lloyds Register Quality Assurance	Preventative Process Mapping
1995	Northern Bank Small Business Enterprise prize	

Sherry Ingham

The School House
West Coast Road, Haddenham,
Buckinghamshire. BU8 BLE

Mobile: 06543 456798   Email: sherry234@goodcooking.com

PROFILE

An experienced Commis Chef, who has worked in a busy hotel for the last 4 years. Experienced at preparing starters, sweets and vegetables, has a good attendance record and enjoys all aspects of kitchen and cooking work. Currently attending Westbury City College for NVQ Level 2 City & Guilds in Multi Skills Catering every Monday.

ACHIEVEMENTS

- Learned to prepare and serve a range of sweets, including crème brulée, pavlova and panna cotta.

- Researched and introduced a new short bread dessert, based on Jamie Oliver's recipe.

- Learned to prepare and serve a range of starters, including twice baked cheese soufflé, mushroom crumble, moules à la marinière and pasta smoked salmon with mushrooms cooked in a vodka-cream sauce.

- Started to work on the stove, making for example: chicken stroganoff and tuna steak with citrus butter resting on a bed of roasted tomatoes.

- Assisted with the preparation and service of buffet food and hot dinners for weddings of up to 150 guests.

- Managed the kitchen on my own for breakfast, including setting up the kitchen, cooking breakfasts, cleaning down and setting up for the lunchtime service.

EXPERIENCE

Commis Chef at The Red Flag Restaurant & Hotel, Wykeham Market 2006 to present

A 16th Century, 25-bedroom family run hotel with a 44 cover restaurant and facilities for weddings and other social functions. The kitchen team comprised: chef, second chef and two commis chefs.

Responsibilities included:

- Preparing sweets, starters and vegetables.
- Breakfast preparation and service.
- Running a section as required, for example on sweets.
- End of service clean down.
- Maintaining hygiene standards.
- Assisting with catering for functions.

Commis Chef at The Shannon Arms, Swallowford 2008

A family owned hotel set in the Borrowmere Valley, which had 10 rooms and a small 20 cover restaurant and pub attached. The kitchen team comprised the owner and two second chefs. I worked there for two weeks to gain additional work experience.

Responsibilities included:

- Making fresh brown and white bread each day.
- Assisting in the kitchen for evening service.
- Cooking sweets, including crème brulée and lemon posset.
- Assisting with reception duties and bar work.

QUALIFICATIONS

2009	Westbury College	NVQ Level 2 in Multi Skills Catering (Ends June 2010)
2007	Red Flag Hotel	In-house NVQ Level 2 in Food Hygiene
2006	Red Flag Hotel	Manual Handling course
2006	Red Flag Hotel	First Aid Certificate
2005 – 2006	Middle College	BTEC National Diploma Level 2 in Retailing
2005 – 2006	Middle College	Key Skills in Numeracy, Literacy and ICT

ADDITIONAL INFORMATION

Marathon running and mountain climbing.

Hold a full driving licence.

THE NEED TO DOUBLE CHECK

Once we have written our CV, the very best thing to do is to put it down and go and do something different for at least an hour. This allows us to return to it refreshed and ready to give it another look, because the process of editing and double-checking all the details, the layout and the spelling requires us to be alert and not be blinded by what we have just written. As you look through your CV, remember to be ruthless with the word count and chop out all the unnecessary 'flowery' bits of detail and the really old jobs that don't help you. People tend not to look past 10 to 15 years so feel free to discard early things that are just cluttering up the space and not really adding anything of value.

With education you can choose how much detail to include. You might have noticed that in the first example above there was no mention of secondary education, which isn't really needed, given that the person has a university degree and relevant industry experience. Whilst you might be rightly proud of your school-based qualifications and certificates, they can clutter up a CV if you've left school many years ago. Naturally, if you're new to the job market then it's likely these will be more important in your CV, so be proud and put them all in.

In order to give our CVs a thorough workout, here are my usual questions and comments that I make on a regular basis:

- ✓ Does your profile contain useful 'hooks' to excite interest in the reader?
- ✓ Do your Aces feature in your major achievements?
- ✓ Have you asked 'so what?' for each of your achievements?
- ✓ Where is the footer with your name on it?

✓ Why have you taken up so much space with your name and address? (Remember the first half page counts most.)

✓ Have you *really* spell-checked it?

✓ Look again at your layout; the indents for paragraphs are not consistent.

✓ Good work! It was worth all the effort, wasn't it?

✱ SUMMARY Writing a good CV can be hard work and it can take several attempts to hone it to a sharp edge, ready to cut through the competition and get us to an interview. The effort is worth it, though, because a surprising amount of people don't produce memorable, readable and relevant CVs and trust to luck to find a job in a crowded and competitive market place. Given that a CV is a piece of *our* work, and is the first piece of work we show to a potential employer, it pays to make sure we have all the right details, in the right order and set out in a neat and tidy manner.

Finally, we need to be happy with our CV for one reason: It has our name at the top.

HOW TO GRAB ATTENTION

The job of a cover letter is to get the person opening our envelope, or email, to read our CV, which in turn will impress them into inviting us for an interview. It's like the starter we order in a restaurant that wakes up our taste buds and makes us salivate for the main course, which we're now looking forward to even more.

If it's a cold-call letter, which means we've sent it on a speculative basis, then it's our way of saying, 'Hello here I am, you need me,' to the person reading it. If it's been sent to apply for a specific role, we need to make sure it ties us to that role from the outset, and if we are emailing job applications then we can treat our email as a sort of cover letter, rather than attaching one with our CV. This is because people don't have the time to open lots of things and will generally ignore our letter and jump straight to our CV, which means we've wasted an opportunity to impress them.

GREAT LETTER WRITING

The secret to a great letter is to use a structured four-paragraph approach, to make sure you have a neat and tidy layout and to double-check spellings. The four-paragraph approach helps you avoid writing too much and makes the information easy for the reader to pick out at a glance. The four paragraphs include:

1. Introduction and application for the job.
2. Specific achievements or information that is relevant to the advertised job requirements.
3. Two or three additional details and mention how much we enjoy this work. Here is an ideal opportunity to be *enthusiastic*.
4. Next steps and ending.

For a cold-call letter the four paragraph approach can be kept, however the paragraphs have a slightly different content:

1. Introduce yourself and say something of interest to them that will grab their attention.

2. Explain why you are writing to them in particular.

3. Showcase your achievements and pick your three Aces which will impress them the most and which *are relevant to their business needs.*

4. Thank them for reading your letter and let them know you will contact them to follow up.

People need to be sold to, which means we need to put in extra effort to build a relationship with them and to establish a rapport and a level of trust. Therefore, if you've said you will call then you need to do so. If they haven't read your letter yet, it doesn't matter; you can still refer to it and make the assumption that as you're talking they're reaching across the desk and hastily sliding it out of the envelope. Often people will be prepared to give someone 10 to 20 minutes for a short introductory meeting because that is an easy amount of time to schedule. Taking the time and effort to go and see them shows commitment and even if they don't have an opportunity for you today (the chances are that they won't) it is likely that your details will be held on file and that you will have made a good impression for the future.

Formal layout styles have changed over the years and people are less fussy than they used to be, but it still pays to make things look neat, smart and orderly. In the UK some people still tut-tut if the opening and ending are not grammatically correct and the rule is: You do not have two *Ss* in one letter. This means that:

✓ If you start with *Dear <u>Sir</u>* (or Madam) you end with *Yours <u>faithfully</u>*.

✓ If you start with *Dear <u>Mr</u> Jones* (or Mrs Jones) you end with *Yours sincerely*.

Once you have a good letter you can keep it as a template and simply tweak it slightly for each job you apply. It helps to keep copies of each letter we send out together with a copy of the CV in case we need to refer back to it at a later date.

> **TIPS:** Good letters include numbers and juicy details and it is perfectly acceptable to copy in an Ace or two from your CV. Repetition between a letter and a CV is perfectly acceptable, because the letter is a digest, a sample of the main course.

SAMPLE LETTERS

The samples shown below have been used to give people a good indication of what to write and how to structure a letter. They are based on real-life examples and the details have been tweaked to make them anonymous. In the same way that a CV is *our* piece of work, a letter is also something we have total control over and gives a recruiter information about our attention to detail and our ability to write succinctly.

In the examples, the use of *numbers* helps to make the letters more memorable and the four-paragraph approach allows us enough space to say just enough to be useful, without drowning the reader in details.

Philip O'Dellfia
The Larches
Fish Hill
LX1 UXB

15th July 2010

The Personnel Manager
Corner Office
A Really Big Catering Company
London

Dear Sir/Madam,

I am writing to apply for the position of Front of House Manager, as advertised recently in the Good Food Gazette, July 2007.

I have three years experience of managing all aspects of a busy restaurant, which seats 40 people and specialises in serving stone-cooked pizza. I successfully managed a team of four waiters, a sommelier and the bar staff of three and was responsible for planning shifts, hiring staff and banking the takings at the end of the day.

In addition to this I have a Higher Diploma in catering management and achieved a Distinction, as a result of producing a marketing project which helped a local café to increase its turnover by £6,000 per annum. This was achieved by introducing toasted sandwiches to its range of products and by opening early in order to sell these to the breakfast trade. I find restaurant work exciting and rewarding and enjoy the hard work and the satisfaction of providing customers with a high quality dining experience.

Attached is a copy of my CV and I would be delighted to have the opportunity to discuss my application further with you. Thank you for your consideration and I look forward to hearing from you.

Yours faithfully,

(Leave about five lines to fit your signature in here)

Philip O'Dellfia

Enc. (This means 'enclosed' and tells the reader there is something included with your letter)

(Just because you have some spare space here doesn't mean you have to fill it. Less is more)

Cynthia Sunnatti
14 Grove Road
East Grinch
Manchester
C3P ODX

15th July 2010

Trevor Bone
Managing Director
Stake Out Consultants Ltd
Perth Street
Edinburgh

Dear Mr Bone,

I am writing to introduce myself to you. I am an experienced Business Consultant, who has delivered over £650,000 of improved profit performance to my clients in the last two years.

I am now looking for my next role as a Consultant and am interested in broadening my experience with your company. This is because you specialise in numerical analysis, which is a key part of my skill set and something which I find interesting and rewarding.

Over the last 10 years I have worked successfully as a Consultant in the UK, France and the USA and my clients have included the NHS, the Civil Service and Primary People Ltd. During this time, key achievements have included:

- Winning a contract worth £850,000 for my company to deliver analysis to the gas industry, by successfully completing a two-day scoping project.

- Designing a process improvement system which saved £200,000 per annum, by using a 'hot switch facility' to reduce in-line delays.

- Convincing the board of Hamill Office Systems to stop the implementation of the Guru2000 accounts package and to buy bigger servers instead, which saved them £160,000.

Thank you for your consideration and I have attached my CV for your interest. I will contact you in the next few days to discuss my letter and would be delighted to have the chance to meet with you to introduce myself in person.

Yours sincerely,

Cynthia Sunnatti

Enc.

The samples can be adapted to match our exact needs and if we only have two achievements, then use those and don't spoil them with a weak third one. If in doubt, always go for a less-is-more approach, where simplicity and clarity will have more benefit to the reader over a letter which is so full of detail and complexity that it is struggling to fit on the page.

✳ SUMMARY A good cover letter is the key that unlocks the potential of our CV. Write a cover letter for each specific opportunity you are applying because if you print off 100 and use exactly the same one each time, they will tend to look mass produced and impersonal.

Check spellings and use bullet points to make the layout easy to read. Be proud of your achievements and use numbers and keywords to grab interest. When you are finished, take a step back, look at your letter and ask yourself:

If this was an appetiser in a restaurant, would I want to eat it or ignore it?

4.5 THE BIG 5: MINUTE TO WIN IT

BUILDING CONFIDENCE

Knowing exactly what to say can be a testing and confusing experience when the pressure is on and we have to perform. At the back of our minds, when job hunting, we're probably concerned about putting food on the table, paying the bills and are generally apprehensive about the future. These feelings and anxieties are perfectly normal and just make us regular human beings. However, because we need to be able to talk to people it makes sense to have some words prepared and ready in our heads.

This is what a *Minute To Win It* is; a pre-prepared introduction about *us* that we can use to get a conversation started.[38] Because we are in control, if we mention something interesting then it's likely that people will ask us a follow up question and look for more detail. We can predict this, which means that we can have a more comfortable start to an interview, than wandering in and wondering what we might be asked about. We know that we're being interesting and when we get asked about *that juicy fact*, we will have the answer *already* prepared.

The previous chapters were concerned with written tools, whereas this one is about a spoken tool. Although a *Minute To Win It* crops up when we're networking, it's actually a more widely used tool than people might at first appreciate, because it can be used when we meet people for the first time, to introduce ourselves at interviews, when socialising at business events, or careers fairs, or simply to have some words in our heads that we can use to get ourselves talking without having to think too hard about what we're saying. This is a good way to build confidence, because having words already prepared means that we concentrate on smiling, making eye contact and engaging the other person.

---

[38] Some people might also refer to them as a 60-Second Sell, a 60-Second Summary or a One-Minute Pitch.

MAKING A GREAT START

People tend to begin an interview, or a conversation, with a 'settler', which is a question designed to be easy to answer and to help us to relax into the environment and feel comfortable. They also do this because in many cases they haven't read our CV, or at best might have given it a quick scan in the corridor on the way to the interview room, so they want to get us talking as a way to get us settled down *and* to give them time to surreptitiously read our CV. After the usual preambles and introductions the classic question to settle people is:

Tell me about yourself.

This is the trigger for us to deploy our carefully rehearsed minute and our conversation is then off to a flying start. If you're in any doubt about the value of a *Minute To Win It*, consider these two opening statements, taken from real life and see if you can guess which candidate went on to have a great interview:

Candidate 1: "Hello Richard, nice to meet you. Tell you something about myself? Well, I've worked in the food industry for 10 years and in my last role I saved £4,000 in a month by using morning meetings to maintain awareness of waste items…"

Candidate 2: "Hello Richard, nice to meet you. Tell you something about myself? Erm, well, I was born in the lovely county of Suffolk and I went to school there and I had a pet dog and I liked cycling…"

The second example demonstrates what I call the 'Short-trousers syndrome' where the candidate panics and begins by painting a picture of his childhood, starting with him walking to school in short trousers. The big danger with this is that after five minutes of helpless jabbering he will have said nothing of value and will simply be plucking out random facts about himself in an effort to fill the space. This is roughly the social equivalent of watching a small boat sinking. You know what the outcome will be, but you watch with morbid fascination as it slips beneath the swell, one plank at a time.

THE VALUE OF 60 SECONDS

A minute is a long period of time. As an exercise, stop reading, stand up and remain silent for one minute, without looking at any clocks. Sit down when you think a minute is up and then check to see how accurate you were. I've noticed that people tend to under-estimate a minute and sit down too early.[39] How well did you do?

A minute is essentially a comfortable length of time to listen for. People often feel good when they're talking so they tend to want to natter on and on, which is boring to listen to. By talking for a minute we give people just enough information to hold their attention for a comfortable length of time and then we give them an opportunity to respond.

PRACTICE

In reality, it doesn't matter if we feel comfortable talking for 40 seconds or 70 seconds, because nobody will be timing us, but if you find it a struggle to *stop* talking, then practise with any watch which has a second hand. Put the watch in front of you and keep glancing at it to remind you that a minute tends to chug round the dial fairly slowly.

Practise making your point and then stopping. The trick for some people I've worked with is to ask a question at the end, as that 'throws' the conversation back to the other person and provides them with a neat ending to their minute. If you ever watch gymnasts they get points for their delicate dismounts and elegant landings and if they land in a heap, miss their footing or simply fall off, they lose marks and can miss out on a medal. Sample questions to ask include:

---

[39] When I have asked groups to do this as an exercise and I've kept time, people have (wrongly) accused me of cheating; they were so convinced that their internal clock was right.

✓ So that's a bit about me, perhaps you could tell me something about yourself?

✓ So, that's me, an experienced and enthusiastic shop assistant; what would you like to know more about?

✓ So that's a potted history of the last 10 years; did that answer your question?

✓ So that's me and I really enjoyed my time at university. What else would you like to know?

When I attended regular meetings at a networking organisation we had a bell that chimed to tell people when their minute was up, which was incredibly nerve-wrecking to begin with as you would be in full flight and then *ding*, the noise would barge in on your senses and you would crash back to earth and silence, like a game bird felled by a hail of pellets from a 12-bore shotgun. However, with practice it was possible to hone my timing and to finish with a couple of seconds to spare, or even to include a lengthy pause in the middle, to let a key point sink in and to enjoy being in control. Every time I was asked how I managed to get such great timing I would reply: *Practice*. Three times the night before, twice in my head during the drive to the meeting and once more, under my breath, before my turn came. There was no mystery to it, or particular skill; I went from a very nervous beginner to a very experienced professional through practice.

EXAMPLES

At normal talking speed we can get through about 150 to 200 words in a minute, although if we pace ourselves at bullet-train speed we could cram in 300 or more. Whatever your natural talking speed is, and the rule here tends to be the slower the better, a minute is plenty of time for us to get out the useful information which we want the other person to have.

Given that interviews and business meetings are different in terms of tone and content it can be worth having several *Minute To Win It* options, that we can use to suit the situation. To illustrate how they look and feel, there are two examples below. However, instead of simply reading them in silence, it's more fun to read them out loud to see how they sound and how it feels talking in a structured way:

EXAMPLE FOR A JOB INTERVIEW

Short introduction (10 seconds)	Okay, well as you can see from my CV I'm an experienced lorry driver and I've spent the last 10 years on the west coast route supplying the Asco supermarket chain.
Quick sketch of your background experience (20 seconds)	I'm licensed to drive all types of HGVs[40] and I also have a licence to operate fork lift trucks, so am able to off-load products if a client needs help. I've also worked as a team leader and I'm used to arranging shift patterns and organising service schedules for the fleet.
Tell a story that will hook their interest (20 seconds)	One of the things I really like about the job is building relationships with clients and when working with Catering Demons I built up such a good relationship with the head chef of a small restaurant, called the Poison Ivy, that she recommended us to a friend, which generated £45,000 of new business.
Summarise and be enthusiastic (10 seconds)	So, that's me, an experienced driver and I'm really interested in this job as your depot manager because it builds on my experience. I've managed people before and I really enjoy working closely with clients.

---

[40] Heavy Good Vehicles; it's okay to include some industry or job specific language, especially if they're common words which the interviewer will know.

Here's a quick quiz for you:

1. What was the name of the restaurant?

2. How much was the new client worth?

3. What does this person really like doing?

EXAMPLE FOR A NETWORKING TYPE MEETING, OR A JOB HUNTING CLUB

Short introduction with an interesting hook (10 seconds)	Good morning everyone and my name is Peter, Peter Piper: I'm a computer software specialist and when you see a banana, think of me!
Quick sketch of your background experience (20 seconds)	I've been working with computers for five years and during that time I've written programmes and managed projects for specific clients, as part of a large consultancy team. Computer software is an interesting field to be in and I've focused on working in the process industry, with the likes of Asco Supermarkets, Picnic Prepared Foods and Tyler's Toffees.
Tell a memorable story that explains your earlier hook (20 seconds)	Why bananas? Well, one of my achievements when I worked for Peck Services was to design and deliver a new computer programme that managed stock levels of fruit and vegetables for the green grocer industry, to an accuracy of 99.9%. This means that if you've recently bought a bunch of bananas, or a pound of potatoes, then it's likely that my software will have controlled their despatch from the wholesaler.
Ask for something specific and repeat your name (10 seconds)	I'm keen to stay working with computers and I'm looking for a project manager role in any large organisation which has a warehouse that needs controlling. So that's me: Peter Piper, the man who moves bananas.

This example has been drawn from my real-life experience and contains a number of specific points to consider:

1. **Be memorable.** This means sharing a fact or a story that people are likely to remember outside of the meeting.

2. **Names build rapport.** Mention brand names, companies and details that help people to connect with you. If I've shopped at the Asco supermarket and you've worked for them, then a tiny connection is built between us.

3. **Stories are interesting.** We tend to grow up with stories and so find them easy to listen to. They also contain information about our qualities which the other person can infer from the stories.

4. **Be specific.** It's easier to remember someone if they ask us for something precise, because our brains tend to move from the specific to the general and being too all-encompassing just means that people remember a mush and we can lose out. For example, asking for 'something nice' for your birthday is more likely to end up in disappointment than if you ask for 'anything by Cartier'.

When we're in a job interview our task is to link ourselves to the role. When we're talking to people more generally, our task is to be memorable. Saying things to be memorable might make you feel a bit uncomfortable at first, particularly if you're not used to selling yourself. And that's fine. Talk about things which you feel safe discussing, which are everyday items and which people are likely to interact with after the meeting and so associate your name with. Without naming the particular brands, I've met:

✓ A person who has his initials on the computer chip at the heart of a leading MP3 player.

✓ A lady who arranged a world conference for a leading computer manufacturer.

✓ A man who tuned the interior of a luxury make of cars to make the stereo system sound like a concert hall.

✓ A lady who saved a pathology lab, in a well-known hospital, from closure.

✓ A lady who worked in Africa supporting small businesses.

✓ A man who set up the machinery that makes a leading brand of ice cream in the UK.

✓ A man who roasts all the coffee for a well-known chain of coffee shops.

Being memorable can last a lifetime and I can still remember, from my childhood, that the father of one of my best friends had invented the dimples on the top of a popular biscuit which stopped the chocolate covering from sliding off. These particular biscuits are still in production and whenever I see one in a shop, I often think of him.

HOW TO CONSTRUCT A 'MINUTE TO WIN IT'

One way to construct a *Minute To Win It* is to write it out along the lines of the examples above. The advantage of doing this is that you will end up with a coherent and flowing set of paragraphs that can be read out with verve and confidence. The disadvantage of this approach is that you will end up with a coherent and flowing set of paragraphs which you need to remember. Many people, including myself, have failed to deliver a *Minute To Win It* once they are deprived of their notes and have to remember whole sentences, which under pressure can become elusive little worms, wriggling cheekily out of our conscious mind, just when we need them the most.

An alternative method of construction is to think of *eight keywords* that can be used to wrap sentences around. Both of the examples above could be boiled down to a list of keywords, which are much easier to remember. If we forget one or two of them in the moment, we still have five or six words left to keep us going and it's a much easier task when under pressure to think of single words than to recall a 150-word piece of prose. The other advantage is that you can swap around the order you talk about them to suit the occasion, whereas written and memorised paragraphs tend to be set in stone and often sound very machine-like when repeated.

We can begin putting together our list of keywords by first answering these questions:

1. How do you introduce yourself at parties or business gatherings?
2. What products, brand names or companies have you worked with?
3. Which achievements are particularly relevant to securing your next role?
4. What numbers feature in your Aces?
5. If you could only look for one job, what would it be?

Then, having answered these, we can extract keywords and put them in either a vertical list or on a circular clock face. This is because different people prefer to work in different ways and for me I find that the clock face approach helps me to go round in a sequence. It's a personal preference and you can choose the method which works the best for you.

EXAMPLE LISTS FOR PETER PIPER

VERTICAL LIST

1. Software
2. 5 years
3. Bananas
4. Programmer
5. Asco/Picnic
6. Fruit
7. 99.9%
8. Warehouse

CLOCK FACE

2. Detail
   • Programmer
   • Asco/Picnic

3. Story
   • Fruit
   • 99.9%

4. Summary
   (Repeat name)
   • Warehouse

1. Intro (Name)
   • Software
   • 5 years
   • Bananas

Start at 9 o'clock
and go round
clockwise

TOP TIPS

A *Minute To Win It* is not something to be feared. With practice and repetition we can all make ours sound natural, interesting and relevant. If we miss out a bit because of nerves, then nobody minds, because they're not timing us. To make us at least 99.9% successful, like Peter Piper, here are my favourite tips for success:

✓ Always repeat your name at the start, as people might not hear the first couple of syllables of what you're saying.

✓ Never read out a telephone number, because people generally struggle to remember a sequence longer than seven numbers.

✓ If your memorable hook makes you laugh, then laugh with your audience.

✓ Get to the end and then ask the other person
  a question.

✓ Write the keywords on your notepad, so that you
  can glance at it to jog your memory if you need to in
  the moment.

✓ If you start to get bored with your keywords then tell
  a new story for variety, but remember the other person
  hasn't heard any of them before.

✓ If you make a mistake or forget a bit, don't worry, just
  keep going.

✓ Practise to make it sound natural and flowing and not
  stilted or contrived.

✴ SUMMARY *A Minute To Win It* is a useful part of our toolkit
and once learned can be used at a moment's notice. With
thoughtful preparation and plenty of practice, we can craft a really
useful 60 seconds that will enable us to speak with confidence in a
range of situations.

If I had to pick out just one tip for success then I would suggest
writing down the keywords on your notepad so that in the moment you
can refer to your notes because, as we've said before, life doesn't have
to be a memory test.

MAKING CALLS THE EASY WAY

Making telephone calls as part of our job hunting activity is something that people often talk about and yet, in my experience, is so rarely done because it falls into the black hole called 'selling', which non-sales professionals often find awkward, embarrassing or just downright scary. We might spend all afternoon on the telephone to our chums, chatting about the cricket or gossiping about the latest celebrity antics, but once we're faced with the prospect of calling a person we don't know, then we can find all sorts of other things to occupy our time. Anything but make that call.

When we're job hunting, we need to telephone people that we have sent speculative CVs to and we need to telephone people to ask for application forms or to follow up on interviews or networking conversations. Talking to someone you already know is relatively easy, but the bit that I used to find really hard was making *cold* calls.

Before we make any calls, we need to be clear that people don't know us, therefore they cannot reject us as individuals worthy of love and respect. Whatever happens during the call we remain *okay* and all of our skills and talent remains intact. This point has already been made earlier in this book, but it is a fundamental part of being successful: People are responding to what they see and hear in the moment and their judgement might be wrong, flawed or misguided. If they really got to know us they might like us, but time pressures don't always allow this.

To get round the feelings of nervousness we can use a template to plan the conversation. This is what we mean by a 'telephone pro-forma'; a standard form of words that we can use, a bit like a script. The advantage for us is that we can do our quality thinking and preparation in relative calm and then when the pressure mounts our words are there to support us. It's the same principle as with the *Minute To Win It*, just tailored for telephone calls.

USEFUL TECHNIQUE

Good telephone technique is a learned skill and the key points that can make a substantial difference to our performance are detailed on the following page, in the form of common mistakes and their antidotes:

1. **Holding the telephone away from your mouth.** The microphone tends to have a limited range, so sit with your elbow tucked in close to your body.

2. **Not introducing yourself.** If people don't know who you are then they might get suspicious, a bit like a sales woman starting the conversation with "Hello, I'm *not* ringing you to sell you anything..." Always start with a friendly greeting.

3. **Not repeating your name.** The first two seconds of each call are lost while the other person 'switches on' their ears, so at least repeat your first name, or spell out your name, in the way people might say "Claire, with an i."

4. **Not asking if the person can take your call.** Always ask: 'Do you have a couple of minutes?' If they have no time now, then ask, 'When would be appropriate?'

5. **Not smiling down the phone.** It takes 26 muscles to smile and 62 to frown. Smiling lifts your tone and increases your 'warmth'.

6. **Not giving signs that you are actively listening.** You need to say 'mmm' or 'uh, huh' or 'okay', otherwise they might think the line has gone dead.

7. **Assuming the other person has heard you and understands you.** Ask checking questions as you cannot see their body language and repeat key details to ensure you both heard the same thing!

8. **Not being precise in what you are saying.** Telephone calls tire people quickly so avoid waffle. Two minutes of telephone time can feel like ten minutes of face-to-face time.

TELEPHONE EXERCISE

To help make use of these tips and learning points, you can have fun by considering these questions in the box:

COLD CALLING PRO-FORMA

A. Refer to the list of poor techniques – which ones do you do?

B. What things irritate you when people telephone you?

C. Do you ever rehearse an important call, either with a colleague or by jotting down some notes?

D. What three things will you do differently next time you make a telephone call?

1

2

3

A pro-forma is a standard form that we can print off whenever we need it. I used to carry a spare copy in my briefcase, so that I could stop and make calls on the way back from client meetings. At first I relied on the pro-forma quite heavily to give me the confidence to pick up the telephone and then, after I had made about 20 calls, I gradually found I didn't need it. I even forgot that there was a copy in my briefcase. Here's an updated example of the pro-forma which I used to call people after I had sent them a speculative CV; it's been written to be spoken out loud and I've included some variations on what to say, so that we sound more natural from call to call:

Sample Telephone Call Pro-Forma 'Script'

Name of Contact:	Company:
Letter posted on:	Speculative role:

Note: The purpose of my call is only to find a time to meet for 10 to 20 minutes so that we can chat about them and their company and start to build some rapport. That's all I want to achieve today.

Hello there, is that _____ ? Good morning/good afternoon.

My name is Richard, Richard Maun and...

I'm calling to follow up on my letter that I posted to you last week...

... regarding your article in the _____ newspaper.

Or   after I was given your name by_____

Or   after we met at_____

Do you have a minute to talk?

YES	WHAT FOR?	NO, NOT RIGHT NOW
Okay, thank you. Do you have the letter to hand? (1) Yes Well as you can see I'm looking for my next role and I'm really interested to talk with you about how I could help you with _____ and _____. Ideally I would like to come and meet with you for 10 to 20 minutes so we can chat about it further. Would you have time this week? (If yes, then pick a day and ask if before/after lunch is better)	Well I'm currently looking for my next role and having read your article in the _____ newspaper I thought you might be interested in my skills as a _____ to help with your _____. So, I was calling to find a convenient time when we could meet up, just for 10 to 20 minutes, to talk more about it. Would you have some time this week on Thursday at all? (1) Yes, Okay. Thank you, would your preference be for before lunch or towards the end of the day? (time and date is arranged)	Okay, when would be a goo time to call you back; befor lunch or towards the end of the day?_____ (This is called a forced clos because it gives the other person little chance to say no; it assumes they will take your call, you just have to agree the time.) Thank you for your time an I'll call back then. Goodbye.

f no, ask which day next week would be convenient)	(2) No	NO, GO AWAY
2) No	Okay, fair enough, which day next week would be more convenient for you?	Okay, thank you for your time and please feel free to keep my letter on file.
kay, that's alright. wrote to introduce myself as m looking for my next role nd as I'm an experienced _____ I was keen to talk o you about how I might be f help to you. What I would ke to do is find 10 minutes f your time when we can neet up face to face, so you nd out more about how I can elp you to...	What time would be best for you? _____	Goodbye.
Would you have 10 minutes his week?		
see above for continuation)		

ould I please have your mobile number or email address in case I need to contact you on the ay, if I get delayed?
mail:_____
Mobile:_____
hank you very much for your time and I look forward to meeting you then.

end an email confirmation to say: Thank you for your time today and I look forward to seeing ou on _____.

HOW TO PRACTISE

An easy way to practise is to call a couple of friends and work through your pro-forma several times. A variation on this is *not* to use a telephone, but to sit back-to-back with one of your supporters and practise. Because you're deprived of eye contact this set-up mimics a telephone conversation and you can stop and start, swap roles and generally explore and experiment more easily than if you're on the telephone. And it's a fun thing to do, which for me is always a good way to learn.

However you choose to practise, people do tend to perform better after they have had an opportunity to work in a safe environment to build up their confidence. In my experience, the more calls I made the easier it became. By making several calls back-to-back and starting with the opportunity that seemed the most remote, (and therefore one I didn't mind mucking up quite so much), I found that by the time I had made six calls one after another I was full of energy and ready to talk to the person in the company that I really wanted to go and work for.

Naturally there were times when I was told to go away and I can remember talking to one personal assistant five times before I decided I was not going to get anywhere with that particular company. That's okay; I kept my smile intact and just crossed them off my campaign list.

TIPS: There are more telephone tips in the chapter about Campaign Management in the section 'Follow Up'.

✳ SUMMARY Cold calling can be one of the hardest things to get started with, so give yourself an easy target to reach, such as to have made five practice calls in the first two weeks of your job hunting activity. Use a pro-forma to give yourself a good process by having a script to follow and you might be surprised at how quickly you develop your skills and your confidence. If you want to get ahead of the competition then being able to follow up on speculative letters or emails is an important skill to have and building in practice time and setting achievable targets is a worthwhile part of your campaign activity.

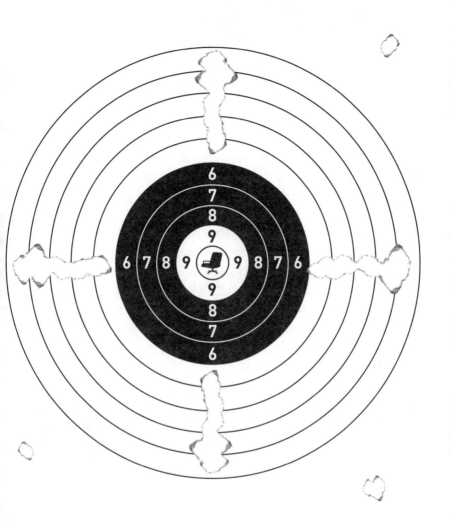

Section 5
SECRET NO. 2
NETWORKING

HOW TO FIND OPPORTUNITIES

Secret No.2 in our job hunting guide is all about a word which we have already encountered, albeit in passing. We're talking about: Networking. The reason why it's a secret is because people seem to make the mistake of putting networking into a business context and thinking that it only applies if you're trying to sell commodities or services and that to go networking you have to be in business. If we shift our focus round a few degrees then we realise that we *are* in business; we're in the job hunting business and we're selling our skills and talents. This means that networking is very much something that we need to do, and we need to do it because that's where lots of jobs are hiding, like tiny fish floating quietly amongst a coral reef to escape marauding sharks. Jobs *are* there, once we know how to spot them and how to gain access to them, and the key is networking.

Networking comes in two parts:

✓ Building a wide range of contacts.

✓ Getting our message out, so people know how they can help us.

This chapter looks at networking, how it can help people and how to build a network. The following chapter is concerned with holding conversations and getting our message across effectively.

The big plus with networking is that it can *increase* our chances of not only finding a job, but also of changing industry, or of staying in a similar industry and changing roles, perhaps from operations to sales or from administration to technical support. Networking can open us up to a hidden world that cannot be found in newspapers or on notice boards. For example, I worked as a consultant for a company which adamantly refused to consider hiring a technical expert to help and stubbornly insisted that I put together a training package for the whole business. My hunch was that a more cost-efficient approach would be to hire an expert and give him an opportunity to demonstrate improvements on a more localised level. Having convinced the company executives that they could have either option, I sent them the CV of a colleague who was looking for work and they asked to meet him. After meeting him, they dropped all notion of a group training plan and hired him within a fortnight. Once they had met him, they realised he was a great fit for them and was just the kind of person they had been looking for all along. From his perspective, it was networking which got him the job, because without it he would never have known that the opportunity existed.

TIPS: Networking is a powerful force for good when we're job hunting and the surprising thing is how little networking people really do. For example, who knows you're looking for work? Your family? Your friends? In my experience, people tell their partner and their best friend and then forget to tell anyone else.

NETWORKS VS NETWORKING

A network is a group of people who are linked in some way, whereas *networking* is an activity aimed at creating tangible opportunities for us by establishing *and* making use of named contacts. Networking is more than 'just talking to people'. To be successful we need:

✓ **Diligence.** To ensure options are considered and contacts slowly accumulated.

✓ **Patience.** It takes time to talk to people, and although we could automate the process this can look like an Internet-spamming activity, which is a quick way to get people annoyed with us.

✓ **Hard work.** We need to drive to meetings, take time on the telephone, update our listings on Internet sites and respond to emails and enquiries from contacts. This requires sustained effort. To use a cliché: You only get out what you put in.

THE NUMERICAL CASE FOR NETWORKING

The following model explains exactly why we need to make networking one of our core activities, and when I show it to colleagues, many of them realise the need to raise their game and put more effort into getting out and meeting people:

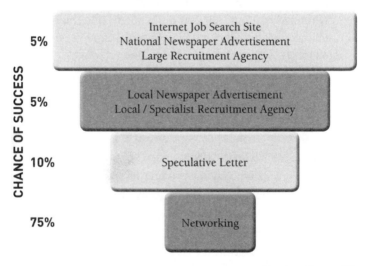

THE CLAYTON PYRAMID[41]

QUANTITY OF PEOPLE APPLYING FOR A PARTICULAR ROLE

CHANCE OF SUCCESS

5% — Internet Job Search Site / National Newspaper Advertisement / Large Recruitment Agency

5% — Local Newspaper Advertisement / Local / Specialist Recruitment Agency

10% — Speculative Letter

75% — Networking

Random Events 5%

---

[41] Named after my colleague Richard Clayton, who was the first person to draw it out, based on his knowledge and experience of sales techniques and the recruitment industry.

The model clearly shows how sharp the drop-off rate is between people applying for obvious jobs at the top, and those who put real effort into networking, at the bottom. There is also a drop-off rate to networking activities as people make a big, impressive start and then fall into the trap of doing apparently 'more productive work' instead of getting out and about. In practice, this means that sending out 20 easy job applications can feel more productive than emailing two contacts to say 'hello'. However, the truth is that, over time, the latter is probably more likely to bring real results. A networking phrase that made *me* take notice and get out of the house was:

Nobody ever got hired by sitting at home with a laptop.

Networking gets us in front of real people who know other real people, and as the following stories illustrate, networking is a great way to use our time.

PEOPLE TRUST PEOPLE

The reason for networking being so powerful is because of the *Third Party Approach* where instead of having to sell directly to a 'cold' contact we are 'warmed up' by someone introducing us when we're not around, which is often known as a 'warm referral'. A personal introduction carries weight because people tend to trust the judgement of friends and colleagues they know well. A friend of mine secured a job ahead of 400 cold applicants because he happened to be friendly with a recruitment agent who, whilst having lunch with the client, mentioned my friend 'in passing' as part of their conversation (knowing that he was a good candidate for the job). The client then interviewed him before seeing any of the other candidates and offered him the job. Had he been in the pile with the others, he would never have been singled out for favourable treatment.

To give us hope that we too can do well, here are three more stories of real-life networking successes:

1. **James' Story.** James had a poor experience working for an owner-managed company and wanted to move into a large blue-chip organisation and forge a corporate career, to take him into senior management. Realising that his industry was suffering a decline and that jobs were scarce, he made a list of everyone he knew and systematically called, emailed or met up with them. Without his knowing it, one of his friends was a business coach to a managing director. When the managing director talked about needing to change his management structure and bring in some new expertise, she mentioned James to him and emailed his CV across. James was subsequently invited in for a discussion and offered a job, which he happily accepted. The managing director didn't interview anyone else. He didn't need to.

2. **Joe's Story.** This story made me laugh. Joe was talking to a group of friends about how he had secured his shiny new job in retail when he paused and said, smiling, "You know guys, I sent out 112 application letters, went to three first interviews and two second interviews and none of that made any difference. I found this job through networking."

3. **Rachael's Story.** This shows how networking can springboard people across a large geographic area. Rachael lived in the north of the country and mentioned to a friend that she was looking for consultancy work. Coincidentally, that friend had learned from the manager of a clinical department in a large hospital in the south, that she needed someone to work as a consultant on a project. Rachael's friend called the manager, recommended Rachael and explained that she was prepared to relocate for a period of time and came highly recommended. With some of the manager's practical concerns answered, the two met up and Rachael was awarded a significant consultancy

contract for an opportunity that previously she had no idea existed and would never have found out about.

HOW TO BUILD A NETWORK

This is easy to do. First grab a sheet of paper and scribble on it the following categories, randomly across the page (to avoid getting stuck in constrained thinking patterns):

- ✓ Family
- ✓ Friends
- ✓ Neighbours
- ✓ Leisure groups
- ✓ Address book
- ✓ Ex-colleagues
- ✓ Your supporters group
- ✓ Recruitment agencies
- ✓ Directors/senior managers you know
- ✓ People who already have the job you want
- ✓ Your partner's address book[42]
- ✓ Contacts on Internet networking sites
- ✓ Local networking clubs

Then systematically write down the name of *everyone* you know who fits into each category. Write down everyone, even if you intend to cross them off later, because they might jog your memory about someone else. We need to have as many names as possible because we don't know who will respond positively to our networking activities. If you've ever used Facebook you've probably found that some people like to chat and others don't. Networking is the same, and to begin with, we don't know who the chatty people are going to be.

---

[42] A good way to be reminded of all the family and friends you've overlooked.

Once you have a long list of contacts, contact each one of them personally, either by telephone or by email. Let them know that you're job hunting, what *specifically* you are looking for and end by asking the classic gold-plated networking question:

Who might you know who could help me?

TIPS: When networking we never ask someone directly for a job, because if he can't help then he'll just feel embarrassed and it could sour our relationship with him. If he does have a job, he will tell us anyway. The purpose of contacting many people is to find more people to talk to because:

A friend of my friend might know my next boss.

Perhaps set a target of 200 people to contact directly in the first month of your job hunting activity. By 'directly' I mean *individual* telephone calls or emails and not mass-mail outs to groups, which can look too much like spam to be of any use. People prefer a personal touch. This group of 200 people might know 50 people each, on average, which means that at the end of that month we've increased the size of our networking footprint to around 1,000 people.

MAINTENANCE IS NEEDED

If you've ever watched a nature programme about birds, you will invariably see some tiny warbler sorting out its nest, replacing twigs and making sure the nest functions properly and has no egg-sized holes in the base. Similarly, our network needs to be tended to. Internet websites need new information from us to keep our profile up to date. We can tell people if we have any news, such as interviews booked, or if we've joined a group and we can send fresh emails to keep our contacts informed of our progress.

We can also say 'hello' to people because that keeps our name in their minds. We don't have to keep asking for things, just be polite and friendly and enquire after them.

As a check question here: How many people in your network have you emailed today, just saying 'hello' to them? A curious fact is that most people do this once a year without fail; at Christmas we send out cards, letters and messages to our family and friends. So, in some ways all we're doing is repeating this on a more regular basis.

Generally, it's quite acceptable to contact someone once a week, or more, if you know them very well, or once every three to four weeks if they're less well known to you. The more conversations you have, the more active your network will be and the more you will have increased your chances of finding a job.

✱ SUMMARY Networking is the smart way to get around. It can feel like it's taking a large effort for apparently small rewards, but it's like the farmer sowing seeds and watering them. Once the seeds grow into crops that can be harvested, then all his work has been worthwhile. Networking works in the same way and it's increasingly being used to avoid the mass of competitors stampeding towards obvious advertised jobs, and to build relationships which deliver real opportunities.

If we get into the habit of asking people whom they might know, we can create new opportunities for ourselves. Networking should be a central part of our campaign activity and we can set ourselves targets to make sure we keep putting in the effort. When we network, we dramatically increase our chances of finding a job, because many of the good ones are hiding just out of our sight.

5.2 DELIVERING OUR MESSAGE

HOW TO TALK TO PEOPLE

A network can only help us if the people in it know that we are actively looking for something and what that something is. This means that we need to decide on our core message and keep reminding people what it is, so that it remains alive to them. When we're job hunting, our core message is likely to be something like, "I'm looking for a job as a surveyor; would you know who can help me?" This is precise and easy to remember, and more useful than: "I'm looking for a job, can you help me?" Being vague might feel like we're increasing our options, but the paradox is that in reality it's decreasing them because people tend to ignore general comments. This is why advertising campaigns tend to focus on *one* clear feature, because the message is stronger and can be reinforced through repetition.

WHAT IS OUR MESSAGE?

This simple question is easily overlooked. What is it that we are asking for? More contacts? Information? To find people in a specific industry? To ask for internship opportunities or to gain work experience? To look for office space? To find work locally as a baker?

In our campaign we identified three horses which we can race and this approach is useful for general job hunting activities. However, we may need to refine it to one horse at a time when networking so that people hear just one clear continuous message and don't become confused. Experiment by asking for one thing only for one month and see what happens. If the response is poor, change the message and ask for something else for a month. Our energy and enthusiasm will generally dictate what we really want to do, so *follow your energy* and let that be your guide.

EFFECTIVE COMMUNICATIONS

To communicate effectively we need to combine both listening and selling skills, because people will not want to pay any attention to us if we don't listen to them. Listening attentively means acknowledging the other person when he is speaking, with nods and smiles and by saying 'uh huh' and so on. Selling ourselves effectively means using our *Minute To Win It* to make sure we tell people our key points, remembering to keep to 60 seconds and to finish by asking the other person a question.

ELEVATOR SPEECH

It can help to have what's known as an 'Elevator Speech', which is sometimes referred to as a Seven-Second-Sell. This is based on the premise that it takes about seven seconds for a lift to move between floors and when you're in there standing next to an important-looking person, you have exactly seven seconds to introduce yourself and get a conversation started. Some networking clubs have an informal coffee-and-chat phase at the beginning to welcome people to the event and this is another occasion to use a quick pitch.

When we're reducing our *Minute To Win It* to a brisk sound bite we need to be memorable, because that's the bait which is going to hook us into a conversation. The way to achieve this is to choose three facts about us in our working life and to write a short 10-word sentence for each one. When we have three, we can choose the one we like best, or mix and match them to see which gets the best reaction from people. They might sound something like this, as you're shaking hands and introducing yourself:

- ✓ "Hi, I'm Helen and I used to make paperback books."
- ✓ "Hello, my name's Lucy and I teach children to play the piano."

✓ "Good morning, I'm Debbie and I've just returned from Poland."

✓ "Hiya, my name's Sarah, I'm a health and safety specialist who likes to lunch!"

In one short sentence we need to grab attention and this can be achieved by being witty or by mentioning one detail that invites the other person to ask you a question, such as:

✓ "How many books?"

✓ "I used to play the piano. What grade do you teach to?"

✓ "What were you doing in Poland?"

✓ "I like lunching too; where's your favourite place to go?"

Being memorable is a great way to differentiate ourselves and our products from a sea of competitors. However, avoid being rude, lewd or revealing something embarrassing about yourself from when you were a child. I once went to a networking event where a builder was asked to tell everyone present something about himself that we didn't already know about and caught in a pressured moment, he snapped back:

"I used to wet the bed. Is that what you mean?"

He was certainly memorable after that.

MINUTE TO WIN IT

Now that we have assembled this as part of our toolkit, we can use it in our networking conversations when we are introduced and the other person invites us to *tell him about ourselves*. The trick to being successful is to make it sound natural by talking at our usual pace, and not to look up and stare at the ceiling, trying to recall the lengthy introduction we prepared. We can smile at the other person and skip through our minute without fear of criticism because he wouldn't have heard it before and would not know which bits we've changed in the moment.

NETWORKING CONVERSATIONS

Whenever we are in a room with people it pays to observe the Three-Feet Rule, which means talking to someone if they are standing that close to us. This is because when our own sense of personal space overlaps with that of another person we both know it and then we have a choice: Either to stand quietly in an uncomfortable silence or to make the first move and say hello. I used to find this difficult to do until I learned some simple tips to help me get a conversation started. Here's an example of a networking conversation to illustrate how it can be constructed out of basic building blocks, which can serve us well as we expand our networking horizons. The scene is a networking buffet in a hotel somewhere near you. Some of the text has been underlined to highlight the kind of questions and techniques we can prepare in advance:

Jackie:	Hi there, my name's <u>Jackie, Jackie Annory</u>. (shaking hands)
William:	Please to meet you Jackie, I'm William, William Ahbong. <u>What do you do</u>?
Jackie:	Well during the day I'm a hairdresser and by night I teach tango. <u>Here's my card</u>.
William:	<u>Thank you; it's very colourful</u>!
Jackie:	Well, colouring hair is my speciality. What about you?
William:	I'm an accountant and I've just moved into this area from Ireland. (He hands over his card)
Jackie:	Thank you and I see that you're CIMA qualified?[43]
William:	Yes, it was hard work, but worth it in the end.

---

[43] CIMA is the Chartered Institute of Management Accountants.

Jackie:	<u>So, what brings you here today?</u>
William:	Simple really, I'm looking to find a finance manager's role with a large company and as I'm new to the area I'm keen to meet people and make some friends. <u>How about you?</u>
Jackie:	I've just started my business so I'm looking to find people who can give me advice.
William:	(Laughing) <u>I could help you</u> with your book keeping to help you get started.
Jackie:	(Smiling) Thanks William, I might take you up on your offer. Right, <u>I need to check my messages</u> so I'll catch up with you later.
William:	Okay, <u>nice to meet you</u>.
Jackie:	You too, bye.
William:	<u>Goodbye</u>.

A conversation needs to flow to be successful and by learning useful questions and set-piece introductions, we can discreetly nudge the chatter along to a friendly and successful conclusion. The example above has been written to demonstrate the following points:

1. Repeat your name when introducing yourself.

2. Look at the other person's card when they give it to you and make a comment, instead of stuffing it casually in a pocket. This makes you look interested in them.

3. Ask questions to keep the conversation moving.

4. Tell people what you're looking for or ask for what you need.

5. Offer things if you can; you never know where it could lead to.

6. Use a polite form of words to bring the conversation to a close. These include things like:

✓ I'm just going to check my emails…

✓ I need the bathroom, so will catch up with you later…

✓ I'm off to get another cup of tea, nice to meet you (smiling)…

✓ Oh, I can see someone I said I would meet, nice talking to you…

✓ Thank you for your time (shaking hands), I really need to be going now…

As long as you smile and are sincere, people don't mind. Knowing how to stop a conversation is helpful, because when we're networking we need to keep moving and avoid getting stuck in one space for too long.

THE TWO-PART STARTER

This is a great way to get a conversation started.

Firstly you ask someone:

✓ Have you been busy today/yesterday? They will answer either yes or no.

Secondly you can ask them an open question to follow up, such as:

✓ (If they say: Yes) What *does* a busy day look like for you?

✓ (If they say: No) What *would* a busy day tend to involve?

The *closed* question at the start forces them to answer in a predictable and confined way, which allows us to follow up with a prepared *open* question, designed to make it easy for them to divulge information about themselves. We can then ask more follow up questions and before we realise it, we've had a successful conversation. Don't worry if it feels like you're doing all the asking, because if they're talking they will tend to feel good about themselves and enjoy your company.

You can soon send them a follow up email and arrange to meet for a second time, where you can do more of the talking.

INTER-NET-WORKING

The world wide wonder web is a good source of contacts because it's full of people who want to have conversations. Whilst many of my colleagues baulk at the thought of spending their days writing to strangers, I've put some effort into doing just that and have found that with a bit of thought it can bring tangible rewards, such as speaking engagements, consultancy work and people I can buy services from.

> **TIPS:** The essential point to remember is not to make your pitch too soon, because nothing stops a conversation quicker than 'buy me'. Instead, have fun building a network of local people, share views, ask questions and generally just pass the time. 'Not selling' in the short term can be the best strategy for longer-term sales success.

I've found that, for example, Twitter[44] can be useful, particularly when you're part of a group who have a shared interest. In my case I've found that what works best is being connected to people who are *local*, because we all have our location in common to provide a point of reference and different things to talk about to keep the chatter interesting. Sometimes I send out a message linked to my website/blog[45] (using Twitter or Hootsuite to shorten the link) which invites people to visit and to look at something specific. Other times I'm just having friendly chats with people, or responding to their questions or requests. By spending half an hour each day on this form of networking, I've generated *hundreds of free visits* to my sites and marketed myself to people whom I wouldn't otherwise know.

---

[44] My user name is @RichardMaun and you're welcome to follow me, if you would like to.
[45] www.richardmaun.com

Remember though, what doesn't work very well is shouting Buy-Buy-Buy at people. I've noticed which messages I respond to and which I really dislike, and use this to guide my own activities.

If you belong to several different Internet groups, such as LinkedIn and Facebook, think carefully before you send exactly the same message to each of them. I made the mistake of sending messages from my mobile telephone, which were automatically forwarded to each group, and when I subsequently visited the sites myself they seemed to jar with the conversations we had had before. I deactivated the service and made sure that the tone and content of each message was tailored to suit each community, because it can sound odd talking like a business professional to your closest friends and vice versa.

By having friendly, chatty little Internet conversations, people get to know us and we them. Trust and rapport starts to build up and then we can gently tell people what we're looking for and invite them to help us.

> **TIPS:** You don't need a website either to achieve this because you can send links back to your LinkedIn page and people will go and read it. All you need is access to the Internet. The rest is free. It just requires our time and diligence to bring to life.

* SUMMARY Holding productive networking conversations is a learnable skill. If we build a good process of learning-practising-polishing, we can have great conversations with a wide range of people and get our message out and about. Everyone can choose to become proficient at networking and to recognise that once we have a job, we often use all these skills anyway when meeting colleagues and clients and building good working relationships with them. Being successful can be easy to achieve and the secrets of success are: To ask questions in order to engage people in conversation, to be memorable and to ask for specific things. Pause for a moment and ask yourself: What is my message? How many people have heard it recently?

Finally, remember that people in your network are just that – people. Treat them with warmth and respect and courtesy and be interested in them, because the more you're interested in them, the more they will be interested in you.

Section 6
SELF-AWARENESS

DEALING WITH OUR DEMONS

Looking for a job is undeniably stressful and is not an activity that many of us would willingly choose to do. If jobs were, like babies, delivered by a stork in the morning, then life would be much easier and our stress levels would be much lower. Different people react to stress in particular ways, and because most of the activities related to job hunting put us under a stress-loading, it makes good sense to pause for a while in our job hunting process and think about what we currently tend to do and, most importantly, what we could do *differently*.

We need to become self-aware by bringing into our conscious mind the bumps in the road which we create for ourselves, and the voices which perch in our ear and order us to comply with their whispered wishes. In the way that society has developed the wheelie bin to deal with the rubbish in our lives, we can develop a simple model to deal with the rubbish in our heads. It's called: The Demons Model.

WHO'S IN YOUR HEAD?

We all tend to have a number of people living in our heads, in terms of the memories we carry with us and the voices who talk to us as we go about our daily activities. For example, when I cross the road I can sometimes hear my first school teacher telling me to "stop, look and listen" and although her voice is faint, there is undeniably a voice in there, which I replay when I get to the edge of the pavement. If I'm being a bit dangerous, I can also hear her admonish me "not to cross between parked cars."[46]

Our model here builds on the principle that we have stored memories of other people in our minds; helping us, hindering us and sometimes tripping us up. The Demons Model suggests that for our job hunting activities we each

---

[46] There used to be a road safety campaign in the UK led by a squirrel called Tufty, so for some people, the voice in their heads will be combined with an image of a giant rodent.

have four cheeky little Demons who are generally asleep in our heads, but when we get stressed they climb out of our ears and perch on our shoulders, where they begin to start jabbering at us. The more stressed we get, the louder their voices get, and we might find ourselves listening to one or two of them more than the others. There may be one or two whom we have never heard at all. That doesn't mean they're not there though, it just suggests that we've filtered them out.

FEARS CONSTRAIN US

The reason the Demons have an effect on us is because they play on our fears. Fears that were laid down, like the keel sections of an oak ship, when we were very young. We've all had to make decisions about how best to fit in with the environment around us, and often we really remember the times that didn't go very well. Pause for a moment and think about which strong memories you might have from your early childhood that have shaped your attitudes and the way you do things. Perhaps you had a parent, or a school teacher, or a big brother who suggested that there was a 'good' or a 'bad' way of behaving, of writing, of being tidy, or of completing tasks such as making a cup of tea?

If we take a step back and think about job hunting, there is no logical reason why some people prefer to use the telephone and others don't and why some people are good at preparing for an interview, whilst others do no work at all. People are complex and part of our complexity is due to the deep-seated fears and concerns which we have that constrain us or push us in a certain direction.

The four Demons play to these fears by *exaggerating* the reality of our situation. They know what to say to prick our nerves and make us take note. We might not want to follow what they are saying, but because they're Demons they worry us that if we don't do what they 'suggest' then they're going to get cross and really shout at us. We really don't want that to happen.

Time to meet the four Demons, all perched on our shoulders and squabbling amongst themselves. They each have little beady eyes, thin hook noses and jutting chins and when they smile, they do so with the warmth and glee of someone who's just thrown a wet sticky snowball in your face and doesn't care that you are blinded and have ice up your nose.

However, it would be tempting to think that these Demons are evil; and the surprising thing about them is that they're *not*. They think they're helping us because their cackling comments are aimed at keeping us out of trouble, like four little parents who all think they know best and that their way is the right way to go about things. This is why we tolerate them and let them live in our heads. We have learned that by following their comments we do stay out of trouble, but in doing so we also get *stuck* in patterns of behaviour that aren't helpful.

THE DEMONS MODEL

We might have a preferred demon, or hear bits of what they are all saying from time to time and as our stress load increases their voices get louder. This means that it's likely that they *will* have an impact on us at some point. Please read the following descriptions and ask yourself: Whom do I tend to listen to?

The **Blue** Demon	The **Orange** Demon	The **Green** Demon	The **White** Demon
Too much **thinking**	Too much **playing**	Too much **helping**	Too much **stoicism**

The Blue Demon likes us to do lots of thinking and to get everything right and he thinks the Orange Demon is a thoughtless buffoon. The Blue Demon wears a blue waistcoat, which is immaculate, without a stitch out of place and for him blue is the colour of a clear blue sky, which represents blemish free perfection and deep thinking. The Blue Demon whispers in our ears things like:

- ✓ Did you check it for mistakes?
- ✓ If you send it out and there's a tiny mistake, you will fail.
- ✓ Don't start that yet; you need to think about it some more.
- ✓ Keep polishing your work, because it's never good enough, is it?
- ✓ If you don't start something you can't get it wrong!
- ✓ Check it once, check it twice, check it a hundred times!
- ✓ Anything less than perfection is a disaster.

Job hunting stress: If we listen to the Blue Demon we can find ourselves paralysed by the need to avoid making a mistake. We might check and recheck our CV and not send it out because it isn't good enough yet. We might not start our campaign for fear of getting it wrong, or we might spend so much time rehearsing our *Minute To Win It* that the end result sounds like a robot repeating a set text; we rob it of all nuance and feeling in our desire to repeat it correctly. Our work might become so methodical that our pace slows down to a crawl and if the phone rings with a networking invitation we decline it as we're not ready yet. We might fret over tiny details that to us seem enormous, but to someone else might be insignificant and perhaps we struggle to accept a job because we worry that it isn't the right one and what calamities would happen if we did say yes?

Coping with stress: The Blue Demon exaggerates the penalties for making mistakes. Our natural attention to detail means that we will work to a good standard and don't need the Demon to push us towards perfection. If we spot a tiny error, we can correct it for the next time; the person on the receiving end probably didn't notice it anyway. We can be good at thinking and we can know that if we just keep thinking we won't get a job; we need to do some *doing* as well. If we miss a bit from our *Minute To Win It*, it doesn't matter because the other person is hearing it for the first time and has nothing to compare it against. A great 30 seconds is still better than 60 seconds of waffle. We know that the secret of success is simply to be *good enough*, which in practice means an accuracy of 70% to 80% and not 150%. We can pause our thinking and get on with doing something. *We are in control.*

The Orange Demon likes us to play and have fun. He gets bored easily and thinks the Blue Demon is dull. His waistcoat is a bright orange, which is the colour of sunshine on a warm and carefree day. The Orange Demon likes to rebel and to do things his way and he whispers comments to us like:

- ✓ Have fun first and second and then work third.
- ✓ It's boring, let's stop and play.
- ✓ You don't have to sit here; you can go and have a chat.
- ✓ Rebel and be creative, no need to be dull and boring like everyone else.
- ✓ Don't finish it now, leave a bit for later.
- ✓ Let's get something else started, because that will look productive.
- ✓ If it's not fun then don't do it.

Job hunting stress: If we listen to the Orange Demon we can find it easy to start lots of things but finish none of them, or we might never start anything as we distract ourselves with little diversions and false starts. We might look like we're working hard, but we know that we have half a CV written, half a cover letter and have *nearly* applied to a few jobs. Whenever we sit down to work, our good intentions disappear and we play, or tidy our desk, or email our friends; anything but settle down to what we think is a dull job. We might enjoy lots of networking conversations and being with other people, but if we're not careful we could just end up talking for the sake of it with no real purpose. We might even ignore what's been written in this book, because secretly we feel that it's all a bit boring and we want to liven things up with a multi-coloured CV and the wackiest shirt-and-tie combination we can find.

Coping with stress: The Orange Demon exaggerates our need to have fun and the need to start lots of things. Our natural playfulness means that we can find ways of making it fun and do the work at the same time. Perhaps by having a colourful campaign chart or by telling a witty anecdote in our *Minute To Win It*. We can have some playtime before *and* after writing a professional-looking CV *and* we can take time to spell-check it. If this is beyond us, then we can ask someone else to check it for us. We can plan our time to balance work and fun, and if we work better at certain times of the day then we can set our own timetable to suit us. Given that job hunting is a continuous process we can also know that it's okay to finish something because there's always more work to do. We can *pause* our playing and do something which adds value and we can work quietly when we need to. *We are in control.*

The Green Demon doesn't like it when we do something for ourselves and ignore others in the process. The other Demons think he's a pushover. His waistcoat is a calm green, the colour of comforting grass and growing spring leaves. He hates it when we ignore other people and barks comments at us like:

✓ Don't be selfish!

✓ If you do their work first they'll like you.

✓ You can play when all the work is done.

✓ Don't say no!

✓ Their needs come first and yours come last.

✓ Look, look! They need your help; you sort it out!

✓ Your job is to make them happy!

Job hunting stress: If we listen to the Green Demon then we put other people and their needs before our own. We might say 'yes' when we want to say 'no' and we might secretly feel undervalued and frustrated. When we're job hunting we can cause problems for ourselves if we're at home because we easily agree to help other people and push our job activities back into the evening, after their, more important, work is done. We might say 'yes' to networking events because we don't want to upset other people, even though we might have had a better use of that time. We might even find ourselves accepting a job that we don't want, on the grounds that it's a job and we don't want to appear fussy or *ungrateful*. When it comes to negotiating with an employer we take the first thing that is offered because to ask for more might upset them and we always want to put *other* people first.

Coping with stress: The Green Demon exaggerates our need to help others and to put ourselves second. This can make us feel that we're being sensitive to others' needs, but the reality is that we're being *over-sensitive*. Job hunting is a *job* and requires us to be alert and energised. If we spend the day doing other people's work and then shoe-horning our activities into the evening, not only do we give ourselves less time, but we are more likely to make mistakes through fatigue. We *can* ask people to respect our needs for time and space, because it's *okay* for us to need things as well. We can avoid the social issues of saying a blank 'no' by replacing it with *'not yet'* on the grounds that we would like to find time at some point in the future. The reality is that we are as important as everyone else. We can put ourselves first and follow our ambitions because that does not make us a bad person or a selfish person. *We are in control.*

The White Demon is dressed entirely in white and prefers to sit apart from the other three, who tend to forget he's even there at all. He wears white because it's the colour of a blank canvas and because it fades into the background when compared to the others. The White Demon will often sit on our shoulders all day without moving, and will snarl things like:

- ✓ Keep going.
- ✓ Don't stop for a break.
- ✓ Don't show your feelings, because they make you look weak.
- ✓ Other people respect your strength.
- ✓ Never ask for help; you can do it on your own.
- ✓ There's always more work to do, so keep going.
- ✓ Hide your emotions because people will hire your skills.

Job hunting stress: If we listen to the White Demon we are likely to isolate ourselves and work in a vacuum. We might want to stop for lunch, or to take time off, but we won't because we are conscious that work comes first and we prefer not to talk to people and will only go networking if we're dragged along by a friend. We might want to ask for help, or admit ignorance, or just feel really angry that we lost our job, but instead we bottle up these feelings and park them out of the way. We might have a supporters group, but we won't call them as that would look *feeble* and we can work it out on our own. The result of this is that we can work ourselves to a state of *exhaustion*, because we don't take proper care of ourselves. Another possibility is that one day we may suddenly explode at the weight of all the unresolved feelings pressing down on our shoulders and smash the place up, or take it out on those whom we love the most.

Coping with stress: The White Demon exaggerates the need for us to be seen as a strong person who can cope. However, the problem with 'coping' is that we tend not to address any underlying issues. If we're angry that we've lost a job, we need to find a person to talk to and share these things with, to release some of the pressure. Asking for help is the sign of a *professional* person and not the sign of a weak one. Using our supporters and friends to guide us is a *resourceful* thing to do. If we prefer to work in a quiet space then we can balance that with networking activities and plan our time so that we can do *both*. If we have worked hard, we can stop and have a break and we can celebrate success. Feelings can help us. For example, if we're nervous about an interview we can practise our interview answers with a friend and do a better job on the day. In a storm the rigid trees break first; the flexible ones survive the longest. We *don't* have to be tough all the time. *We are in control.*

DEALING WITH THE DEMONS

The four Demons reveal common ways that people's behaviour becomes exaggerated when they are under stress, and it's likely that all of us will listen to one or more of the Demons at some point. In doing so we overlook the reality of our situation and narrow our field of vision, which hampers our progress. However, we can be clever and use the Demons to our advantage by stripping away the exaggeration and updating our self-awareness with the following positive statements:

✓ **We can choose to be good enough.** Our CVs and cover letters can be written to a high standard and we can do a great job of our *Minute To Win It* and of making great telephone calls.

✓ **We can have fun and meet people.** Job hunting doesn't have to be dull and we can stop and play sometimes. Meeting people can be fun too and we might make some new friends along the way.

✓ **We can have ambitions and needs and can put ourselves before other people.** Job hunting is work and this means we can treat it like having a proper day job, even if we're working from home, where we might be tempted to do household chores first.

✓ **We can feel our feelings.** If we're nervous we can get help at no cost to our personal credibility. If we're fed up with our job hunting work, we can stop for a day and go and do something else to recharge our batteries and to put a smile on our faces.

* SUMMARY The Demons Model is there to help us acknowledge some of the things that can get in the way of successful job hunting. Knowing about campaigns and CVs, for example, is important, but needs to be supplemented by *self-awareness* about ourselves and what we tend to do when we're under stress. A degree of light stress can be helpful in motivating us to achieve our goals, but if it becomes overwhelming then we tend to resort to 'safe' patterns of behaviour which we don't necessarily like, but which we're comfortable with. The Demons Model gives us an opportunity to see our behaviour for what it *really* is, and we can decide to keep the good bits and get rid of the things that get in our way. We can stay safe *and* we can find more productive ways of working; we don't need the Demons to keep tripping us up.

The bonus is that because many people focus only on the technicalities of job hunting, such as CV writing, we can gain an advantage over them. This is because to be *really successful* we need to marry technical skills with good ways of working, so that we can avoid the pitfalls which other people are more likely to fall into.

HOW TO CONNECT WITH PEOPLE

Job hunting involves selling ourselves to new people, and one of the differentiators between success and failure can be how good we are at building rapport with the people we meet. The theme of 'people buy people' is repeated in this book because people often make decisions based on emotions and not based on objective reasoning, even though they often present it as the other way round.

If humans were purely objective beings, there would be no need for brand names and we would buy the jeans, the sunglasses, the car or the wrist watch which did the best job for our budget. However, a quick look around our house, or our wardrobe, will remind us that some of the items are there because of their styling and because of our emotional response to them.

> When we're job hunting, building rapport is an essential way for us to build our brand value and to market ourselves well at an emotional level. We don't have to like doing it, but we do need to recognise that doing it well is an essential skill and one that can get us a job. I've met many people who focus solely on the technicalities of job hunting and ignore the emotional side, so being able to do the following activities well can make us stand out from the crowd.

Therefore, this chapter is written to raise our awareness and give us some handy pointers so that we can sell ourselves effectively when we're face to face with people when networking, during an interview or when making a presentation.

FINDING OUT HOW SPARKLY WE REALLY ARE

Many people I've worked with come across as deeply dull. This might be due to nerves, or a lack of skill, or perhaps because they really are very dull indeed. Whatever the reason, they always come off second at interviews, or when networking, if they happen to be alongside someone who sparkles. We've seen this already with CVs and it's the same when we meet people face to face. In order to do well, we need to ask ourselves the two key questions:

✓ What do I do currently?

✓ What do I need to do differently?

This might require feedback and my suggestion is that you get it from your supporters and your close friends and your partner and children, if you have them. Children see the world as it is and, although their feedback can be devastating, it will be honest and free from the varnish of social politeness. The best way to get feedback is to ask people to complete the following score sheet. *You may photocopy this page if you need to:*

RAPPORT BUILDING FEEDBACK SHEET
How often do I do the following things? (Rate them 0 for 'never' and 10 for 'all the time'. Please circle the number that feels right to you.)

1	Make eye contact	0 - 1 - 2 - 3 - 4 - 5 - 6 - 7 - 8 - 9 - 10
2	Shake hands readily	0 - 1 - 2 - 3 - 4 - 5 - 6 - 7 - 8 - 9 - 10
3	Smile	0 - 1 - 2 - 3 - 4 - 5 - 6 - 7 - 8 - 9 - 10
4	Show active listening (e.g. nodding)	0 - 1 - 2 - 3 - 4 - 5 - 6 - 7 - 8 - 9 - 10
5	Ask questions	0 - 1 - 2 - 3 - 4 - 5 - 6 - 7 - 8 - 9 - 10
6	Vary the tone of my voice	0 - 1 - 2 - 3 - 4 - 5 - 6 - 7 - 8 - 9 - 10
7	Pause	0 - 1 - 2 - 3 - 4 - 5 - 6 - 7 - 8 - 9 - 10
8	Dress appropriately	0 - 1 - 2 - 3 - 4 - 5 - 6 - 7 - 8 - 9 - 10
9	Keep to time (e.g. punctuality)	0 - 1 - 2 - 3 - 4 - 5 - 6 - 7 - 8 - 9 - 10
10	Offer compliments	0 - 1 - 2 - 3 - 4 - 5 - 6 - 7 - 8 - 9 - 10
11	Say please/thank you	0 - 1 - 2 - 3 - 4 - 5 - 6 - 7 - 8 - 9 - 10
12	Use people's names	0 - 1 - 2 - 3 - 4 - 5 - 6 - 7 - 8 - 9 - 10
13	Follow the pace of the other person	0 - 1 - 2 - 3 - 4 - 5 - 6 - 7 - 8 - 9 - 10
14	Sit in a purposeful position (not slumped in a heap) And finally...	0 - 1 - 2 - 3 - 4 - 5 - 6 - 7 - 8 - 9 - 10
15	Notice areas of commonality	0 - 1 - 2 - 3 - 4 - 5 - 6 - 7 - 8 - 9 - 10

Once you have collected scores from at least three people, look at them and see what they tell you. Are there any consistently high or low areas? Are people in agreement? Do the scores match your own perception from other comments you may have had previously?

The score sheet is there to make other people's perceptions clear to us and if we disagree with them that's okay; we just have to remember that *they* could have been interviewing us. If we've scored less than 7 for any item then read the relevant part in the numbered sections below and make a positive decision to do at least one thing differently, because:

> When we meet people we have about *90 seconds* to make a good impression because they will tend to form *90% of their opinions* about us in that time. They will then build on those impressions for the rest of our time together, either building up a positive impression or mining down to a negative one. This is what is often referred to as The 90/90 Rule.

1. MAKE EYE CONTACT

We can be really technically proficient, have written a great CV and yet struggle to get a job if we find it difficult to make eye contact. It won't make it impossible, but it's one of the key indicators of nervousness; people find it disconcerting if our eyes are everywhere, but looking at them. I realise that direct eye contact is considered rude in some cultures, but this book has been written from a UK/European perspective, where eye contact is generally regarded as a fundamental part of building relationships with people.

We can learn a couple of tricks to make it easier to look at others. The first trick is to use something called social gaze. This means focusing on a notional triangle stretching from the outside ends of a person's eyebrows and pointing to the tip of their nose. When we look at someone, we can concentrate our gaze *inside* the triangle and that person will feel we are making eye contact *without* his being stared at. If we're really close then look at the area around the bridge of the nose, or he might wonder why we're scrutinising his eyebrows.

This technique works because people tend not to notice exactly where we're looking and so as long as we're looking in the general area, they feel that we're making eye contact with them. When presenting to a large audience, a variation on this technique is called 'zoning' where we look at a block of people and shift our gaze around to give the effect that we're looking directly at them in turn, even though we're not.

The second technique is to look at someone for a count of three and then to look down at our notepad and make a note or shift our gaze. Doing this is socially acceptable, whereas staring at the ceiling or over their shoulders is not. In our heads, we can look in the 'triangle', count 1-2-3 and then look down and write a single word. We can then look up again and repeat the process. A suggestion is to vary the count and length to between three and six so that it feels natural to the other person.

2. SHAKE HANDS READILY

When I've been to networking meetings I've often been surprised at just how many people don't know how to shake hands or are reluctant to make physical contact. Offering a hand to someone makes you look *assertive* and, when accompanied by a smile and direct eye contact, is a wonderful way of confirming your confidence right from the outset.

However, a good handshake is where you actually grip someone's hand firmly, shake it a couple of times and then *let go*. This might sound blindingly easy to follow, but it's worth practising because you won't know if you:

✗ Have a vice-like grip, which is uncomfortable.

✗ Have a grip like wet lettuce, which is embarrassing.

✗ Have a tendency to grip their fingers, not their hand, which is painful.

Avoid these three pitfalls by practising, because a good handshake is an easy win to achieve.

3. SMILE

They do say 'smile and the world smiles with you, frown and you won't get the job', or something close to that, because people like people who smile, as this portrays a sunny disposition. Overdo it and you could look a bit unhinged, so remember to be natural. A genuine smile requires us to smile with our whole face. If we just flash our teeth, we could look like a fox about to pounce on a cute little bunny.

There are three occasions when a smile is particularly effective:

✓ When we are meeting and greeting people.

✓ When we are telling a story which we're proud of, or using keywords to show our enthusiasm, such as 'great', 'enjoy' and 'really like'.

✓ When we're saying 'thank you' and 'goodbye'.

Practise smiling at yourself in the mirror and practise flicking a smile at people as you go through your day-to-day activities, so you can switch it on at will. Use keywords to trigger it, as suggested above and it will be surprising how often people smile back and automatically begin to think of us as a 'nice person'.

4. SHOW ACTIVE LISTENING

People can't see inside our heads, which thankfully is a good thing, or the world could be a much more intimidating place. This means that they can't see us hearing them, so we need to acknowledge their presence by using listening signals. We've already seen these during the chapter about making telephone calls and here they are again, with one addition:

- ✓ Nod.
- ✓ Say 'uh huh', or 'okay', or 'that's interesting'.
- ✓ Smile.
- ✓ Make a note of a keyword.

I've found that looking down briefly and writing a word is a good way for the other person to feel heard, but you do need to look up quickly and not get stuck scribbling on your notepad. Similarly, if you're fond of playing with a pen it can be really irritating for the other person to hear click-click-click whilst he's talking; put the pen down and stop waving it around.

5. ASK QUESTIONS

If you're not listening you won't know what to ask, so asking questions is a good way to show that you *are* paying attention, which always helps to build a relationship. Closed questions invite a binary yes or no type of response, whereas open questions encourage the other person to share information and to keep talking. They all begin with one of Kipling's 'Six Serving Men': *What* and *why* and *who* and *how* and *where* and *when*.

Ask a couple of questions from time to time to show your interest, but don't bombard the other person in a rapid-fire sequence, because you want to look friendly and not like a member of the secret police.

6. VARY THE TONE OF YOUR VOICE

If-we-talk-in-a-continuous-monotone-we-can-sound-really-really-boring-and-people-will-tend-to-lose-interest-in-what-we-are-saying-and-might-even-fall-asleep-zzzzzz.

We can raise our volume to show interest or lower our tone slightly to indicate thoughtfulness. Either way, it pays to practise and the best way is for us to record ourselves reading out a story from a newspaper. Keep going for at least two minutes and when you listen back to it, pay most attention to the latter half of the recording as when we're fatigued we're more likely to revert to standard voice patterns. We can soon hear if we're monotonous and can then have a second attempt; this time raising and lowering our voice.

If we have a habit of tailing off at the end of sentences, we might come across as a bit disinterested because when our voice drops, it suggests that our thoughts have moved on. If that's the case, then take a deep breath at the start of each sentence so we have a lungful of air to propel us smoothly all the way to the end of our sentence. As a tip here, we can watch a newsreader in action on the television and notice how he controls his breath in order to hold our interest in the story.

7. PAUSE

If we 'machine-gun' people with our views, they will tend to get bored with us. People need time to assimilate what we're saying, so taking a *pause* when we've made our point is a good way to help them follow us as it gives them an opportunity to talk. Generally speaking, people prefer talking to listening, so giving them a chance to join in helps to build rapport with them.

8. DRESS APPROPRIATELY

Often the first thing we notice about people is the way they dress and the way they style their hair. In job hunting circles, the general code is to dress smartly and to dress 'quietly', which means sober, muted colours. Our personality can still peek out, like the sun edging round a grey cloud, but at least we won't have offended people when they sized us up during the long walk across the office to greet them.

As a case in point, I worked with a computer expert who sported a natty gold ring in his left ear. He liked it. I liked it, but I advised him to remove it for interview purposes, in case the interviewer had strong opinions. Although he said he would, in his hurry to make it to the interview, he forgot all about it. When I met up with him the following day, he looked very sheepish:

"How was your interview?" I asked.

"Well, okay-ish," he replied, looking guilty. "The second I sat down he asked why I was wearing an ear-ring and how that wasn't within the dress code for the company."

Unsurprisingly, he had struggled to build a relationship with the interviewer, who had clearly marked him down as a 'dangerous non-conformist' from the first moment they met. He wasn't invited back for a second interview to that particular company and the ear-ring disappeared. It has yet to be seen again.[47]

9. KEEP TO TIME

I was nearly late for a crucial job interview once, having been stuck in traffic during the long drive. When the interviewer asked about my journey and I remarked that I had just squeaked in to reception with seconds to spare, her face fell and, fixing me with an unexpectedly steely stare, she snapped:

"Well Richard, that wouldn't have been a great start to the interview. Would it?"

"No," I gulped, like a naughty school-boy. "You're right."

The opportunity might be lost due to poor time-keeping, particularly if you make no effort to inform the person with whom you're meeting where you are and why you're going to

---

[47] Anything which goes against the norm can be a 'reason not to like'. Although that might grate on us, we have to remind ourselves that we are trying to get a job and not to win any awards for street fashion.

be late. If the interview is more than four hours' drive away, then my tip is to travel the day before and find somewhere to stay close to the venue. Not only does that eliminate the risk of a delay, it can also make you look keen and organised, particularly if a fellow candidate is late.

10. OFFER COMPLIMENTS

When was the last time you paid a friend a compliment? We often take people for granted and yet when someone remarks positively about how we're dressed, or the work we do, then we get a little surge of pride and feel well-disposed towards them.

A consultant friend of mine had to assess the needs of people's business as a precursor to selling them a package of products and he fell into the trap of criticising each owner's business because he was *asked* to point out problems. However, once he realised that the businesses were really like the owners' babies, which they loved – wrinkles and all – he changed his tack. He would find some good things to say and *blend* those with his other observations and he soon noticed that his conversion rate of visits-to-sales increased. By finding things to like and by making a point of sharing them with the owner, he had warmed up the relationship between them, because nobody *really* wants to be told they have an ugly baby.

When we meet people, a good tip is to find things we like and to say so. It doesn't matter how small the things are because if they're meant well they will be taken well, assuming you're not complimenting your host on the great plastic coffee cups that came from the vending machine. There are limits here! Suggestions can include the location of the office, the size of the meeting room, the fact that you felt welcomed by the receptionist, or that you were sent some great directions. Compliment the client on their interesting products, or services, or décor, or professional working environment. If you believe what you say, it will help to build rapport.

11. SMILE AND SAY 'PLEASE' AND 'THANK YOU'

There's an urban myth that when children reach their teenage years they lose the power of speech and simply grunt odd syllables to us to indicate hunger, or a need for clean clothes, or for the bus fare into town. Grunting is *not* a spectacularly good way of communicating and a friendly, smiley 'thank you' is a low-cost way to build rapport with people. Not everyone bothers to do it, but if we do, we radiate warmth and charm because good manners can impress people.

As an example, I can still remember the day we had a busy assessment centre with 20 candidates all milling around. At the end of the day I asked the office manager how she had found the candidates and she singled out one particular person for praise; this person had been the *only* one to say thank you for lunch.

12. USE PEOPLE'S NAMES

I used to have a bad habit, but I've been cured of that now. I used to refer to colleagues at work, rather casually, as 'mate'. I did this until one day a supervisor took me to one side and politely, but firmly, told me that his shift thought I was a poor manager because I didn't know any of their names. This was shocking, because although it was true, I hadn't realised that I had been covering up my lazy ignorance quite so badly. Since then I've used people's names and found that they prefer it.

When I'm meeting someone I write their name *in advance* on the top of my notepad so I can glance at it if I need a prompt. In a networking meeting I might hold his card, to allow me to refer to it if I forget. In general I repeat his name at least three times, so that it begins to get stuck in my conscious mind.

A person's name is part of his or her identity and so by using it we're affirming that we have taken notice of them; this feels good.

13. FOLLOW THE PACE OF THE OTHER PERSON

This is where telephone sales people often get it wrong; they have 30 seconds to get your attention and to pitch their product before the sand runs out of their egg timer and they have to make another call. However, we all work at slightly different speeds; some of us get straight to the point, others like to meander for a while and collect their thoughts as they chat. When we're networking with people it can be tempting to say 'hello', mug them for a business card and then move straight on the next person, which can be productive, but unsatisfying for the people left gasping in our wake.

We can follow the pace of the other person by using these guidelines:

- ✓ Notice when they have tired of greetings and want to talk about more business-related topics.
- ✓ Notice when their eye contact breaks, which is a sign of them losing concentration and means it's time for us to stop, or change the subject, or ask a question.
- ✓ Match their speech patterns so that we're talking at the same speed and volume.
- ✓ If we make a shift and they *don't* follow, then shift back and wait a minute before trying again, such as when offering a card as part of closing the conversation.

Matching speech patterns and subject changes is a subtle way to 'walk in step' with them and helps them to feel comfortable with us.

14. SIT IN A PURPOSEFUL POSITION

I interviewed a young graduate once who sat skewed on his chair, so that his body was facing the window. As a result, he had to turn his head to look at me. This meant that when he wasn't concentrating, he delivered his answers to my questions to the car park and not to me. He looked as if he was too good for the job and although he was probably unaware of this it didn't help him to appear as a friendly character and not as the know-it-all he seemed to think he was.

After much discussion among my colleagues, the consensus we reached is that the best 'starting position' is to sit at a desk with the chair pushed back slightly from it and turned to an angle of about 10°. This means that we're sitting facing the person, but not directly. It enables us to cross our legs, put our hands on our lap and sit comfortably with a straight back. It's hard to cross our legs when they're jammed under a table.

Although we can lean forward when the other person does so, and lean back when they do, to build rapport, it's good to have a starting position to return to. This will help us avoid getting stuck in one position or unconsciously slumping into a heap. When we match or mirror the other person's posture, we signal rapport to them and if they follow our posture changes, it confirms that we're in step. However, if we lean forward and they lean back, then we need to take the hint that we're creating an unwelcome 'bulge' in their personal space. This signals a lack of rapport, and, if it happens, return to the 'starting position' for a while and try again later.

15. NOTICE AREAS OF COMMONALITY

I've kept this one to the end because it's one which can make a lasting difference, but is the least-used technique I've seen. When we meet someone for the first time we're *strangers*. Humans are naturally tribal animals – think about football supporters or how wars get started. We like to find out if the other person we're with fits into our tribe. One way to achieve this is to notice areas that we have in common, because that's a match for one of the groups we're in. When the other person is talking, listen carefully for anything which matches elements of our own life and when the opportunity presents itself, exclaim with a smile:

✓ I do that!

✓ I've been there!

✓ I like that too!

When we do this it sends out a tiny invisible thread that binds us gently with the other person and we cease to be a stranger, because now we both fit into the same group. I mean, if I like red wine and you like red wine then you must be a good person. Or perhaps you like Italian food and that's one of my favourites; we must both be okay sorts of people then.

When we find areas of commonality and notice them, we tend to smile and relax because we fit together in a small way. Of course if we fit together in a big way then we may end up getting married, but that's another story.

✳ SUMMARY Building great rapport gives us the power to bind ourselves to people at an emotional level. It may not guarantee that we get the job, but it can help the other person to overlook some of the gaps in our CV, or to take a chance on us if we have a slightly different background to the one they were looking for. In the example about the graduate who sat looking out of the window, he was more qualified than the other candidate we saw that day, who had earned a degree in a different discipline than the one we were ideally looking for. However, she smiled and was friendly and built a great rapport with myself and my colleague. We offered her the job because we knew that if we had a good rapport, we had a solid base which we could build on and could easily teach her the bits that were missing from her CV. We were right; she was good at her job and great fun to work with.

We need to be self-aware of what we do well already and what we really need to do differently, because if we can get the small details right we can sell ourselves successfully and increase the chances of securing a job.

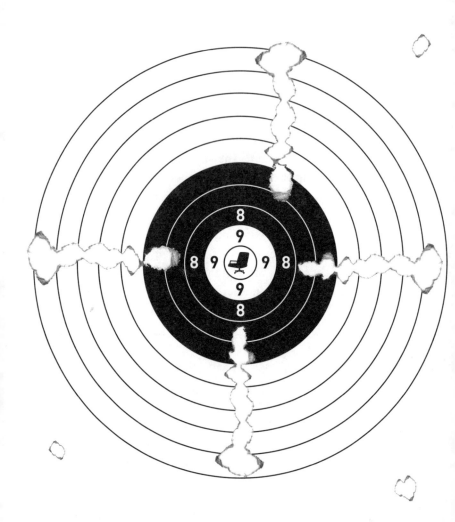

Section 7
INTERVIEW SKILLS

7.1 MANAGING THE PROCESS

ANATOMY OF AN INTERVIEW

The culmination of our job hunting activity is when we get invited to an interview. Because it's a barrier which separates us from our next job, we need to pass it in order to be invited to join the organisation. We have already encountered some of the tools needed to do well at an interview, such as a *Minute To Win It* and rapport building skills. This section builds on these and looks specifically at the major elements which make up a modern interview:

1. The process
2. Questions and answers
3. Presentations
4. Assessment centres
5. Contracting

When is an interview not an interview? Answer: Never. We need to be aware that whenever we are meeting someone who might buy our skills and abilities, we are in a live interview situation, whether it's at a networking event, or talking over the telephone, or meeting with a recruitment agent. Some people try to play tricks by inviting us in for an 'informal chat'. There's no such thing; it's an interview and normal interview practice still applies, because whenever we're selling ourselves we need to keep our guard up and our senses tuned to the reality of the environment.

We will all have different experiences as we go about our job hunting activities, for example we might not have to make a presentation or attend an assessment centre, so please read the chapters which apply to you. However, I would suggest you re-read the chapter from Section 1 about mistakes as well, as it never hurts to learn from those who have gone before us.

THE PURPOSE OF AN INTERVIEW

At a fundamental level, an interview is our chance to sell ourselves to an organisation by demonstrating clearly how *we* can add value to what *they* do. Adding value means that we can help them to solve problems, to continue servicing their customers, or to help them build up or to improve their business. It doesn't matter what level in the organisation we're applying for because everyone has to support the organisation's quality, cost and service goals.

An interview is a conversation; it's not meant to be an interrogation on a hard chair under a spotlight. Like all conversations, both parties start to generate an opinion about the other side and it's okay to have your doubts overturned or, conversely, to feel uncomfortable and to wonder if you want the job. During one interview I asked about holiday entitlement and the owner replied with a sneer:

"You young people don't need holidays; we work hard and play hard, that's our motto."

Although I was the favoured candidate, after this reply *my* motto was: If that's how you treat people, then I don't want to work for you.[48]

The purpose of an interview is for us to meet each other and to make decisions about how we feel, whether we like what we see and whether we can do business together. Our potential employer can judge if we really are as good as we claim to be in our CV. They can test us and prod us and see if they like the results. An interview is in many respects like test-driving a car. You'd be foolish to buy one without doing so. In the same way, an interview reduces the risk for both parties. It helps us to find out if we are a match and enables us to get a sense of what it would be like to work together. If we don't like the way we're being interviewed and we feel that something doesn't feel right, we have choices and we can exercise them, remembering to be polite at all times. We can:

---

[48] I was much younger then, but that's irrelevant really; we all need a break sometimes, whatever we do.

✓ End the interview and ask to leave.

✓ Continue and then write a polite letter afterwards withdrawing our application.

✓ Stop the interview and ask to speak with another manager, particularly if we feel we're being interviewed in a manner which is discriminatory or patently unfair.

In the above example, I chose to continue and politely answered their questions until I was asked if I would like the job, when I smiled and said, "No, thank you." I explained my reasons and we left on good terms. My feeling was that if I felt uncomfortable during an interview, what would it be like to work there? We always have choices and we can always exercise them.

INTERVIEWS ARE PREDICTABLE

Most interviews follow a pattern: A greeting, an introduction to the organisation, some questions about us and our CV, a chance for us to ask questions, a thank you and a goodbye. This means that we can predict what we are likely to be asked about and can prepare our answers accordingly. For example, if you claim to know how to type, or cook, or sell, or drive, or have any specific skill on your CV, *be prepared* to demonstrate it during the interview. If your CV talks about your love of reading books be prepared to talk about at least *three* which you have read. (Anyone can read just one book, but to have read three shows more depth.) If your CV mentions your medals and awards, be prepared to tell the stories about what you did to win them. If your CV mentions that you speak a foreign language then be prepared to speak it at interview. Multi-lingual interviews are more common than people realise and are an easy way to be tripped up.

Many people don't appreciate how predictable an interview can be, so it pays to prepare thoroughly. The next chapter contains a selection of standard interview questions for which we can learn answers. Combine this with being able to talk fluently about the contents of our CV and we've already prepared for about 70% to 80% of the interview time. It can be that easy, and we can help ourselves to do a good job by recognising this fact.

PEOPLE BUY PEOPLE

This has been said before, but it's worth repeating. Interviewers often work hard to remain impartial, even-handed and objective, in order to be fair to many candidates. This is a reasonable and professional way of conducting an interview, but it overlooks one thing: Humans are emotional animals and much of our decision-making is based on deep-down feelings of like or dislike, trust or caution, respect or disgust. People like to hire people who are:

- ✓ Enthusiastic
- ✓ Good learners
- ✓ Smiley
- ✓ Passionate about the job or the industry
- ✓ Hard workers
- ✓ Reliable

All of these attributes can trump a lack of experience, missing qualifications or underdeveloped skills: This is because you can't train 'enthusiasm' or 'flexibility', so if you have them in-built they're worth talking about and are of value to a potential employer.

WARNING

When you're being interviewed, the organisation is on show

too. If the people you meet seem unpleasant, or highly disorganised, or they move your time or date without a decent explanation, you need to ask yourself what that might hold for the future if they aren't able, or can't be bothered, to make a good impression at this stage.

Several years ago, I was interviewed by an owner and his sister for a management job. I wanted to be a manager, and so felt flattered to have been invited to the interview. I ignored the fact that the two of them squabbled for an hour, were inconsistent in their questioning and generally seemed at odds with each other. The sister was pleasant, but her elder brother was clearly a trainee tyrant. However, I persuaded myself that 'things would work out alright' and accepted a job with them. The consequence of my decision was that I had a thoroughly miserable six months as a manager and was eventually sacked on the grounds that I was no good. They were right too; the brother undid all the work I had done and I was powerless to stop him, because I didn't know how to; I had had no training. I learned my lesson, though, and have since walked away from opportunities if I felt uncomfortable with the people sitting in front of me during the interview.

Beware: If it looks wrong, smells wrong and feels wrong, it's likely to be wrong.

THE INTERVIEW PROCESS

People often think the 'interview' is only the time spent answering questions, but in reality it spans a much wider band of time because we're being assessed in some form during all of these stages:

✓ **Acceptance**: Are we polite in our emails?

✓ **Arrival**: Have we turned up at the right time in the right clothes?

✓ **Greeting**: Do we appear friendly and enthusiastic?

✓ **Discussion**: Can we ask and answer questions to a good standard?

✓ **Other activities**: Did we do well at related exercises?

✓ **Summing up**: Are we asking questions that pin us to the job? (See the next chapter)

✓ **Exiting**: Do we remain polite and professional until we're clear of the building, when we can finally relax?

Beware: The UK Foreign Office had a reputation for salting their waiting rooms with dummy candidates who were there to engage real job applicants in conversation, note how they conducted themselves, which newspapers they read and so on. In effect the interview had started the moment the candidate walked through the doors and *not* at the appointed time given on their invitation letter. In my experience the interview really encompasses all the times when we 'touch' the organisation. It's no good being polite on arrival and rude on exit; we need to be consistent.

Knowing that an interview is a process with a beginning, a middle and an end can help us, because if we practise the *whole* process we can do better than the next candidate who has only rehearsed his answers to a couple of obvious questions.

GREETINGS

How we greet people sets the tone for our resulting discussion, so at an interview we want to say 'hello' with warmth and interest. Here are some sample greetings for us to try out, as we smile and shake hands:

✓ Hi [name], thank you for inviting me here today.

✓ Hello [name], it's great to be here and thank you for seeing me today.

✓ Good morning [name] and thank you for the opportunity. I've been looking forward to meeting you today.

ENDINGS

No matter how well the interview has gone we can still pick up points with a warm and sincere ending. Try these options, which we can say with our best smile:

✓ Thank you [name] for your time today, it was good to meet you.

✓ Thank you [name] for the opportunity to talk with you. I'm really interested in this role.

✓ Thank you [name] for seeing me and I look forward to hearing from you next week, as I'm really keen to do this kind of work.

Notice how you want to leave on a high note and reminding them of your enthusiasm and energy always leaves a positive impression as *people tend to remember the last thing they hear.*

RESEARCHING THE ORGANISATION

Many companies expect us to know about them when we arrive, which is not unreasonable if we want to convince them to spend money on us in the form of wages. It always pays to spend some time researching them by:

✓ Reading their website.

✓ Looking up your interviewer on LinkedIn.

✓ Researching related industry subjects and issues by reading appropriate magazines or journals.

✓ Doing a Google search for related press releases and news items.

✓ Talking to people who already work there.

Doing any research in the first place helps to convince people you're interested in them. Knowing what their issues and future plans are enables us to demonstrate to them how we fit in with their ambitions, or how our style matches with their core qualities. Understanding something about our interviewers' background means we can build rapport by making links with them.

Remember that they might do a Google search on us too. What's out there which is embarrassing or controversial? There is a difference between having fun and enjoying ourselves and being offensive or irresponsible. Given that in an interview situation most people are conservative, it might pay to Google yourself and see what comes up and then to have a tidy-up of blogs or website content.

CHOOSING OUR CLOTHES

Different colours have different properties. Red is dominant, which means that it projects itself forwards, whereas green is recessive, which means that it tends to fade into the background. Darker colours convey more authority, whereas lighter colours can imply creativity. Plain shirts can be easier on the eye than crazy colourful ones. Novelty ties and socks are great at parties and pointless at interviews. Jewellery and accessories need to match our clothes, not fight with them.

Therefore, when dressing for an interview it helps to wear *darker* clothes, plain blouses, or shirts and ties, and to have black shoes. Some people still scoff that a person who wears brown shoes with a dark suit is going to be a bit unreliable. This might sound like nonsense, but if you're dressed to look smart and authoritative you're going to make a much better impression than if you wear a clown suit with big floppy shoes. Conformity counts because anything other than a sober and smart appearance could give an interviewer a reason not to like us. We need to let our sparkling personality shine through and not our chunky gold medallion.

DEMONSTRATING PRACTICAL SKILLS

Several years ago I was hiring for a sales role which required the candidate to be able to write reports and build simple spreadsheets on a computer. During the interviews I specifically asked each candidate whether they could do both of these tasks:

"Oh yes," they all replied with unshakeable confidence.

"That's great," I replied with a chuckle, "because I'm going to pause the interview now and give you 20 minutes to write a letter and 20 minutes to compile a spreadsheet on this computer we've already set up."

At this point several candidates went white and started to say that they hadn't had time to prepare, which is a dubious excuse, given they had just claimed they could do the work. I've always been surprised how people tell little lies at interviews, and it's not unusual to ask a candidate to demonstrate his abilities.[49] In the example given, what the candidates didn't know was that I had previously hired a person who couldn't use a computer. He had lied during his interview and we *hadn't* given him a practical test. It took me six months and cost the business £10,000 before we could remove him and re-hire someone else.

If you have practical skills listed on your CV and they have rusted up with under-use, spend a day or two practising them before you go to an interview. It could make all the difference on the day.

PRACTISING THE PROCESS

Practising interviews is a good way to increase our confidence. Even 10 minutes talking to yourself in the car on the way to one is time well spent, because interviews are one of those occasions in life, like weddings and childbirth, where emotions run high. People get nervous, palms begin to sweat and our brains helpfully empty of all useful information,

---

[49] A recent survey suggested that about 30% of all candidates tell a few lies during an interview. However, this requires them to have told the truth to the researcher and they could have been lying again.

like a stream of water gurgling down the plughole after a pleasant bath.

> **TIPS:** The best way to practise our interview skills is to sit with one of our supporters and do a dummy interview, but the trick is to make it as *formal* as possible. I've found that holding it on neutral ground, such as in a hotel, wearing formal business clothes and bringing a copy of our CV and job advertisement makes a big difference. It might be practice, but it's *realistic* and that helps people to perform in a similar way to how they will on the big day. One other key tip: Don't just ramble on for 30 minutes. If either one of you thinks it's going badly, stop, take a deep breath, work out a better response, practise that item specifically and then move on again.

In order to have something to aim for when practising interviews, here is a score sheet you can use (*you may photocopy the page for your own use*). Give your 'interviewer' a copy and ask him to tick or cross the things you do. If you can get most of them right, then you're in great shape and will tend do well at your next interview.

PRACTICE INTERVIEW SCORE SHEET

COMPETENCE	BEHAVIOUR		SCORE *Please circle*	COMMENTS
Initial Impressions	☺ Smile & say thanks ☺ Confident handshake ☺ Tie straight, hair combed ☺ Appropriately dressed ☹ Scruffy clothes ☹ Inappropriate jewellery ☹ No eye contact ☹ Late arrival		4 Very good 3 Acceptable 2 Below standard 1 Serious concerns	
Demeanour	☺ Consistent eye contact ☺ Enthusiastic and interested ☺ Confident voice ☺ Smiles ☹ Poor eye contact ☹ Distant, remote ☹ Quiet or hesitant ☹ Arrogant, dismissive		4 Very good 3 Acceptable 2 Below standard 1 Serious concerns	
Answers	☺ Concise, detailed & relevant ☺ Uses STAR for impact ☺ Can answer follow up questions ☺ Thinks before speaks ☹ Waffles on and on ☹ Poorly prepared ☹ Lack of detail or clarity Doesn't know own CV		4 Very good 3 Acceptable 2 Below standard 1 Serious concerns	
Technical	☹ Knows useful details relevant to role applied for ☺ Knows basic technical terms ☺ Is able to talk about technical terms used in CV ☺ Is able to give examples of work done ☹ Poor technical knowledge ☹ Lacks examples of usage ☹ Muddled answers ☹ Forgets items from own CV		4 Very good 3 Acceptable 2 Below standard 1 Serious concerns	

COMPETENCE	BEHAVIOUR		SCORE *Please circle*	COMMENTS
Show Stoppers (*Stereotypes and high-performance indicators which can really influence the interviewer*)	☺	Demonstrates drive, flexibility and great communication skills	4 Very good	
	☺	Confident about personal learning and future challenges	3 Acceptable	
	☺	Builds rapport with interviewer	2 Below standard	
	☺	Asks future-paced questions	1 Serious concerns	
	☹	The hesitant leader		
	☹	The narrow techy-type		
	☹	The one-trick expert		
	☹	The arrogant bore		
ONE THING TO REALLY PRACTISE:			OVERALL RATING: Good enough Needs more work	OTHER COMMENTS

INTERVIEW TIPS FOR THE BIG DAY

We've learned about the interview process and we've practised so that we can smile and make eye contact. On the day itself we can still continue to help ourselves by considering these tips:

1. **Take two additional copies of our CV.** We might need to give one to an interviewer and it helps to have a copy for us to refer to.

2. **Re-read our CV.** It pays to remind ourselves of our achievements and to be prepared to answer questions about obvious gaps or deficiencies.

3. **Practise our *Minute To Win It*.** Say it out loud in a conversational style, as if you're answering the question 'Tell me about yourself.' Re-read the relevant chapter in the Toolkit section if you need to.

4. **Rehearse our key achievements.** This will help us to tell the right stories under pressure and not to blurt out something inappropriate (see the chapter about mistakes).

5. **Choose our favourite three tips for rapport building.** It always helps to bring these things back into our conscious memory. Re-read the last chapter for the tips.

6. **Take a smart notepad and a pen.** On your notepad write down the interviewer's name, keywords from your *Minute To Win It* and any questions you would like to ask.

7. **Arrive *early* and wait around the corner.** We can park up a side street, or pop into a café and re-read our CV, straighten our hair and put on our jacket. The interview starts the moment we go through the main entrance and you never know who might be watching.

8. **Eat a banana just before we go through the gates.** Bananas are great for slow-release energy, which can help our sugar levels to remain constant during the interview. The sugar in chocolate is released in a burst, so we feel great for a minute and then need a boost quite quickly, which is why we need another one. Eating porridge is also another option if you're not a fan of bananas.

9. **Read the literature in the reception area.** This makes us look interested in the company.

10. **Go to the toilet when we arrive.** This might sound dumb, but needing the toilet in the middle of an interview gives you a dilemma: Waiting in discomfort or asking to be excused, which risks breaking the flow of the conversation. We can also use it as an opportunity to smooth out any travel creases in our clothes and to comb our hair.

11. **Take three deep breaths.** This is a classic way to calm nerves because we take control of our body and force it to release the antidote to adrenalin. This physically slows our heart rate and calms us down. Take a deep breath, hold it for a count of five, let it out slowly through your mouth and then repeat twice more.

12. **Ask for a glass of water.** Tea and coffee tastes bitter when it cools down and also dehydrates us. If we

need some thinking time or are nervous, we can sip the water to give us a couple of seconds to compose ourselves.

PSYCHOMETRIC PROFILES

These are frequently used to give interviewers objective information about behavioural styles and preferences. Some people use them in unfair ways, for example, by drawing wrong conclusions from incomplete data or by using them to support their own likes or dislikes. These people give psychometric tools a bad name. Luckily, they're often used appropriately and respectfully and can assist organisations in finding differences between candidates who seem to have similar CVs, or they can provide prompts for interviewers to ask particular questions about us. When they're properly administered and assessed by competent and trained people, they can be very useful tools and so if we get asked to complete one, the only thing we can do is to smile and go for it.

We need to be honest with our answers because if we do what's called 'socially responsible answering' where we put down what we *think* the other person is looking for, we're likely to be picked up by the profile as being inconsistent. For example, people going for a management job might want to be seen as a great leader, but the point here is that we *don't* know what the other person is looking for and if we don't fit, well, we don't fit. Trying to second guess these things and be smart about it is always counter-productive.[50]

Profiles are not tests. Tests are tests. Profiles contain batteries of questions which have no inherent right or wrong answers, or good and bad answers. Tests have defined answers to their questions, which can be used to measure our performance and assess our cognitive abilities. Some people mix the two up and feel that they've 'failed the profile'. This is not the case. Whatever happens, we remain good people at

---

[50] I tried it and it back-fired. The organisation did hire me, because I had enough experience, but my wonky profile then prevented me from being promoted, which I only found out when I left the organisation.

all times and a profile cannot rob us of our skill and talent; it just tells us what we tend to do most of the time in certain situations. We all have a wide range of responses to a wide range of situations and a profile is simply a picture of our most and least used styles of behaviour and ways of responding to people and activities. When faced with any kind of profile or test, all we can do is:

✓ Take a deep breath.

✓ Read the instructions twice.

✓ Work quickly.

✓ Answer honestly.

✓ Go with our first answer (if in doubt it's more likely to be the best answer).

✓ Keep going until we have finished.

Sometimes we might be given the results to take away and, if not, it's always a good idea to ask for a copy, if only so we can learn something about ourselves. However, profiles tend to have a shelf life because they're often a mix of *state* items (how we felt on the day) and *trait* items (deep-seated behaviours which tend to remain static). If we were to repeat the exercise a few months later our lives might be different, the weather will have changed, our mood altered and so on, which means that there is a likelihood that some of the answers might change. This means that if we are given a set of results, good practice is to tear them up after a *maximum* of 12 months because they've gone out of date and are not fully representative any more.

TIPS: If we've not completed a profile before, then it can help to do one in order to practise the process and to get a feel for some of our preferences so that we can anticipate possible interview questions. It might be worth paying for a professional to administer a profile. There are also plenty of books and resources available either for free or at a low cost. Things to research first might include:

1. *Team Role Profiles* (Belbin), available on the Internet at www.belbin.com

2. *Learning Styles Questionnaire* (Honey & Mumford), available at www.peterhoney.com

3. *Conflict Mode Instrument* (Thomas Kilmann) available at www.opp.com

4. *Myers-Briggs Type Indicator* (Myers-Briggs). This is a more in-depth profile and is widely used. I recommend the book *Life Types* by Hirsch & Kummerow as a good way to find out more about yourself.

In addition, the *British Psychological Society* has information about profiles and tests and can be worth contacting, if you find this area interesting and would like more information.

PANEL INTERVIEWS

Sometimes we might be interviewed by two or more people. This can be to our advantage as it will give us the chance to impress several people and perhaps reduce the likelihood that one person is biased against us. Greet each person in turn on arrival and thank each person in turn on departure, if you can, because we need to impress all of them with our good manners. Sometimes that's not possible, if we're waved to a chair in the middle of the room. In this case simply smile at everyone and give them your warmest *good morning* or *good afternoon*.

If we have a panel interview, we need to look at all the members of the panel as we're answering each question, so that we can see who is listening, smiling or frowning. If we look at just one person during the whole interview, then we will probably be marked down by the others, who will feel ignored. We need to keep shifting our attention and make regular eye contact with everyone on the panel.

When one interviewer asks us a question, we can address the beginning of our answer to that person and then look round as we continue to explain. If anyone holds our eye, follow his lead and look back at him. One of the disadvantages of a panel interview is that there can be a constant barrage of questions directed to us. This can be intimidating. Sipping water, pausing to look thoughtful or writing ourselves a note can be used to break their flow and give us a moment to catch our breath.

SECOND INTERVIEWS

A first interview is often used to see whether we match up to our CV, whereas a second interview is there to probe deeper and to be more searching. Organisations often use second interviews as an opportunity for us to meet lots of people, complete more time-consuming exercises or answer more technically searching questions. They use them to bottom out any risk-issues that might be associated with us and to see if on a second meeting they *really* do like us.

This means that we need to be careful.

If we're asked to prepare something in advance, then we need to *check and check again* to make sure we've answered the brief. Many people don't; they think a 10-minute presentation means they talk for 10 to 20 minutes, for example. It's essential to stick with what you've been asked to do as nothing irritates an interviewer more than a candidate who decides to be creative and follows his own agenda.

In our first interview, we will have told some of our stories and we need to make sure we have different ones in hand for the second interview. Repeating the same one is likely to be met with:

"You said that last time; what *else* have you done?"

The other thing about second interviews is that people use them to confirm their concerns, and the reason why many people fail at the second interview stage is that either:

1. They don't have sufficient technical knowledge to withstand scrutiny, or

2. They don't build a rapport with the interviewer.

A second interview is there to build on the first one and where people might be generous and overlook poor eye contact at a first interview, the chances are that they won't the second time around. This means that it's essential to practise and to take on board any feedback that is given, either by the companies we've visited or by our supporters who are doing their best to help us out.

Preparing for a second interview means revising our *technical language and skills* because if the job requires specific skills then it's highly likely we are going to be asked a lot of searching questions by an in-house expert about the depth of our technical knowledge.

It also means having fresh stories and examples about our past activities and it requires us to really think hard about why we want the job and what we're prepared to do to make a success of it.

When you have a second interview it's also worth reading ahead to the chapter in this section about negotiating and contracting, which looks in more detail about talking with your potential employer to construct a mutually agreed contract.

SALARY PACKAGE

When do you talk about the package on offer? When you feel the time is right; which usually means either when the interviewer raises the issue, or towards the end of the second interview. The assumption is that if you have come for an interview, then you're interested enough in the package for it not to be an issue, so if your first question is:

"What sort of company car can I have?"

then you're not going to make many friends. The package is important because if we're going to work hard then we need to feel we have a fair deal. There's more about how to discuss our salary and benefits with an employer in the chapter about negotiating and contracting, later in this section.

DISCRIMINATION

The law in the UK and in many other countries is very clear on issues of race, gender, age, religion and disability: You can't use them to discriminate against people and there are tough penalties for doing so, if your case is proven. If you think an interviewer has been discriminatory in the way he has conducted himself then you need to consider how to respond. Write down a *verbatim* (word for word) note of what he has said and include the date and time. You can then ask for the interview to be suspended and to meet a personnel representative, or you can write to the organisation afterwards to express your concerns.

Most organisations will take accusations very seriously, so be polite and factual in your correspondence. They may offer you another interview with a different person as they will not want their process to be flawed and unfair. If you think there's been a serious problem and you've suffered as a result, it's up to you whether you want to seek legal advice. You can often get the first hour of consultation for free with a solicitor.

Discrimination can be subtle, but questions that an interviewer would be very wise *not* to ask include:

✗ Do you have children?

✗ Are you planning on having children?

✗ How will you do the job and look after your children?

✗ How old are you?

✗ How long before you retire?

✗ Where were you born?

✗ Do you think you're old enough to do this job?

✗ How do you think someone of your race/age/sex will cope with this role?

These questions all point towards discrimination, which even if unintended, is still against the law. A polite answer to this kind of question is:

✓ And how is that question *relevant* to my application for this role?

This will either make the interviewer think twice or will reveal crucial information that we weren't previously aware of, as some roles have genuine aspects to them which mean the organisation has to ask about particular personal details. However, if they do, they need to be very clear about the purpose for needing that information.

REFERENCES AND APPLICATION FORMS

Although we will have supplied a CV, it is likely that we will be asked to complete an application form. This is to ensure the organisation has the right information about us. If we don't want to rewrite our CV then it's okay to ask if we can append it to the form. Similarly, if we haven't already lined up at least two people to be referees for us, we can ask to supply that information at a later date. Although many organisations do take up references, they are often only used to double check that we are who we say we are and to find out factual information, such as our attendance record or to confirm our date of birth.

A suitable referee is probably someone we know and trust, who is of professional standing. Senior managers, ex-colleagues, old teachers and previous employers can all make excellent referees for us.

When filling out forms, we need to be honest and if we need to take them away to check dates or details, then it's better to do that and ask for more time than to rush it and get things wrong. A wrong answer can count as a lie and might get us sacked later on for misrepresentation, so be careful.

COMMON MISTAKES

Here are seven of the main things that people do with depressing regularity during an interview to ruin their chances of securing a job:

- ✗ Turn up late, or fail to turn up at all.
- ✗ Appear rude, arrogant or superior.
- ✗ Avoid eye contact.
- ✗ Sound bored.
- ✗ Appear more interested in the salary and related package than in the job itself.
- ✗ Don't provide enough relevant detail when answering questions.
- ✗ Waffle, bluster or talk nonsense.

* SUMMARY An interview is our chance to sell ourselves by demonstrating how we can add value to an organisation. Success at interviews is all about having a good process and practising typical questions in order to reply with thoughtful answers. However, just knowing answers isn't enough; we need to manage our way through the whole process from acceptance and welcome through to goodbyes and thanks.

If we practise and use the score sheet to give ourselves structured feedback we can do well on the day. If we add in the rapport building skills from the previous chapter we can do even better. If we remember our *Minute To Win It*, then we are starting to perform at a high level and if we make a few notes and re-read them before we go in for our interview then we're really flying.

Interviews don't have to be a test of memory; a structured approach can help us to give a good account of ourselves and with *planning, practice* and *preparation* we can be really confident that on the day itself we will sell ourselves effectively to our next potential employer.

HOW TO BE A STAR

The meat, vegetables and gravy of any interview is undoubtedly the question session because past performance is one of the strongest indicators of future behaviour and future potential. The interviewer's mantra runs thus: *If they've done it before, they can do it again. For better or for worse, for good or for ill.*

In our modern job hunting world, we need to assume that the person interviewing us has been trained to be skilful in asking questions and in listening carefully to our replies. If he hasn't, this default position will still keep us safe. Sometimes, interviewers have a standard set of questions, compiled by their personnel colleagues, so that each candidate is given the same interview to maintain standards. Their job is to gather objective information from us about how we can add value to their organisation.

Our job is to answer their questions fluently, confidently and, most importantly, *honestly*, because we need to sell ourselves successfully, by showing how we fit in with their values and their culture and by confirming what skills and experience we have that are worth hiring. Honesty does *not* mean telling an interviewer about our worse faults and dangerous habits; we can *decide* what to tell them and what to hold back. *Choosing* our answers and being selective with what we reveal is not the same as telling an untruth. The former is common sense, whereas the latter is dangerous.

We need to answer the questions we've been asked and not ones we've invented for ourselves, like a politician who is being given a grilling by a leathery old journalist and who tries to dodge his forensic cross-examination. Answering questions can be made much easier by anticipating in advance what we're likely to be asked and then rehearsing our answers. This seemingly impossible task is, in reality, surprisingly simple.

PREDICTING QUESTIONS

Interviewers often draw their questions from relatively standard categories that will tend to include:

- ✓ Likes and dislikes.
- ✓ Competency and incompetency.
- ✓ Past experience.
- ✓ Gaps or inconsistencies in our CV.
- ✓ Current constraints.
- ✓ Future potential.
- ✓ Technical abilities.
- ✓ Personal qualities.

What this means is that many people will tend to ask the same questions, no matter what the role is or who the organisations are. Clearly there will be some differences at a technical level, but we can still prepare to be asked the same questions on a reassuringly repetitive basis.

There are *five types* of interview questions and we can make the assumption, as part of our preparation, that an interview will touch on each category. The types of questions are:

- ✓ **Classic**: To gather basic information.
- ✓ **Critical incident or competency based**: To find out what we can really do.
- ✓ **Cutting**: To put us off balance and make us think hard in the moment.
- ✓ **Killer**: The one question we didn't want to be asked, which can stop our interview stone dead.
- ✓ **Closing**: Used by us to help seal the deal at the end of the interview.

Knowing these types of question means that we can work out what we're likely to be asked, and the smart people *prepare an answer to each question.* This is one of the best ways to sell ourselves effectively and to increase our confidence on the day. Not doing it can be a terrible mistake: I've seen all sorts of people thrash themselves into a sweaty mess, or be rendered mute, in their efforts to remember even simple facts about themselves and their life, through poor preparation.

ANSWERING QUESTIONS

To successfully answer a question we need to hear it and to understand it. If we miss one, we can ask the interviewer to repeat it to us. If we get asked a long rambling question, we can politely ask the interviewer to tell us *precisely* what they're looking for.

If we get stumped and stare at the ceiling, the interviewer will notice it and we'll lose points. It can take a couple of seconds for our brain to process the question and to dig out the answer from one of its banks of filing cabinets, so taking a sip of water or repeating the question in our head, or writing it down on our pad, bridges that gap in a thoughtful way. I think of this as 'interview theatre' and it's okay to use props like this to help us out.

If in doubt we can use part, or all, of the mnemonic TRACT to help us, but use it sparingly, as repetition can make us sound like a robot. The mnemonic goes like this:

✓ **Thank** the interviewer for his question.

✓ **Repeat** the question to check we have heard it correctly.

✓ **Answer** the question concisely.[51]

✓ **Confirm** you have answered it by asking: *Does that answer your question?*

✓ **Thank** him for the question.

---

[51] Answer the question and then stop talking. Rambling is for weekends, not for interviews.

This technique is used mainly in handling questions at the end of presentations, but it can help us here, particularly if we repeat the question by saying:

"So, what you're asking me is…?"

Interviews tend to last for a set time, such as an hour, and the longer our answers are, the fewer the questions the interviewer can ask us. This is a fatal mistake to make and can lead to the following exchange when our interviewer is reporting back to his colleagues:

"She was a nice lady, but she wouldn't stop talking. I only managed to ask two questions, so she only scores 2 out of 10."

"Oh well never mind, let's hope the next candidate does better."

DIRTY TRICKS

Some interviewers will ask us 'evil' questions or try to provoke an argument in order to unsettle us. (Sample questions come later in this chapter.) All we can do is to answer the questions thoughtfully, or ask about the purpose of their comment. However, one 'dirty trick' which I regularly use when working with clients in practice sessions is to nod and say 'uh huh' a lot. I do this to sensitise them to what can happen in a live situation.

This is a dirty trick because I'm not particularly listening to all the good things the candidate is saying; I'm encouraging him to continue, to keep walking past all the bits he's prepared and to keep talking. To keep walking out of his comfort zone and to start digging around in his memories for additional information. To keep walking until he says something really interesting, which is probably the *truth* about how he felt at the time, or what he *really* did to resolve the problem.

A variation on this is to remain silent, which has the same effect on a candidate, who inevitably breaks the silence because he doesn't know that the interviewer is playing this game. If you spot an interviewer doing this, or encouraging you forwards over the cliff by saying 'more please', *stop talking* and say to them:

✓ You look like you want me to say more. What would you *specifically* like to know about?

or

✓ Sorry, did I not answer the question?

Either of these will make them think and will stop your headlong plummet. In sales circles the dangerous habit of over-talking is called 'buying it back'. This means we keep selling and selling and selling until either the other person gets really bored with us, or he begins to see flaws and inconsistencies in our pitch. Either way, he will tend to move from 'like' to 'dislike' and then it can be an uphill struggle to change that perception, because his perception becomes his reality.

CLASSIC QUESTIONS

These are the ones which are used to find out basic things about us and they often come at the start of the interview because they're straightforward and relatively easy to answer. A list of classic questions is given below and for some of them I've included sample answers afterwards, which you can use to guide your preparation. Read each question and then write keyword answers next to it:

Classic Interview Questions

(Questions in italics have sample answers afterwards)

- *Tell me about yourself...*
- *Why do you want to work here?*
- *Give me three strengths and three weaknesses...*
- *Why did you leave your last role?*
- *What have you been doing whilst looking for a job?*
- *Whom else have you applied to?*
- What salary are you looking for? *(This is covered in the section about negotiating with employers)*
- What do you know about our organisation?
- What skills or experience make you suitable for this role?
- Describe your current working day.
- How would you feel about relocating?
- What was your previous salary?[52]
- Why did you choose to study for that qualification?
- Which tasks do you find difficult to do?
- Which tasks do you enjoy doing or do you find boring?
- Which achievement at work have you been most proud of?
- What are your three best achievements to date?
- What do you like most about this job?
- What do you like least about this job?
- Where do you want to be in two or five years' time?[53]
- What have you learned from your last role?
- What do you think of your previous employer?
- What sort of a person are you?

---

[52] Answer honestly, because it's a matter of record. However, that doesn't mean we can't ask for more or less money in our next job, because we might be looking for a promotion, or changing careers.

[53] Never answer 'in your job' because that sounds threatening. Instead talk about the role you would like to do.

GREAT ANSWERS TO CLASSIC QUESTIONS

1. Tell me about yourself. We've already encountered this in the toolkit section and this is the opportunity to deliver a concise, informative and interesting *Minute To Win It*. We can anticipate what sort of follow up questions will come from the details contained within it. For example, if we mention that we delivered a project in Spain we might be asked how we found working in that country, or what was our greatest challenge working there? What would you ask if you wanted to probe deeper?

2. Why do you want to work here? (Or why have you applied for this job?)The truth is in many cases we don't; we'd rather be a millionaire on a yacht in the Mediterranean, but telling them this is not a great way to impress. Neither is talking about our love of their office décor. This question is a way of finding out how much we know about that organisation and the job and this is where our research counts. It might be that the job is one we love doing, that it's in a great location, that their career opportunities or training programmes are second to none, that they have a reputation for looking after their staff, that someone recommended them to us, or that it's a logical next step on our current career path. All of these are perfectly acceptable reasons for wanting to work there. Be careful if we use strong words such as 'love' and 'passionate'; we need to be prepared to defend them and to make sure that our tone of voice, our smile and our body language also convey enormous energy and enthusiasm.

3. Give me three strengths and three weaknesses. This question is so banal that it ought to be outlawed, but is a trusty old piece of kit, so needs to be taken seriously. The trap here is that we might talk about strengths which we don't really have, or mention weaknesses which fatally undermine our chances of getting the role. For example, saying that our timekeeping is appalling, or that we have this terrible pent-up rage which boils over once a week could kill off our job prospects. A good way to handle this question is to think of three things that we have previously been praised for and three weaknesses that have either been resolved or are completely understandable. Here's a classic example:

"In terms of strengths I would say that I'm great with details, I'm good at selling products and that I work really hard."

"In terms of weaknesses, sometimes I can work too hard and I need to be reminded to take breaks, my desk can get scruffy and I've learned to plan my week to make sure I keep important tasks in sight."

These are honest answers and in each case I have plenty of examples and stories to back them up. My weaknesses are not in themselves ones which are going to cost me a job, at least the weaknesses I'm prepared to admit to in an interview! The person interviewing us will be checking our answers against what they have seen and heard from us already, which is why we need to be honest, as gross inconsistencies are hard to maintain in front of a skilful interviewer. They will also tend to follow this question by asking:

"Can you give me examples of your strengths in action?"

Of course we can. We're great. And thoroughly well rehearsed.

4. **Why did you leave your last role?** There's no shame in redundancy, so we can admit to this easily. If we were sacked, then in many cases the fine detail is worth explaining in an interview, because we can highlight grey areas and inconsistencies with the previous company's policy. For example, I coached a manager who had, on the face of it, been sacked for sending in a false expenses claim, but when we looked at the detail he hadn't done anything wrong. He had fallen foul of a technicality, which the company had used to

get rid of him, and once I knew about the detail I was greatly reassured that he was a decent and trustworthy person.

If you've run your own business and it failed, then be honest and explain how you successfully managed its closure in an orderly fashion and can talk about what you've learned from the experience. People don't mind if you have a failure on your CV, as long as you can talk about it in a friendly and thoughtful way. Appearing as a sour-faced victim, or a thoughtless buffoon, is a great way to ruin your chances of success and if you still have lingering resentment then talk it through with one of your supporters and park it firmly *outside* the interview room.

5. **What have you been doing whilst looking for a job?** This is a loaded question because the interviewer is looking to see how proactive (self starting) we are. Just because we don't have paid work doesn't mean we can't do things that have relevance and value to our next employer. Doing nothing, apart from slobbing out on the sofa and watching daytime soaps and property programmes isn't going to sell us very well. Likewise, a gap year, when all we can talk about is drunken parties in Australia, sun bathing in Hawaii or youth hostelling in Thailand, isn't necessarily a great use of our time. A long holiday is nice, but if everyone else has done it too, how does that help us to differentiate ourselves from the competition?

We need to be active and do *value-adding* work because it shows how motivated we really are and how we have kept our skills sharp. Some things to consider doing might include:

✓ School governor.

✓ Charity shop work.

✓ Intern work for an organisation.

✓ Volunteer for community projects.

✓ Sports coach for local children's clubs.

✓ Working as a freelance consultant or a sole trader.

✓ Temporary work abroad to improve language skills.

✓ Further training; continuous personal development adds value to you and to your CV.

6. Whom else have you applied to? This is a great question because the interviewer is looking for what's known as a *convincer*. If we are really keen on working in a hotel, for an advertising agency, or as a solicitor, for example, then applying for only one job isn't going to make us look genuinely enthusiastic. It's okay to talk about other companies we've applied to because that's one way of convincing an interviewer that we're genuinely interested in the role and the industry.

TIPS: Practise answering all the questions in this chapter. Practice allows us to talk nonsense in a *safe* environment and then develop useful answers which can highlight our good points and make light of our flaws, or gaps. Recording ourselves is a great way to learn because we can listen carefully and then consider the question: *Would you hire you?*

CRITICAL INCIDENT QUESTIONS

These were originally developed by the police as a way of dramatically increasing witness recall. They work by inviting us to remember key details about an event in order for us to be able to tell the 'truth, the whole truth and nothing but the truth', so that the person listening feels that they could be watching a film of us in action. Their two great advantages are that they're very difficult to lie about, because we're recalling actual events and can't easily make up small details, and they give a very clear picture of us in action, which allows the interviewer to probe deeper about what happened and how we responded. *Our past behaviour is the best guide to our future performance;* so it's important to be familiar with this questioning technique.

Being able to share clear and relevant stories, which paint us in a good light, really impresses people because they can 'see' our competencies[54] in action. Failing to do so often implies we don't have the depth of experience needed or have exaggerated our abilities.

Critical incident questions tend to follow a pattern, which often falls into three parts:

---

1. Questions to start us thinking about a situation:

- Think about a time when you had to solve a *complex problem.*

- Think about a time when you had to be *really creative.*

- Think about a time when you had to *improve a process.*

- Think about a time when there was a *crisis.*

- Think about a time when you had to *change course radically.*

- Think about a time when you had to *overcome resistance.*

- Think about a time when you made a *bad mistake.*

- Think about a time when you solved a *very difficult problem.*

- Think about a time when you showed *great perseverance.*

- Think about a time when you showed *exceptional leadership.*

- Think about a time when you *worked hard to get someone to adopt your idea.*

- Think about a time when you *changed someone's mind.*

- Think about a *significant setback you've had.*

- Think about a time when you *felt out of your depth.*

Notice how each question is asking about a significant, meaningful event and not just 'any old time'.

---

[54] The skills and abilities that we use to do our work, for example, to solve problems or resolve difficult situations, to lead people, or to communicate effectively.

2. Questions that invite us to set the scene (like watching a virtual video):

- Please set the scene for me; who was present?

- Where were you situated? Where were the other people situated?

- What time of day was it?

- Now tell me what happened first?

- How did you respond?

- And then what happened next...?

- What did you do then?

3. Questions to dig deeper (where the really valuable information is hiding):

- What was your thinking behind that action/decision?

- How did you do that?

- How did you feel at the time?

- How did you feel afterwards?

- How did others perceive you?

- What have you learned?

- What would you do differently next time?

These can be tough questions to deal with, but with preparation and practice we can do really well at answering them. Indeed, once we have the stories in our heads we can use them to answer classic questions and so remove the need to be directly asked critical incident questions at all. The advantage of this tactic is that we can take control of the interview, because the interviewer, being curious, will ask us predictable follow up questions, which we've also prepared.

The technique for answering critical incident questions is called the STAR technique and it looks like this:

Answering critical incident questions:

Think of a story to illustrate each of the commonest critical incident questions, which tend to be asked as "Tell me a time when you..."

1. Showed great perseverance.
2. Showed great personal flexibility.
3. Showed brilliant communication skills.
4. Changed someone's mind.
5. Showed great leadership of others.
6. Handled a disagreement with someone.
7. Solved a complex problem.
8. Recovered from a setback.

Write down your answer by putting key words only to each part of STAR:

- **S**tate the issues at hand, or the situation, in only two sentences.[55]

- **A**ctions taken by you and why you did them.

- **R**esults for both you and those around you (make it a win:win).

Tips:

- Preparation is key. Start with a story. Write it out. Condense it.

- Tell it confidently. Practise painting a picture in two short sentences.

- Talk from genuine experience as people can spot a fraud.

- Use "I" not "we". People need to know about what you did, not about others.

- Include numbers and key details to be memorable.

- Be prepared to discuss your thoughts and feelings about an incident.

---

[55] There's a dangerous trap here. People can lapse into 'book at bedtime' mode and lose track of time, which is fatal, because it eats up valuable interview time and sends the interviewer to sleep. We need to paint a picture with a couple of quick, broad brush strokes and some juicy details and then move on to describing what we did and the results we gained.

Example of a critical incident question and a STAR answer:

So, Richard, can you <u>tell me about a time</u> when you changed someone's mind?

(State)
Yes, I can. The situation was this: I was in the middle of a sales visit, to win a £2m contract and my technical manager disagreed with the customer's health and safety policies and was adamant that he was going to tell them what he thought they should be doing. The danger was that he could have deeply offended the customer with his views, which although correct were not what the customer wanted to hear, due to cultural and political differences.

(Actions)
So what I did was to spend two hours with the technical manager and listen to his concerns so that he felt heard. I then took him through the detail of our client contract, including the political situation and the likely consequences of his actions and what would happen if we lost the order. I also suggested that he could write to me with his concerns and his proposed solutions to them and that we would find a way of sharing them with the client in the future. I did this so that he had the same facts as I did and could feel that he was being taken seriously by me.

(Results)
The result was that he accepted my view that the visit was to win business and not to tell the customer what to do. He concentrated on his technical task, which the customer was delighted with and we duly won the £2m order and repeat business worth a further £4m.

All critical incident questions will ask about how we performed under pressure, so think about the times at work when you were really working effectively under a high stress load. If you don't have a suitable work-related story, choose something from your home life or leisure time. For example, a colleague of mine was stuck for something to say about leadership as she had never led a team at work, until she remembered a story about skippering a yacht in the fog with an untrained crew. Suddenly she had a great story to tell and even though it wasn't work related it still made for a great STAR answer. If you're stuck for an answer to any of the typical critical incident questions, these prompts might help your thinking. Don't worry if you spot overlaps between some questions; that just means you can use your answers in different ways:

- ✓ **Showed perseverance.** When did you have to *push hard* to make something happen? When did you show sustained energy over a long period? When did you overcome obstacles or show high levels of sustained motivation?

- ✓ **Showed flexibility.** When did you *choose to* do something different, special, tough, to start a new task or to willingly have a go at something that initially you weren't too keen on? When did you willingly adapt to a new situation or respond positively to a difficult change at work? When did you *instigate* a change? When did you choose to learn a new skill?

- ✓ **Used brilliant communication skills.** When did you choose your words carefully to get your *message across* to people? What *successful negotiations* have you had with colleagues, or customers, or suppliers? When did you make a great presentation, or perhaps work in a foreign country and had to make yourself understood?

- ✓ **Changed someone's mind.** When did you *move* somebody from a 'no' to a 'yes', or sell a new idea to them? When did you persuade them to change an old way of working, accept change or do something they really didn't want to do? How did you overcome their doubts?

- ✓ **Provided leadership.** When did things get difficult and you had to take charge of the team, task or project and successfully resolve things? When did you have to step into a vacuum left by others? When have other people followed your instructions, or when have you motivated them to achieve new goals?

✓ **Handled a disagreement.** When did you act in self-awareness and respond positively in a hostile situation? How did you calm an angry person or use facts to win an argument?

✓ **Solved a problem.** When did you puzzle out a solution to a tricky question, or did some detailed thinking to find a new or innovative way of working? What methods have you used to solve problems? When have you made tough decisions or had to establish a priority between competing tasks?

✓ **Recovered from a setback.** When did you have to really work hard, or start over again, or showed initiative, or courage to keep going. When did you remain calm and work out a plan to get where you needed to go?

Take the time to think up your stories and don't worry if you feel like you're struggling at first, because it may take a few days to collect them. Perhaps you can talk though your CV with your supporters, or ask your partner to remind you of when you were really tired. Fatigue is a sign of stress, which can be a clue to the fact you were doing great things at work.

Being prepared with crisp, informative stories is the only way to deal with critical incident questions; it's no good remembering our really fantastic story when we're driving home, because that's too late to do us any good. Remember that we've already spent time assembling our achievements in the Toolkit section so all we have to do now is choose the ones we like most and angle them towards answering a particular question. I could also have used the above example to talk about leadership, problem solving or communication skills by emphasising different aspects of it, which means that with one story I'm able to answer *four* questions, giving me great flexibility during an interview.

TIPS: Once you have collected some STAR answers, check that they are in your CV as you could have missed including them in and so miss the opportunity to list even better key achievements than the ones you already have.

CUTTING QUESTIONS

Some interviewers like to ask tough, direct questions that require us to sit back and really think hard (as if critical incident questions aren't bad enough). Generally, they're doing this not to be unfriendly, but if an interviewee looks very confident, this is a good way to increase the pressure and really see if he can perform to a high standard. Alternatively they might have some concerns about us, particularly about our transferable skills (if we're coming from another role) or about the accuracy of our CV, if there are oddities in it. Our job is to anticipate these concerns and be able to provide the evidence that can reassure them. If we're unprepared, getting one of these questions can be the interview equivalent of sitting on a generously spiked cactus. Here's a selection for us to ponder over and to think of suitable answers to:

Examples of Cutting Questions

(I've asked all of these at some point to check information, pick up on holes in a CV or to test people's ability to think on their feet. (Tips to answer questions in italics are given below.)

- What's your biggest mistake and what did you learn from it?

- If I telephoned your former colleagues/team right now, what would they really say about you?

- If your ex-boss was outside and was seeing me next what would he say about your past performance?

- How can you convince me to take you on in this role?

- Why do you have that gap in your career history?

- Why did you leave your last role so quickly?

- Why did you make that sudden career change?
- What does 'passionate about change' on your CV really mean?
- What really happened?
- What other options did you consider?
- You said the 'team did the work' so does that mean you made no real contribution to the result?
- How do you think that qualification will help you in this role?
- *How do you perform under stress?*
- *You have talked about 'people' being an organisation's primary resource, but none of your CV achievements are people-related. How do you explain that?*
- *You said you were 'passionate about people'. How can you justify that comment?*
- *Here's a ball of wool (or pen, or mobile telephone, or rubber band). You have three minutes to try and sell it back to me, starting now.*
- *Why should we take a risk on you?*

How to answer some of the most common cutting questions:

1. How do you perform under stress? This is a trick question because you are performing under stress during the interview. It's designed to test your self-awareness, because if you say 'I'm a high performer' when you're clearly floundering, then the interviewer will spot the lie. A good way to handle this question is to tell one of your prepared STAR answers, to demonstrate your coolness under fire.

2. You have talked about 'people' being an organisation's primary resource, but none of your CV achievements are people-related. How do you explain that? There are many versions of this question and an alternative is: "You said you were passionate about people. Can you justify that comment?"

Being caught reciting a cliché is, to use a cliché, like skating on thin ice. It's fashionable to make glib comments about people being the most important resource in an organisation, and interviewers are becoming wary when they hear this platitude trotted out. If you're claiming to be a great manager, or a wonderful leader, then rehearse great answers to this kind of question. Focus on how you developed, trained, mentored or coached people and what the *benefits* of this work were to the organisation. How did the team's work improve? Who was promoted? What conflict situations were amicably resolved? How did the business metrics change? Who made real progress under your supportive guidance?

3. Here's a ball of wool (or pen, or mobile telephone, or rubber band). You have three minutes to try and sell it back to me, starting now. This is a 'spot exercise' to see how we cope under stress and think through a problem. This is a common question for many roles and not just sales jobs. Answer it by describing three or four features, or uses for the item, which are practical or imaginative. For example, if you get handed a pen, talk about how it can help you communicate with people, the fact that it will last for 1,000 pages of writing and the fact that the casing has been ergonomically designed to make it comfortable to use.

If you're tempted to write on your CV, or say at interview, that one of your strengths is *being able to think outside the box*, which is such an old and overused statement that it should have its feet up in a retirement home, you can bet that this question, or something similar, is heading your way. Saying something bland and clichéd is going to incite an alert interviewer to pounce on it. I would, wouldn't you?

4. So why should we take a risk on you? This is often asked as a final question and can bring confident candidates crashing to the floor with surprise as they panic and attempt to answer it. The best answer to offer is based on this:

"Well, Richard, *hiring anyone is a risk*, but this role requires (for example) sales experience and an eye for detail and *I've already demonstrated how* I won 10 contracts in 10 days and fixed the difficult problem with the circuit board. *So, the evidence is that* I have the skill and experience to do the job."

The key is to acknowledge the risk and then to kick it away by repeating two key attributes you have which demonstrate you can do the job.

KILLER QUESTIONS

A killer question is one that kills off your chances and ends the interview, a sort of 'I'll get my coat' moment. When people ask me to give them a practice interview, I like to work out what's the *worst question I could ask them*, which is the one that's going to make them gasp and say with a sigh:

"Ah! I knew you'd ask me about that!"

"Well, what's the answer then?" I ask calmly.

Most people have *one question* that they dread; perhaps it's to do with a gap in their CV, a poor exam result, a sudden change of career, a business failure, or several jobs in short succession. Whatever your killer question is, you need to work with a friend to come up with a neatly polished and acceptable answer.

> **TIPS:** There is always an acceptable answer to be spun out of any situation. If you're struggling to explain parts of your career history, talk to your supporters, or a local executive coach, or a friendly recruitment agent and seek their advice on what to say.

As an example of a killer question in action, I can draw on

my own experience. When I was much younger I saw a job advertisement for a workshop facilitator in the local newspaper, telephoned the managing director and talked my way into an interview on the back of my rampant enthusiasm. I even prepared a sample presentation, so that when the interview started to go off track I whipped it out and offered to deliver it. My carefully rehearsed five minutes went really well and, seeing my confidence rising, the MD leaned forwards and said:

"Imagine you're a tutor. You walk into a room to start your day, introduce yourself and a much older man at the back puts up his hand and says: I've got twice your experience, so why should I listen to you? Now then: How would you handle that?"

An obvious question, given my youth. I thought about it – I laugh at the memory now – my mouth worked but no words came out. At the time it felt like my brain had tripped, cutting the power to my vocal chords. After a couple of minutes had creaked past in stupefying silence, whilst I gulped like a goldfish, I finally knew what to say:

"I'll get my coat," I croaked, through dry lips, and walked out.

Don't be scared about your killer question: Be prepared for it.

CLOSING QUESTIONS

Towards the end of the interview we will be invited to ask questions. This is our opportunity to find out how well we've done and to look well prepared and confirm our interest in the role. It's also a great way to *demonstrate our assertiveness* by speaking up and being inquisitive.

Simply saying 'you've already answered all my questions' is to miss an opportunity. Instead, choose your favourites from these examples below and write them at the bottom of your notepad so that you don't have to remember them at the end of a searching interview.

Examples of Closing Questions:

- What would my challenges be in the first three months?
- What would be my priorities on day one?
- Are there any questions which I've not answered to your satisfaction?
- Is there anything about my application which you are concerned about?
- How would you describe the culture of the organisation?
- How would you describe your style of leadership?
- What's the next step from here? (Look for buying signals.)

The first two questions are future-pacing, which means they take the interviewer into the future, where they can 'see' us doing the job. Once people can see us in the role, it can dispel any doubts they have and we can become the preferred candidate. The next two questions give us an opportunity to make up for any earlier deficiencies, because we can't make corrections once we've left the room.

Asking about the *culture* gives us an insight into what it would be like to work there. Similarly, asking about *leadership style* tells us about our next boss, and my tip is if they talk about being 'firm but fair' then that can reveal a bully. After all, why be *firm*? What's wrong with reasonable and fair, friendly and encouraging, or coaching and questioning?

Finding out about the *next step* gives us useful information and we can get a sense of whether we are liked and might be coming back, or if they've had enough and want to be rid of us. Smiles and warmth and a conversation about what our first few weeks will be like are called *buying signals*, because they show that the interviewer is interested in us.

Asking intelligent questions can help us to confirm that we're a strong candidate for the role and can end the interview on a high note. Aim to ask at least two questions per interview and note down the answers, for future reference and to make us look interested. More examples of questions to ask are in the chapter about contracting and negotiating.

✳ SUMMARY Interviews are a test of how we perform under pressure. Many great candidates have slipped up, revealed serious flaws and floundered under scrutiny. Conversely, 'weaker' candidates have performed to a high standard, surprised the interviewer and got the job. Because an interview is a sales meeting by another name and we are our own product, we need to know about ourselves and talk fluently about our strengths and skills. This is easy to do once we have answers to the kinds of questions we're likely to be asked. It also means our performance during an interview is greatly affected by how effectively we prepare.

We don't have to memorise answers to every question because we can use our stories in different ways and be flexible in the moment. STAR answers are particularly good for this because telling a concise story is a great way to sell ourselves in an informative and robust manner that impresses people and makes us memorable. We can all do it and we can all be stars on the day.

FIVE SLIDES AND A SMILE

Dear Candidate,

You have been invited back for a second interview, where we would like you to deliver a five minute PowerPoint presentation. Your presentation will be timed and once you have finished, we will ask you questions about it. Your presentation will need to address the following areas:

1. The needs of the business.
2. How you meet those needs.
3. Other relevant information or success stories.
4. What have you learned from your previous role?
5. Why should we choose you in preference to other candidates?

We look forward to seeing you next week.

Kind regards

The Personnel Department

This is a real brief and whether we're being invited to an assessment centre, or to an interview, or are handed this as a surprise exercise on the day (which has happened to me) the same guidelines and structure apply for a successful outcome for us. They also apply whether we are using a laptop, or flipcharts, or have been asked to simply stand up and talk for five minutes.

STRUCTURE: THE FIVE-SLIDE FORMULA

A good rule of thumb is to allow for *one slide per minute* as an average. However, this assumes we have three bullet points per slide and spend only 20 seconds on each one. If we have a slide with more than that, we need to trim the next slide to keep our average time-per-slide to one minute. If we don't, then it's a certainty that we will run out of time. Curiously, if we have a 10-minute presentation to deliver, having five slides still works well, because we will have a natural tendency to talk more about each slide. Timing is crucial because we need to take advantage of the time we have been given without running over. Think of it as landing an aeroplane; we need to land smack on the runway. If we fall short we crash and burn. If we overshoot we crash and burn. We are the pilot and we have control, so we need to exercise it well.

To answer the brief on the previous page, our five-slide formula should be prepared like this:

1. **Title slide:** Give our presentation a title that links to a story we're going to tell, to grab the audience's attention.

2. **Linking slide:** Link the needs of the business directly with what we can do.

3. **Expansion slide:** Tell one or two key stories that illustrate why we're good for the role.

4. **Supporting slide:** Tell the audience something about ourselves that is related to the questions we've been asked in the brief.

5. **Summary slide:** Explain why we're a strong candidate and include a 'questions' prompt at the bottom. It's pointless to click to a blank slide with the word 'questions' floating on it, because the audience can't then see our summary. Combining these two slides into one means that the audience has our summary burned into their retinas whilst we answer follow up questions.

SAMPLE SLIDES FOR US TO CONSIDER

1. Title slide. On this one I've put the amount saved from a key achievement without explaining what it was, because it encourages curiosity in people and gives them a memorable number to remember.

PER PRODUCTS

Office Manager

£25,000 Saved

Jim Teakirke
December 2009

---

2. Linking slide. Use two columns to link the first two questions together and to provide a neat summary of our suitability for the role. Include numbers and keywords to avoid blandness. Notice how each line contains a relevant business need (or job requirement) and next to it how we meet that need. This layout is a very powerful way to get across the message that we can do the job.

THE BUSINESS NEEDS:	HOW I MEET THESE NEEDS:
• To organise the payroll	• 2 years of experience
• To manage the 3 clerks	• Managed 2 assistants
• To effectively respond to customer enquiries	• Confident, organised and polite
• To improve the back office processes	• Reduced paperwork by 25%
• To improve customer service standards	• Increased performance from 65% to 98%

---

3. Expansion slide. We can talk more about two of the points from the Linking slide and the story we put up as a title on the first slide. The bullet points are prompts for us – do not be tempted to write a paragraph for each one, use keywords only.

INFORMATION & SUCCESS STORIES
- Handled £120,000 of payroll cash each year
- Performance increases through staff training and regular meetings
- £25,000 saved by introducing an electronic archive

---

4. **Supporting slide.** If the brief asks us a specific question, such as 'what have we learned' then we must answer it. The interviewers will expect an answer, so if we duck the question it can make us look sloppy in our preparation, which could lead them to believe that we will be sloppy in our work for them.[56]

PREVIOUS LEARNING
- Need to stay polite at all times with customers
- Visual wall charts make for a tidy office
- Savings can be made if you go looking for them

---

5. **Summary slide.** This is not a space to sneak in new information; it's an opportunity to make a graceful exit by highlighting key points already made. In terms of the brief, this is where we answer the question: Why should we choose you? Even though we have only just talked through our stories and key achievements, we still need to repeat them. We can't assume people were listening because people's attention can easily wander, and even if someone is looking directly at us, he might *actually* be thinking about what to have for dinner that evening.[57]

In this example the candidate has restated two of the major business needs and highlighted his previous experience and the achievements that meet them. He's also taken the opportunity to restate that he likes this work, if anyone didn't hear it the first time around, in order to confirm his enthusiasm.

---

[56] Our behaviour on this task is likely to mirror our behaviour in the role. If we fail to answer part of the brief, then what does that really say about us?

[57] I was meant to be timing a candidate's presentation once, as part of a panel, and was distracted by the sight of a yellow digger trying to manoeuvre outside. It was only when the candidate had finished that I realised I hadn't heard anything he had said for the final few minutes. Was I embarrassed? Yes.

SUMMARY: WHY ME?
The business needs to improve:
- 65% to 98%
- £25,000 saved

The office needs professional management:
- 2 years of experience
- Track record of excellent customer service

I really enjoy this kind of work

The next slide is the one to use right at the end. We can create a copy of the summary slide, with the additional text, and click to it when we finish our presentation. To the audience it will look like the summary slide has remained static and the new text has appeared. This is a useful technique to end a presentation without needing to use complex animation.

SUMMARY: WHY ME?
The business needs to improve:
- 65% to 98%
- £25,000 saved

The office needs professional management:
- 2 years of experience
- Track record of excellent customer service

I really enjoy this kind of work

Thank you for listening. Any questions?

In five slides we can give the interviewers a clear picture of what we can do and why we are a great candidate for them to consider. As we have seen throughout the book, particularly with networking, the art of sales is about getting a clear message across, which is why each slide has only a few main points on it. Three is a good number to use because landing our aeroplane on the runway is more important than strafing the audience with details; if the interviewers want more information they will ask for it.[58]

TIPS: The whole point of the exercise is to complete the presentation in a professional manner. Success is down to us having a good process *and* great content. The Five-Slide Formula gives us a good process to follow and we can work hard to pare down the content to the essential minimum.

HIPS, EYES AND VOICE

A great set of slides is easily ruined by poor performance on the interview day and we can be marked down for a mumbling style of delivery, a lack of eye contact or a body which thinks it's been hired to be an Elvis impersonator, and wiggle to its own rhythm.

Hips. This is the place to start because if we get this right, the rest will follow. The absolute golden rule for good posture, in my experience, is to stand with our hips square to the audience so that we are facing them directly. Keeping our hips in line will keep our head straight and our eyes facing forwards. We can trust that the big screen is working, so we don't need to keep looking at it.

Eyes. The same rules apply as for interviews. We must make eye contact with people and if we have a panel in front of us we need to keep our eyes moving. A useful trick is to practise counting: one-two-three-*move*, one-two-three-*move*... and so on. Playing 'find a friend', where we concentrate on the first person to smile at us, means ignoring the others and is a sign of nervousness.

Voice. We need to be loud enough, to vary our pitch, to emphasise keywords and to pause at the end of each slide, just for a moment, in order to keep the audience's interest. If

---

[58] If you find it hard to leave things out then go back to the section about Self-Awareness and re-read the Demons Model. Someone is telling you to keep going when you don't need to.

an assessor can't hear what we're saying, she can't score us. If you're not sure of how you sound, record your voice and listen back to your performance. This might give you some painful feedback, but it's preferable to failing miserably on the interview day.

DEALING WITH NERVES

Many great presentations are spoiled because of nerves, which can make us talk too fast, miss out sections or forget to watch the clock. Here are my favourite tips to combat them and I use them all the time:

- ✓ **Practice.** If we practise to an imaginary audience, we will be more comfortable on the day itself. I practise presentations in my kitchen at home, and have delivered some cracking 10-minute talks to a bowl of fruit, James the gerbil[59] and a potted plant. We can also make sure that our timing is spot on and we can practise answering imaginary questions (using TRACT from the previous chapter).

- ✓ **Stopwatch.** I always use a stopwatch or put my wristwatch on the table in front of me with a sticker on it to point to when my time runs out. There's no excuse for poor timing and knowing the elapsed time means that we can speed up or slow down, depending on how well we're doing.

- ✓ **Write down the first sentence.** I'm not a fan of summary flip cards, unless they're used to replace PowerPoint completely. Trying to do both at once gives us a higher workload than we need and more things to shuffle, drop and generally get in the way. However, I often write down my welcome and first sentence, so that if I feel nervous I can read it out and get off to a good start.

- ✓ **Water.** Sip water to moisten your mouth and provide a natural pause.

---

[59] Sadly now departed. He never seemed to mind my practising, although that was probably because I bribed him with sunflower seeds.

✓ **Avoid animation.** One click for one slide is my motto. If we have to click to get each bullet point to appear or if we have clever whirling text that stretches in and out, we will spend valuable seconds waiting for things to happen. If a slide appears on one click and we're running out of time we can also say: *"As you can see, there are three reasons why I'm a good fit for the job, but what I want to draw your attention to is…"* We can then talk briefly about just one point before calmly moving on to the next slide.

✓ **Three deep breaths.** This has been covered before, but in case you missed it what you do is: Take a deep breath, hold it for about five seconds and then slowly expel it through your mouth. Repeat this twice more and you will start to feel calmer.

✓ **Take a copy of your slides with you.** You can read through them one last time before you stand up. Also, don't rely on the organisation to have sorted out your PowerPoint file. Take a hard copy and a soft copy, on a disc or a memory stick. Remember also to save it as a *PowerPoint 97-2003 Presentation*, as more recent software is not always backward compatible. (See the chapter on mistakes for a related story.)

TIPS FOR SUCCESS

After watching many assessment centre presentations, here are my favourite tips, which show us how to perform to a high standard. When we're practising, we can have them in front of us and tick off each one when we're satisfied we have learned it:

✓ **Show people the evidence.** Don't just say 'I did it well'; give facts and figures and tell interesting stories.

✓ **Be prepared to justify 'weasel' words.** "I am *passionate* about dogs." What does this mean? How is it manifested in my working life?

✓ **Stand still and keep hands out of pockets.** Also put down the pen that you love to wave about, or click repeatedly, as it can be really distracting.

✓ **Add your name to the bottom of each slide.** In case someone enters the room late and wonders who you are.

✓ **Use assertive language.** Instead of saying "I'm a pretty good leader," which sounds rather vague and uncertain, say "I *am* a confident leader."

✓ **Use upbeat words to create a positive atmosphere.** These include: *great, successful, enjoy, rewarding* and *committed.*

✓ **Use your hands to emphasise key points.** If you're in any doubt about how to use your hands, park them behind your back, which will at least pull your shoulders back, lift your head up and improve your volume.

✓ **Smile.** If you're enjoying it, then they'll enjoy it too.

✳ SUMMARY Interview presentations are often timed, to ensure each candidate is treated fairly, and are scored to make sure the brief has been fully answered. This means we're being asked to do a real piece of work in real time and if we do well, it can add lustre to our CV and set us up for a great interview. If we rush it, or ignore parts of the brief, we can look sloppy and incompetent. Although there's always room for first-time nerves, or for the odd mistake, people assessing interviews will score us based on what they see and hear. (See the next chapter for an example of a score sheet.) We can use the Five-Slide Formula to keep things crisp and concise and we can practise until we're confident.

If you are reading this and have never made a presentation before, then a suggestion is to use the briefing 'letter' given at the start and to practise anyway, in case you're in for a surprise when you go to your next interview.

Delivering a great presentation is a classic way to persuade people that we're worth hiring because many assessors, or audience members, will be saying to themselves: "This is what they will be like if they work for us." I've seen people who were previously unknown to the presenter come up to him afterwards and offer him a job, based on the strength of his performance. So, if we get asked to present at a conference or at a networking event, our answer should always be: *Yes, please.* The opportunity a presentation can create is too good to miss.

THE SECRET WORLD

If you're a graduate, a manager, or someone applying for a role with a large blue-chip company, the chances are quite high that at some point you'll be invited to an assessment centre. These centres are becoming increasingly common because they make good use of time, allow organisations to bulk-process many candidates and are an efficient way of making employment decisions quickly. They often focus on assessing candidate competencies because seeing people perform a set of tasks under pressure is an accurate indication of how they're likely to perform if they're hired. Some people I've worked with have complained that they're 'not like real life', but they *are*.

We can trust that they do put people under a stress load and can reveal what they tend to be like when stripped of job titles and left to perform on the basis of skill and talent. This can affect people who have been used to managing by title, rather than by aptitude, who can find it hard to command attention and often struggle to make themselves heard in group work. This is, of course, *precisely* what the assessors are trying to find out: Who can lead people and solve problems by being skilful and who relies on success by wearing their 'I'm the boss' badge and being arrogant?

Assessment centres are naturally competitive, as candidates know that only a few of them will be offered a job at the end of the process and this means they tend to be tough, searching and mentally exhausting. I've known many people fail to turn up on the day because nerves have got the better of them, which is a pity, because just like interviews and presentations, with *knowledge* and *preparation* we can demystify assessment centres, increase our confidence and perform to a high standard on the day.

To achieve success at an assessment centre we need to be good at interviews, confident in presentations, build rapport with ease and be able to ask and answer relevant questions. All of these things are covered in the preceding chapters, so here we're going to take a walk through a *typical* assessment day from an *assessor's perspective*. The exercises described have all been adapted from real life and are exactly the kind of things which are used to find out how talented we are. However, if we know what's happening behind the scenes and how we (as candidates) are being monitored, then we're in a great place to deliver a gold medal performance and earn ourselves a job.

THE TIMETABLE

As *assessors* we'll have more information about the day than the candidates because often the exercises are kept secret and only revealed to them at the last minute, but we'll know what's coming up so that we can read our briefing notes and prepare our score sheets. Some assessment centres ask people to bring prepared presentations, which the previous chapter covers, so in this chapter we're going to concentrate on 'surprise' exercises on the day.

TIMETABLE	
8.00	Assessor briefing
9.30	Welcome to the day – outlining the activities and the organisation
10.00	EXERCISE 1: Personal Introductions
11.00	EXERCISE 2: Psychometric Profile
11.30	Break
12.00	EXERCISE 3: Time Management
1.00	Lunch – food and culling time
2.00	EXERCISE 4: Forced Leadership
3.30	Break
4.00	Application Forms – candidates complete paperwork
4.30	EXERCISE 5: Panel Interview
5.30	End of day for the candidates
6.00	Assessor review meeting

8.00AM ASSESSOR BRIEFING

At the start of the day, or perhaps the day before, we will be briefed about the timetable, what to look out for, how to score candidates and so on. We may be asked to follow one candidate for the whole day so that we gain a continuous picture of him, or we may be scoring different candidates during different exercises to avoid a candidate being disadvantaged if an assessor takes a strong dislike to him. As assessors we're being monitored by the centre manager, who runs the day, and we want to do a good job, because it will reflect well on us.[60]

In our assessor packs, it's likely we will have some basic guidance notes to remind us of good practice, which can include the following things:

ASSESSOR BRIEFING NOTES:

- Your role during the assessment centre is primarily to collect evidence, both positive and negative, which will enable us to make a judgement about the candidates at the end of the day.

- When completing score sheets for an exercise, remember to collect evidence for the duration of the whole exercise and only write in your score at the end.

- If you haven't seen it or heard it then don't infer it. It's easy to give people strengths or weaknesses which they don't actually have by making assumptions on the information available to you.

- There is nothing wrong with finding no evidence. No evidence is not necessarily a negative; it just means there was no information at the time.

- As assessors you will be asked to justify your scores during the end-of-day review session, so make sure you record evidence of what your scores are based on. Note down exactly what people say or how they react.

- Listen to the thoughts in your head. Just because you disagree with a candidate doesn't make him wrong. Are you saying to yourself 'what a load of rubbish' when they're actually giving you good evidence?

- Beware of horns and halo, which means taking an immediate like or dislike to a candidate and then finding further evidence to support your view, whilst ignoring evidence that would provide a balanced picture.

- Good evidence gathering means: 1) Observe and listen; 2) Write notes; 3) Organise notes into categories relevant to the score sheet; 4) Score the candidate's performance.

---

[60] Assessors are often drawn from across the whole organisation. Being careless or biased can reflect badly on them if their performance is reported back to their departmental managers.

Our assessor packs will also contain blank score sheets for us to use. Although there may be some detail variation, or overlap, with what we're specifically looking for in each exercise, all sheets will tend to be linked to the same core competencies. This means that as the scores are compiled, a picture emerges of each candidate's performance, his highlights and his weak spots. Here's an example of a score sheet (which has been adapted from a real assessment centre pack):

ASSESSMENT CENTRE SCORING SHEET

Candidate's Name: Exercise:
Assessor's Name: Date:

Score each competency up to 5 points based on the evidence you have seen. Write down any supporting comments next to each line you have scored.

(A) Communication Skills

1. Talks clearly and precisely.
2. Displays active listening skills.
3. Makes eye contact.
4. Asks purposeful questions.
5. Waits for others to finish before speaking.
Score:

(B) Thinking Skills

1. Thinks before he or she speaks.
2. Bases decisions on available evidence.
3. Is able to support any assumptions made.
4. Is open minded and adjusts thinking to account for other people's ideas.
5. Is able to sift out irrelevant or unimportant details.
Score:

(C) Time Management

1. Plans use of time effectively.
2. Is aware of the elapsed time.
3. Completes all parts of the brief.
4. Takes time to read the brief before answering.
5. In groups, reminds others of the time remaining.
Score:

(D) Assertiveness

1. Is prepared to take the lead in group work.
2. Holds people's attention and makes himself or herself heard
3. Organises other people in a friendly way.
4. Asks people questions to keep them involved.
5. Controls the conversation so that people can all contribute.

Score:

(E) Energy

1. Encourages other people to keep going.
2. Maintains own performance to the end of the exercise.
3. Overcomes setbacks or difficulties.
4. Persuades people to his or her point of view.
5. Makes a consistent contribution.

Score:

TOTAL SCORE:

The competencies mean that we will collect *specific* evidence. It's worth noting that most of the evidence is about *process* and *style* and not about outcomes. This is a bit like when we did a maths exam at school and were given marks for our working out, even though we might have reached a wrong final answer. Most organisations will expect to teach people technical details, particularly if they're from a different industry or lack experience. However, they will tend to look for minimum standards of communication skills, thinking ability, adaptability, energy and assertiveness from day one. This is because if there's plenty of competition for jobs, an organisation is not going to waste time and money training people in basic competencies if it doesn't have to.

TIPS: Read the score sheet and make a note of any items you need to remember on the day. You will be under a stress load so you need to avoid bad habits showing up. Candidates who often score badly are those who keep repeating poorly thought-through ideas, are argumentative, dogmatic, monosyllabic or who withdraw and stay quiet. If you are thinking good thoughts, then you *must* share them with people because an assessor cannot see inside your head. People who often score well are those who speak up and verbalise their thinking, take part and seem bright and bubbly.

9.00AM CANDIDATES ARRIVE

The candidates arrive and we mingle with them, say hello and sip coffee. Although the candidates aren't being *formally* scored at this stage we, as assessors, are noticing who greets us politely and confidently and who doesn't. We will also notice who seems relaxed and is asking us questions and who is withdrawn and quiet.

As assessors we need to be careful; being withdrawn at the start of the day is not necessarily a negative as some personality types take time to warm up to their environment. However, if someone is consistently withdrawn as the day unfolds, then we need to ask ourselves why that might be.

TIPS[61]**:** Arrive on time, be polite and use your networking skills to engage people in conversation. Smile and appear enthusiastic. You're in for a long day so you need to make sure you have had a good night's sleep and a decent breakfast to start the day well. The environment is a *live* one, so until you go through the gates at the end of the day you are being assessed *at all times*. As you walk in through the door to begin your day it can really help to remind yourself of these things:

✓ *You have a right to be there. You've been invited for a reason.*

---

[61] These tips are to help us anticipate the problems and pitfalls we're likely to encounter. Good technique improves confidence and scores points. And points make prizes.

✓ *If you're nervous, you're normal: You're still okay.*

✓ *You don't have to be a perfect expert. You can have some gaps in your knowledge and experience and still pass the day.*

✓ *You have already done well. Only a small minority of applicants are invited to assessment centres.*

9.30AM WELCOME

This is where we will be formally introduced to the candidates and where the centre manager will welcome them to the organisation and explain the purpose and structure of the day.

> **TIPS:** Look interested, smile at people and take note of any particularly useful details or questions that occur to you which you can ask during the day, or at your interview later on.

10.00AM EXERCISE 1: PERSONAL INTRODUCTIONS

Most assessment centres want to start with an easy exercise to give candidates a chance to settle into their environment, and the classic one is some kind of introduction. Candidates will either be asked to introduce themselves or to introduce the person sitting next to them, after having been given a few minutes of preparation time. If they have been asked to prepare a formal presentation, delivering it is also a typical option for this slot.

When I was a candidate at an assessment centre, another candidate made a complete disaster of the first exercise because he didn't listen to what was being asked for and when it came to his turn, he wasn't able to introduce *his neighbour* and had to sit in silence. Afterwards, on the way out to get a cup of coffee, one of the assessors tried to be friendly by saying to him:

"Don't worry, you haven't *ruined* your chances already."

I overheard this and winced; personally I don't want reassurance that early.[62]

TIPS: Write down the key things you're being asked to do on your notepad and the *time* you have available. Put your wristwatch on the table in front of you so you can keep track of time. (Remember you're being watched for what you do as well as what you say.) Write keyword answers to the questions, not long sentences, because the aim here is to capture the information. If you have to introduce your neighbour make sure you have written down his *name* and use it as you introduce him.

Remember that your *Minute To Win It* probably contains most of the information you've been asked for so quickly jot down your eight keywords on your pad to jog your memory.

Allow yourself at least 10% of the available time for a quick rehearsal at the end, even if that means muttering quietly to yourself.

11.00AM EXERCISE 2: PSYCHOMETRIC PROFILE

This takes place early on because it gives the administration team time to collate and process results for the interviews later in the day. Sometimes candidates are asked to complete a profile before they arrive, but the problem with this is that the centre manager can't be sure they've been completed in the right environment. As assessors we can use this time to read candidates' CVs and to discuss our early perceptions about the candidates.

---

[62] When I tell this story I'm always asked if he passed the assessment centre. He didn't.

TIPS: In the chapter about interview skills there is a section on profiles and tests. Remember that we just have to do our best and not worry about the results. If we know our achievements and we have answers to classic and critical incident questions then we will have a fair idea of what we like, why we're here and what our preferences might be. Remember: If in doubt we can trust our intuition and go with our *first* answer.

11.30AM BREAK

As assessors, we are interested in how the candidates make conversation because these are always great opportunities to see who looks a bit lost, who drones on and on, and who is polite and friendly.

TIPS: Go to the toilet *first* and then get a drink as this means you're set up to get back to the main room on time. Nobody wants to be late for the start of the next exercise. Also if there are biscuits or fruit on offer then it might help your energy levels if you eat something and have a glass of water to keep yourself hydrated.

12.00NOON EXERCISE 3: TIME MANAGEMENT

Being successful at work means managing our time and this is a good way to see how people work under pressure, use systematic thinking to organise and solve problems and to justify decisions taken. These exercises are often referred to as 'in-tray' exercises, but with the rise of email we can also think of them as 'inbox' exercises. Here is an example:

THE INBOX EXERCISE

You have 10 minutes to complete the following exercise.

You are the supervisor of a team of five reception staff, in a large hotel. It's 8.30am and you have a regular review meeting each day at 9.15am that lasts for 15 minutes, where you allocate tasks and share information. You have just checked your inbox and have the following messages:

1. Your manager wants to see you urgently to discuss a disciplinary issue involving two of your staff.
2. The payroll office reminds you to collect the payslips for your team by 10.00am.
3. A coach party of tourists from Austria is due to arrive at 9.20am and will need to be checked in quickly to clear the reception area.
4. A junior chef has emailed to say she's sick and won't be coming in.
5. Your night porter has emailed to say the credit card machine is out of order and he's used up all the spare paper payment slips and that the occupants of room 101 have complained that the shower isn't working properly.
6. A regular client wants room 103 reserved for him.
7. A customer looking to arrange a wedding has moved her meeting with you from 11.00am to 9.30am.

Question:

How do you plan your time and tackle these items?

Write your answers on a separate piece of paper and be prepared to present them to the assessors afterwards for discussion and questioning.

Stop: Have a go at doing this exercise for real before you read on.

As assessors we are looking to see how the candidates deal with the following issues, some of which relate to our score sheet and all of which show how they process the information and exercise their own judgement to good effect:

1. There is a clash between the meeting and the arrival of the tourists. How do they handle it?

2. The broken credit card machine is a priority as clients can't pay when they check out. The exercise is set in the morning because there's likely to be a flood of residents leaving at this time.

3. Some tasks can be delegated to other people and the supervisor doesn't have to do them all.

4. Some items are time-specific and can't be moved, whereas others *can*.

5. All actions have consequences. For example, not telling the head chef that his junior is off sick could have a knock-on effect for breakfast and lunchtime services.

6. There are no right and wrong answers, but there might be a better set of priorities. For example, putting customers first and solving their issues might be preferable to collecting the payslips.

7. People can use their initiative and can change things. They could shorten the 15-minute meeting to five minutes or hold it earlier.

8. The manager's urgent request is misleading because 'urgent' is inviting people to make an assumption. What does it really mean? Do it now or do it later? Will people check out the details or will they make an assumption and slavishly follow it?

9. Some tasks are related to each other. For example: If room 103 isn't reserved first, there's a chance that one of the coach party could be accidentally booked into it.

10. Did the candidates allow any time for *planning* the tasks? In reality it would have taken them a few minutes to sit and think and work out a plan. This is a hidden task. It's not directly mentioned, but it is a task in itself which needs to be added to the list.

These points are embedded in almost any time-management exercise. Often the exercise is there to test candidates on what's not been said as much as what has. There may be some red herrings to distract people, but often people don't bother to read the question thoroughly and don't give themselves time to assimilate the information; they jump straight into answering it. If they do, they're in trouble.

TIPS: Draw a vertical *timeline* and block out chunks of time for tasks or highlight specific points of time. This can help us to see how the tasks flow throughout the period, if any are connected and even if we have enough time to complete them all. At first sight there is always a mass of information, so a good *sorting and drawing process* can help us to see it and get to grips with it. An alternative to the timeline is to decide whether tasks add value or are 'nice to have' things that can be postponed.

Then we need to make a quick *list of assumptions* and what our thinking is about them. Finally, we can use our initiative and see which items are *fixed and which are flexible*; it's up to us to decide what to do first, what to do second, what to delegate and what to dump.

Managing time invites us to demonstrate our process-thinking skills, challenges us to check our assumptions and be creative with our solutions. Once we know the tips and the hidden secrets we can work quickly and efficiently to come up with a coherent and defendable answer that will withstand scrutiny.

1.00PM LUNCH – FOOD AND CULLING

As assessors we will join the candidates for lunch and mingle with them. Who complains about the food or thanks us for providing lunch? Who is eating happily and who is looking nervous and picking at his food?

In some assessment centres the assessors will have a lunchtime review and decide who will leave the day at this point and who will go forward to the afternoon session. They will have seen the candidates perform at two exercises and will have the results of psychometric profiles and tests.

If candidates have performed poorly and the evidence is consistent then they may be asked to leave now as the organisation won't want to waste time interviewing people they're not going to hire.

> **TIPS:** A professional assessment centre manager will have already told you if there is a lunchtime 'sort out'. All you can do is to enjoy the food, keep smiling and keep asking the assessors intelligent questions about the work they do and the organisation in general. If you've done well enough you'll be staying for the next part and if you haven't, you can't change it, so there's no point in worrying.

2.00PM EXERCISE 4: FORCED LEADERSHIP

This is a significant exercise because it shows how the candidates can work with people and work with a group of strangers. It's called *forced leadership* because there is no appointed leader and candidates have to assert their presence, listen to their colleagues and work through a complicated task as *equals*. This exercise is a great way to find out who has in-built leadership ability because quieter types will often stay quiet, bullish arrogant types will trample others and people with a warm disposition and confident problem-solving skills will shine through. Remember: It's *not* the group which is being scored; a group can do badly and an individual candidate can still perform to a good standard. You're being scored on your own contribution.[63]

The exercise is often set in the realms of a business case, where candidates are presented with a large volume of information and expected to collate it, understand it, sift it and come up with some practical solutions. There might be a dilemma to resolve, a problem to advise on or a decision to make. There is always enough time to complete the exercise

---

[63] A group I was in at an assessment centre did appallingly badly. However, I kept going, asked questions and persevered even though I knew our ship was sinking and I was the only one out of our group to pass the centre.

and the apparent complexity is designed to test people's ability to stay calm and work methodically. Groups who follow a simple logical process will tend to do well. Groups who make hasty decisions, ignore key facts or who succumb to stress and argue will tend to do badly.

Here's a typical example of an exercise. Once you've read it, stop and have a go at answering the questions before you read on:

SMITH & JONES MOTORS

You have 50 minutes to complete the exercise. You must work together as a group. You may use any of the resources present in the room.

Team Brief:

You are business consultants hired by a local business called Smith & Jones Motors. The business was purchased six months ago by your client, Mr Melton, and he's asked you to advise him on how to run the business, as he's never run a dealership before.

Specifically he wants to know:

1) What are your top three recommendations to increase profits?

2) Should he buy the land next door and expand his business? He would like to know the thinking behind your decision.

You visit the business to find out more information and this is what you learn:

1) Mr Melton has three staff who work in the business full time. Mr Norris works five days a week and sells two cars a day. Mrs Jones only works on Tuesdays and Thursdays and rarely sells any cars. Mrs Wilding only works on Saturdays and once she sold 10 cars in a day, when she had an assistant to help her complete the paperwork.

2) Mrs Wilding's assistant left and hasn't been replaced. She now sells six cars on average on a Saturday.

3) Mr Melton doesn't speak with the customers because he's 'too busy' running the business. Mr Norris complains that Mr Melton takes two-hour lunch breaks each day in the restaurant across the road. Mrs Jones complains that as the wife of the previous owner and the longest serving employee she is really in charge and not Mr Melton. She likes to tell Mr Norris what to do.

4) Mr Melton tells you he has no debts and has a healthy £20,000 in the bank. He buys all his cars on a sale-or-return basis and it only costs him £100 handling fee per vehicle to do so.

5) Each car makes on average £500 profit after the sales team has given buyers' a 'special discount'. The forecourt can hold stock of 50 cars and when you visit there are 20 family hatchbacks, 10 estate cars, three sports cars and a 4x4 off-roader that Mr Melton has offered to sell for a friend. Each car costs about £4,000 to buy and is priced at £4,999. Mr Melton's motto is 'Your car's fine when the price is £4,999'. The cars are all clean and shiny, although the seats on one of the sports cars is wet from a leaky sun roof and the 4x4 is obviously rusting.

6) Mr Norris secretly tells you that he's going to leave soon because he's been poached by a rival dealer.

7) Next to the forecourt is an empty parcel of land and Mr Melton is wondering whether to buy it and sell more cars. He thinks there would be enough space for 30 more vehicles. The land is priced at £15,000 and the vendor has given Mr Melton first refusal, but wants an answer within seven days or he will put it up for public auction.

8) Mr Melton thinks that Mrs Wilding has become lazy and is wondering whether to get rid of her and ask Mrs Jones to work on Saturdays instead.

9) Mrs Jones is supposed to look after the accounts, but she's fallen behind. She knows the tax is due and estimates it to be about £7,000. She asks you not to tell Mr Melton and promises that she will be up to date within a couple of months.

As assessors we will position ourselves in the room so that we can see the one or two candidates whom we're scoring. We've also read the brief and we're keen to find out whether the candidates all make the same mistakes as the previous group, in last month's assessment centre. At the end of the exercise, once we've handed in our score sheets, we're going to give the group a 10-minute debrief to test their thinking and the candidates will think the exercise is over, but it's *not*. We can collect evidence at all times because we know that some people will relax at the end of the exercise and tell us what they really thought about it, argue with us or tell us they thought it was stupid or unrealistic: All of these things can lose points.[64]

---

[64] I've experienced this for real as an assessor, when a candidate argued fiercely that our suggested answer was wrong and totally refused to acknowledge that his thinking might be flawed. Do you think he passed the day?

Here are the commonest mistakes made in forced leadership exercises:

- ✗ **Not answering the brief.** For example, the above brief asks for three options, not six. It also asks people to explain their thinking, so there are really *three* tasks to do and not two.

- ✗ **Not using data.** There are facts and figures in the information and people often don't use them at all to support their thinking. This can make their answers look weak and subjective under scrutiny. *Always aim for a 'data-rational' answer.*

- ✗ **Not using all the information.** Some of the boxes contain more words, which are easy to skim-read and ignore. Also different stakeholders might be more or less important than others or have personal agendas that are clouding the real issues. *All information can have value* and needs to be read at least once before it is discarded.

- ✗ **Not exploring options.** Candidates often readily agree with someone who tells them 'they've done this before' and are reluctant to suggest alternatives for fear of looking silly. *It's okay to speak up if you have a point to make or an alternative option to suggest.*

- ✗ **Not asking: What are the real problems here?** There are always lots of things going on and this exercise has all sorts of issues, any one of which could have an impact on long-term profits.

- ✗ **Not considering the consequences of their decisions and recommendations.** Anticipating what happens next is a great way to make sure ideas are practical and have been thought through properly.

- ✗ **Not following a simple process.** Some candidates think it's great to use a set-piece tool to answer the questions and I've rarely seen this done well. Smart groups collect all the information, make sense of it, suggest some solutions, test them and then choose the best ones which they can support with a data-rational argument.

TIPS: You're probably not being scored on the actual outcome. You're being scored on how you *personally participated.* Here's how to do well in this kind of exercise:

1. *Never grab the marker pen.* Let someone else go to the flipchart and be the group's writing donkey. The scribe often becomes isolated from the group because he's physically distant and when the group huddles to discuss a point he's cut off and exposed.

2. *Speak up if you have something to say.* You will not score points if you stay silent and think great thoughts.

3. *Ask questions to bring other people into the conversation.* What do you think? What's your idea? What do you think about this suggestion? What would you do first? How do you see the problem? This approach suggests you are assertive and consultative, rather than being strong minded and a bit bullying.

4. *Be heard exploring options and using numbers.* You're scored on what you say, so even if a bully dismisses you, you will have said the right things to score points. For example: What else could we think about? How could we do it differently? Let's explore the arguments for buying the land and not buying the land.

5. *Position yourself to be in the group.* With a slight angle of your chair you can face people and be included, or isolate others and cut people off. Use both to good effect.

6. *Apologise if you talk over someone.* Good communication skills are a must and an apology makes you look self-aware and polite.

7. *Avoid words like 'should, ought and must'* because they are too directive and can inflame people. Swap them for: 'I wonder if...' or 'Would you consider...' or 'The evidence suggests that...'

8. *Be open-minded and don't rely on your real-life experiences.* If you say 'I've done this for real and know the answer' then you're heading for trouble, because the exercise is to get you thinking. Focus on the information you've been given and base your answers on it.

9. *Use a pause button* to gain control of the conversation. This is my favourite tip for looking assertive. In order to break into a conversation, or to stop it and take control, you reach out your hand and push down on an imaginary button on the table, whilst saying, 'Can I just pause you all for a moment?' It sounds like you're asking, which is polite, but you're not; you're telling them to be quiet. This interrupts their flow and will create a silence that you fill by saying: 'Thank you... what I think we need to consider is..."

Practise these points, or note some of them on your pad, so you can discreetly refer to them before the exercise begins. Mining gold during a forced leadership exercise is about your self-control and about making a thoughtful and active contribution because there are no right and wrong answers; it's all about *what you say* and *what you do.*

3.30PM BREAK

As assessors we're looking to see who complains about the exercise and who has enjoyed it and found it an interesting opportunity for them to learn something, who is grumbling that it 'wasn't like real life' and who is talking about what they've learned and how much they like solving problems?

> **TIPS:** Get a drink and nibble a biscuit because forced leadership can be really draining and you have an interview coming up and need to re-energise yourself. Read your notes quickly, look at your CV and think about your performance during the day as it's highly likely that you're going to be asked about it.

4.00PM APPLICATION FORMS – CANDIDATES COMPLETE PAPERWORK

This is our opportunity to prepare for the panel interviews which are next. We can read through CVs, look at the results of the profiling and compare score sheets to generate a list of useful questions to ask.

> **TIPS:** Complete any paperwork quickly and quietly. If you're asked to re-write your CV, find out if you can clip a copy to the form. If you're asked for references and don't have any yet, ask if you can supply that information at a later date.

4.30PM EXERCISE 5: PANEL INTERVIEW

This is an opportunity for us as assessors to double-check the evidence we've been gathering during the day so far, or to make sense of conflicting scores, or to ask about a stop-go performance where a candidate has had some real highs and some real lows during the day.

The panel format is deliberate because it means we can keep up a constant stream of questions between us and make good use of time. We can also compare our comments afterwards to make sure we're in agreement, or understand differences of opinion, so that we can be confident of the decision which is reached at the end of day review.

TIPS: Normal interview rules apply and the process and questions will be similar to those covered in the preceding chapters. However, because you've already been invited to the centre, your CV has already been read, so you may not be asked too many questions about it. It's more likely that you will be asked a series of critical incident questions because your answers can be *scored* and then added to the rest of the scores collected during the day.

In addition you might be asked about the day itself and here are some sample questions and answers:

1. *How have you found the day?* Answer: Hard work, great fun, really enjoyable. I enjoyed the problem-solving exercise.

2. *Oh, why was that?* (A predictable follow up question). Answer: It was good fun to work through the problem and it reminded me how much you can achieve in a short space of time.

3. *If you were doing the problem-solving exercise again tomorrow, what would you do differently?* Answer: I think I would draw a big chart and put all the key facts and figures on it, or I might break us into two smaller groups and task each one with looking at a part of the problem.

4. *If we were to offer you a job after today would you accept it?* (This is to test how interested you are.) Answer: Yes, that would be great!

5. *So why do you want to work here?* Answer: Because today has shown me a bit about what

it's like to be here and I like the people and the products and am keen to join you.

6. *What will you do if we don't offer you a job?*
(This is to really test your interest.) Answer: I will apply again next year or write to your managing director and ask if I could have three months' intern work, for free, so that I can get some experience.

The interview is unlikely to be adversarial (unfriendly) because you've already been put under pressure during the day. However, it might be searching and your reasons for wanting to join the organisation will be probed to see how genuine you are and to make sure that if you're offered a job then you will take it and not waste their time. Confidence comes from preparation and the answers given above are classic ways to sound interested, demonstrate your learning mindset and score bonus points.

5.30PM END OF DAY FOR THE CANDIDATES

We ask the candidates if they have any final questions and wish them well on their journey home. The assessment centre manager will give them a copy of their psychometric profile and will cover any final points of administration. Then we can all begin to prepare for the assessors' review meeting.

TIPS: Thank people for their time, thank them for lunch and leave with a smile on your face. If you have a long drive home be careful; it's likely that your system has been flooded with adrenaline all day and is now starting to crash as it wears off. Take a break on the way home and get something to eat and drink in order to keep your sugar levels up. You can relax once you're home safely.

6.00PM ASSESSORS' REVIEW MEETING

This is where we get to discuss each candidate in turn, review his combined scores and make a decision about him. The centre manager will chair the meeting to ensure we have a fair and evidence-based process and do not lapse into subjective, or prejudiced, comments and decisions. Each candidate will be made an offer, or declined, or in extreme cases be asked to reapply once he's gained a bit more experience. Once we've finished we can go home, because we're just as tired as the candidates.

> **TIPS:** If you're offered a job, then great. However, if you're not and you're really unhappy about it, say so and ask if there is a way to come back for another interview or if there is an *appeal procedure*. You might not always be told about these things because if you're a borderline candidate the organisation might just be testing you to see how passionate about working for them you really are.
>
> I know several people who 'failed' an assessment centre, appealed, passed a second interview (because their passion was evident) and went on to do really well. If you're prepared to fight a bit for your job, some companies will respect that and you can convince them you're worth taking on. Be careful not to keep on and on, though, because that can become irritating and might ruin your chances for the future.

That's the end of our day and as assessors we can congratulate ourselves on a thorough job well done. We have weeded out some poorly performing candidates and we've hired some future stars. We also know that it's *just one day* so that people who haven't passed are still good people at heart;

they just didn't have enough of what we were looking for, that's all.

✳ SUMMARY Assessment centres are searching. They do mimic real life and they do give us a good sense of how we will perform under pressure and what our temperament is like. A properly run centre will take into account if we're 'late bloomers', who had a slow start and then did well at the end, so whatever happens during the day we need to keep going and do our best.

The tips and guidelines in this chapter have all been taken from real life and have all made a difference to candidates' scores. We can all choose the tips that most appeal to us, remember them and use them to enhance our performance on the day; because we can highlight our strengths, be confident and give a good account of ourselves.

YOU HAVE POWER

You have all the power until you sign. So says a colleague of mine and I heartily agree with him, because in many organisations our first negotiation over pay and rations is also likely to be our last. We have the power to ask questions, to clarify the fine details, to ask for what we want and to choose whether to say *yes* or *no*. When an employer wants to hire us we can find out how much latitude they have with the package on offer and get ourselves a deal that we feel comfortable with. In many cases they don't have much room for manoeuvre, but it's always worth asking questions, because if we don't then the answer is always *no*.

We negotiate to reach agreement, and a contract is a collection of all our agreements. Until the ink is dry on the contract, the way we go about contracting and negotiating might be used as a final test of our character. Do we stick up for ourselves, ask intelligent questions and gently, but firmly, push our case? Or do we act like a petulant child who's had his ice cream confiscated and make demands, stamp our feet and get angry? In our process of job hunting, which is after all a sales process, we don't want to fall at the final hurdle and be left gasping for air as another horse thunders by, passes the post first and takes our job with it.

CONTRACTING IS KING

A contract is a mutually satisfying agreement between two or more people. If a contract of employment isn't mutually satisfying then we need to ask ourselves why we're going ahead with it? We might just need the money, and that's fine for a short while, but it could be the beginning of a tough patch in our lives.

To contract successfully we need to explore the hidden things which both parties may want to talk about, but haven't had the time to do so yet, and we need to bring them out into the open where we can see them. By doing this we create a clear set of expectations for all parties, so that when we start in our new role we're setting off in the right direction. In my experience the issues fall into two categories; hard and soft.

Hard issues are all about the pay and rewards that we get in return for offering our labour. In our contract it's okay to test the boundaries and ask about:

- ✓ **Basic salary.** Getting a few extra £s now is worth it, even if that means a smaller pay rise in the future. Some companies will offer to increase your pay once you've completed a probationary period, which mitigates their risk. If they offer this then it makes sense to ask for the rise to be backdated to your starting date so that you don't lose out.

- ✓ **Bonus.** Many job packages contain a bonus element as a way of mitigating the risk of paying us too much and then not getting the right results. It's good to check out what the bonus element is and ask for one if a higher salary cannot be achieved. However, actually getting paid a bonus can be fraught with difficulties if the organisation decides to change the rules or rig the profit results halfway through a period. A company I worked for had to scrap its bonus scheme completely one year because our plant was doing so badly, and we were so far away from the trigger point for the year-end payment that people were becoming actively de-motivated by it. Be careful if a bonus is based on *net profit*, because the managing director might decide to buy himself a new car, or similar, which you have no control over and which reduces *net profit* and hence your bonus. It's preferable to have a bonus based on *gross profit* performance, which is easier to keep track of and less open to manipulation by unscrupulous bosses. A good tip with any bonus is to ask for it to be *guaranteed* during your first year (or at least a percentage of it) on the basis that you're going to need time to settle in or that you're agreeing to take on a new and as yet untried project or product (that was conceived by someone else and could be flawed) and don't see why your bonus should carry 100% of the risk of things not going to plan.

✓ **Pension.** This is often held in a different budget to our pay, so that even if a company cannot increase their salary offer they can often increase our pension contributions by a percentage point or two (I have benefitted from knowing this myself). Over the longer term this can be much more valuable than a pay rise and it's always worth asking for a few extra points.

✓ **Holiday entitlement.** This is often based on length of service, but if you've just been working as an intern, then ask for that period to be included in your total service so far, as that can hasten the addition of extra days. Also, find out if any untaken leave can be carried forward at the end of the year.

✓ **Training and continuous personal development.** If you need to develop a skill then it can be a good tip to agree a budget for this *during* your negotiations so that it becomes part of your starting package. Companies can be more willing to agree to expensive courses *at this point* as a way of incentivising you to join and to prove that they do care about their staff.

✓ **Hours of employment.** Are they fixed or flexible? Find out what the rules are and how accommodating the company can be.

✓ **Sick pay.** The law covers statutory sick pay, but it's worth knowing what the company's rules are in advance.

✓ **Location of work.** Could you work from home sometimes? Many organisations recognise that not everyone works well in a nine-to-five pattern and that working from home and choosing your times to suit you can make for increased productivity.

✓ **Equipment.** Do you need a laptop, printer, toolkit, mobile telephone, van or car? Ask now when they're much more likely to agree to your requirements. Company cars can be expensive luxuries, due to levels of personal taxation, so if you don't really need one for business, consider if having one is more to do with your ego, than it is to do with necessity.

Soft issues are to do with the work we will be doing and what is expected of us. In my experience many people spend time picking over the details of what mobile telephone they can have and ignore the job content. This can be a big mistake because no matter how much we're paid, agreeing to do a job that is beyond our abilities can be draining on our physical and emotional energy. When talking with our next employer we can make sure we both have a clear set of expectations by asking about:

✓ **Goals, targets and KPIs.**[65] However hard we work, in some organisations the only thing that matters is achieving the targets. We need to understand them in advance and what our role is in meeting them.

✓ **Why we're being hired.** We might be hired because of one or two core skills that we have, and it's good to know which bits of our CV are the ones which we will be using, in case they're not ones we feel confident about. For example, being expected to be an assertive leader when we always prefer to work quietly on our own is not setting us up for success.

✓ **The daily or weekly content of the role.** Although some companies provide candidates with lavish and over-specified job specifications, many don't. I took a job once as a production manager in a small factory, which meant doing all the jobs that the director didn't want to do, including using my own car for collecting raw materials. Needless to say that was the last time I took on a job without knowing what it would really

---

[65] Key Performance Indicators: These may be related to the performance of the business, the team we are part of, or our own performance or a combination of all three.

entail. If people find it hard to tell you what the role looks like in detail then ask them to describe a typical day or the sort of things your predecessor did.

✓ **Why this role needs to be filled.** Perhaps it is a new role that has been created or perhaps we're filling someone else's shoes. Either way, it's good to know in case we're being set up as an 'expert', or going to be chewed up as office fodder, like the previous five incumbents.

✓ **What does success look like to our boss?** This is a telling question because we get to find out what our boss' view is and his view is all that matters. Similarly, asking him what really annoys him or what the previous post holder struggled with can be equally revealing.

✓ **Particular work-related dislikes or gaps in our experience.** Most roles have many parts to them and it's likely we can't always do all of them. If this is the case we need to share them with our next boss so that that they can be aware of any issues which may arise and, more importantly, not criticise us for them subsequently. If we've told them once and they said, "Okay, fair enough" then that's part of our contract.

✓ **The need for a particular support or training.** Same as the above point. It's healthy to talk about these issues before we sign so that we can agree on a plan to resolve them.

✓ **Our priorities.** This question may have already been answered during our interviews, but if it hasn't then we can find out what's expected of us in week one, month one and the first six months. When we begin our new job we will know what to focus on and what to leave until later.

When we're contracting it's quite normal to be nervous and to wonder if we really can do the job. The way to test this is to ask ourselves the following question:

Is there one thing that we can do on day one in order to get started in the job?

If there is, then we can build up to the rest of the tasks on our to-do list and if there isn't, we're better off finding another opportunity to go after.

Clear contracting is all about asking questions and agreeing on the fine detail to our mutual satisfaction. Once we have a contract that we're happy with, we know that we have completed our job hunting process. We can indulge in a small celebration and look forward to starting our new job, smug in the knowledge that *we've set ourselves up for success.*

VERBAL OR WRITTEN?
A verbal contract is often enforceable in law, but it's preferable to get terms and conditions in writing *and* signed by all parties concerned. This needs to include our job specification so that we are clear about what is expected of us on day one. If a company is reluctant to write one then my suggestion is that we write our own and ask them to approve it. Also, keep notes of any relevant interview conversations in case you need evidence to support a breach of contract in the future.

HOW TO BEGIN CONTRACTING AND NEGOTIATING
Sometimes we need to take the initiative and get the discussion started. Waiting for an offer to plop through our letterbox may be too late for us to influence its contents. We can either raise the issue during our second interview, or if we leave that and are subsequently offered the role, we can ask to come back in and talk about the detail, before our contract is prepared unilaterally without our involvement.

When you feel the time is right you can try one of these openers to get things started:

✓ I'd like to talk through the package that's on offer. Would you like to do that now or later? (If they demur and say later, then they're either running out of time, or they want more convincing that you're suitable for the role.)

✓ I would like to discuss the salary package as I'm interested to find out what the budget is for continuous personal development.

✓ I'm interested in the job and would like to discuss the terms and conditions. Is now a good time?

Remember to smile and make eye contact in order to be assertive and to be taken seriously. Notice their immediate reaction: Did they smile or frown, lean forward to engage you or push back and put some distance between you? Does their reaction feel cool? Do you need to soft peddle, or does it feel friendly, making you look forward to a spirited and productive negotiation? These are all *buying signals* and you can adjust the pace and strength of your negotiations accordingly.

Negotiating Tip (1) *Tell them you want the job.*
Stating your interest makes it clear to the other party that you are serious and are not going to waste their time. If they want to hire you, the interviewer will work harder – if the sale has been closed *in principle* – in order to make sure it's closed *in practice*. If you say, "I would *really* like to do this job and I would like to discuss the salary package on offer." then you're making a commitment, stating your intentions clearly and sincerely and are starting the following discussions by looking assertive and confident.

Negotiating Tip (2) *Talk about the salary when they look like they want you.*
If someone has decided you're the person he has been looking for, he begins to make an *emotional commitment* to

you and starts to feel distanced from the other candidates. This means that you're in a stronger position to gently and politely negotiate for what you want, because he is more likely to concede ground in order to ensure you do take the job. Knowing when this moment occurs can be tricky, but in practice wait for a second interview and watch out for buying signals that might include: Relaxing, smiling, nodding enthusiastically at your answers and starting to talk about what your first week *will* be like, which office *will* be yours and going into detail about the job itself. Detailed discussions mean that he is investing time in you because he is starting to see how you *will* fit into the organisation, what it *will* be like working together and how you can help to solve problems.

Negotiating Tip (3) *Suggest a 'range' to allow room for discussion.*
Using a range approach is the equivalent of asking open questions, because it generates discussions and people can move about inside it to find a place where they are comfortable. If you're asked: *What are your salary expectations?* Then express your answer as a range, for example:

- ✓ Well, the advertisement talks about a £10,000 salary and I was looking for somewhere between £10,000 and £12,000. Or you could say:

- ✓ I'm not sure what salary you had in mind for this role, but I was looking for something between £30,000 and £35,000, based on what you've said the job involves.[66] Or another way is to go for the 'package' approach:

- ✓ I'm looking for a £50,000 package, and happy to talk about how the salary and related items are structured. Perhaps you could sketch out your thinking?

---

[66] Our earlier research will help us out here because we will have a rough estimate of what similar roles in other organisations have been advertised at. Picking a number at random could be embarrassing and might even be a fatal mistake.

I often use a vague term like 'sketch out', because it gives the other person the opportunity to be cautious in their response, as it's likely they will want to test our reaction. Being blunt and telling people, "If I can't have a car then I'm not interested" is a good way to annoy them. I've seen this happen before and a colleague was deeply affronted once when a candidate insisted he had to have his own car, which was against company policy for his grade. It cost him the job, because he looked stubborn, unrealistic and self-centred, which were not traits we wanted to hire.

Negotiating Tip (4) *Solve problems.*
Reminding employers about how you can solve their issues is a good way to strengthen your case, because essentially recruitment is about solving problems. If you're part of the solution then you're worth hiring and that can generate leverage for you during negotiations. Remind them of tangible past successes you've had and draw their attention to particular skills which make you eminently suitable to take away the pain for them.

Negotiating Tip (5) *Make an objective case based on past performance.*
Many people negotiate for a compromise, because that's what they learned as children; to ask for a bit more, knowing they will settle for a bit less. As grown-ups, this kind of horse-trading can make both sides feel that they've won and lost something, which can feel a bit crude and develop into an argument, particularly if the employers feel they've offered you a fair deal to begin with. In a job hunting context it's preferable to link negotiations to past performance so that you can make a convincing case for your salary and related package because, as we have already observed, *past performance is the best guide to future behaviour.*

Negotiating Tip (6) *Have a 'minimum walkaway'.*
A salesman friend of mine introduced me to his concept of a minimum walkaway, which means knowing what the smallest thing is that you want to get out of a meeting so that you can have a minimum target to aim for. In some networking meetings our minimum walkaway will be that we want to set a date to meet up for a second time; that's all we want to achieve in order to claim success. As a job hunter it can mean deciding what our lowest salary or smallest package will be and ideally we want to know what our minimum walkaway is before we go into an interview.

For example, in the process of being offered a job during a second interview, I discovered that the holiday entitlement was only 15 days a year, whereas my previous role had 25 days. The salary on offer was £21,000 and *on the spot* I decided that for 15 days leave I wanted a minimum salary of £26,000 to make up for the extra work and said so when asked what my salary expectations were. The interviewer was not at all pleased when I stuck to my figure and it quickly cost me the job. He wasn't prepared to move up and I wasn't going to move down because £26,000 with 15 days leave had become my minimum walkaway.

Negotiating Tip (7) *Close the deal.*
When you think you have pushed enough, or have achieved your *minimum walkaway* and are happy, then it's prudent to stop and say:

Thank you. If you were to offer me the job on those terms I would be happy to accept.

Knowing when to stop talking and to smile and close the deal is an easy trick to overlook, but sometimes that's all it takes to get a job. If the interviewer has other people left to see and they know they have you as a confirmed candidate, it may change their attitude towards them. Knowing what *you* want and *asking* for it is an *assertive* thing to do and could be the evidence of your behaviour that prompts them to hire you. And, as the saying goes: *If you don't ask, you never get!*

A FINAL WARNING: DON'T BE SEDUCED BY MONEY

Working for a bad boss who bullies you and makes it difficult to do your job can ruin your health or trample through your happy home life. I know; I wrote a book about bad bosses and how to survive tough times called, rather cuttingly: *My Boss is a B@$T@*D*. My suggestion is to work for someone whom you like and respect, even if the job has its downsides. If we like the people we work for and they treat us well then that can be more rewarding in the long term than earning a big salary and being thoroughly miserable. We only have one life, and although money is necessary to get through it, we can't take it with us when we die.

✳ SUMMARY Contracting and negotiating is a good opportunity to demonstrate how we can be assertive, state our case and remain polite and calm. It shows employers that we have mettle and are to be taken seriously, even if we don't move them an inch from their opening position. What we won't know is whether or not our ability to sell ourselves has impressed them enough to offer us the job, and if we already have an offer in principle then we need to be able to close it to our satisfaction so that we are heading for a great time at work and not stress-laden disaster. *Once we have a contract that we're happy with, we can relax because we've succeeded and can enjoy the glow of being a professional job hunter who has beaten the competition.*

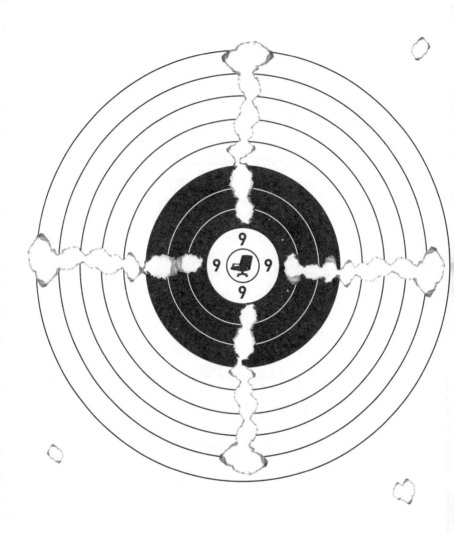

Section 8
SECRET NO. 3
PRACTICE

8.1 MY FAVOURITE TIP

IT MAKES ALL THE DIFFERENCE

I'm often asked for *one top tip* that people can take away from a workshop or a coaching session to help them get a job. Although I have several that can make a difference, the one which I've noticed has consistently made the *most* difference is: Practice. Job hunting skills are all there to be picked up and polished and no one is born a job hunter. We can all learn how to do well and if we really want to be successful *we can be*. It might take a while and the road might be hilly and have a few potholes in it, but we will get there.

This book is full of practical skills, tools and secrets and knowing them is only *half* the story; we have to be able to put them into practice and deploy them when it counts. Throughout this book, various chapters have included sage advice to practise that particular skill and with good reason: I've seen talented people dry up at interview, talk nonsense to employers and succumb to nerves at presentations and networking events. In all cases they could have made a better impression if they had practised a bit harder beforehand, and most of them have ruefully admitted as much. *Not* practising key skills makes for a *higher risk* approach to job hunting than we need to have, because it makes it much harder for us to sell ourselves effectively when we're put under pressure.

Job hunting skills are basic life-skills and practising them means that we have the skills for life.

WE'RE GOOD AT PRACTISING

It's worth reminding ourselves that we've had to learn how to walk and talk. How to hold a pen. How to tie shoelaces. How to read and write. How to be polite. How to ride a bicycle or how to drive a car. We were born with *none* of these skills; we've had to learn them and practise them in order to be proficient.

Job hunting is about selling ourselves, and if we want someone to pay us thousands of pounds then we have to realise that we need to be good on the interview day in order to persuade them to invest in us and part with their cash. However, I also know that understanding the need to practise *and* actually doing it can be two different things for some people. As we've already seen with the Demons Model, people can be very good at getting in their own way. So what can you do to be successful?

FOLLOW YOUR ENERGY

People have a tendency to avoid doing things which really don't interest them, and if we're applying for jobs that we don't really want, human nature is going to gently sabotage our efforts by delivering a poor performance. We look like we're doing what we need to, but secretly we know we're limping along when we could be running. A phrase that I carry about in my head is: *Energy flows where thought goes.* If you think a task is boring you're less likely to do it, or conversely if we really want to achieve something then it's surprising how much energy we can create for ourselves. We might choose to work weekends, work late into the night, drive long distances, spend our money on training courses or equipment, talk to people and do what it takes to get where we need to go.

So a basic question to ask ourselves if we're not practising things is: *Are we looking for the right job?* If we're not then we need to stop, talk to a supporter or two and tell them our secret desires and what it is that we *really* want to do. We can then bring our energy and thoughts into line and we can really get going with our practising, because now we're heading in the right direction. It's okay to have an ambition and it's okay to make one of the horses you're racing a particular job, business opportunity, career break, masters degree or any other project that makes you want to jump out of bed and run to work each morning.

IF YOU THINK YOU CAN OR YOU CAN'T, YOU'RE RIGHT

So said Henry Ford, who in between making cars found the energy to have his useful quotations recorded for posterity. I like this quote because it's right. We limit ourselves and often do so based on what we think, rather than what the evidence actually is. We make assumptions that we can't do *that* job because we don't have *that* skill or we couldn't run a business because we don't have an MBA.[67] Many of the very top people in industry have little or no formal qualifications; they just got on with it and learned on the job. When I started out as an executive coach I knew very little about what to do, but I *so* wanted to do the job that I decided I could learn as I went along. I read books, took a distance learning course in psychometrics and attended regular training sessions. I paid for coaching supervision time to enable me to reflect on my practice and find ways I could improve. I invested hard cash and long hours and successfully changed careers; I made it happen.

HOW TO PRACTISE

There are several ways in which we can practise our skills that don't have to take up lots of time, cost money, or be complicated. They can be simple, quick, cheap and, most importantly, *fun*. Parts of this book contain exercises and if you haven't had a go at them then perhaps that might be a good place to start. In addition, I've found that the following pointers can help people to get things worked out and parked firmly in the forefront of their minds, where they can more easily retrieve them when the time comes. Try these and have a laugh and a joke when you do:

---

[67] Grrr… anyone can be successful in business, with the right motivation and guidance. MBAs can be useful and can be completely superfluous, depending on your situation.

✓ **Hold weekly or monthly meetings with a coach, or supporter, or friend, or fellow job hunter.** Talk about specific aspects of your campaign or rehearse particular skills.

✓ **Telephone someone the day before an interview, give them a list of seven questions and ask them to give you a quick practice session.** This might only take 30 minutes to complete and can make a substantial difference to your ability to recall answers the next day.

✓ **Record yourself.** Often we don't accurately hear what we say so it can help if we practise by asking and answering questions, by talking through our *Minute To Win It* out loud. Listen to the tape and then have a second round to see how you have improved. Most mobile telephones have a dictaphone function so we probably have the kit to do this in our pocket already.

✓ **Repeat tasks.** Repetition creates a metaphorical groove in our brain; it's a bit like pouring hot water onto jelly, which creates an indentation on the surface. More hot water in this dimple creates a deeper hollow. This might sound odd, but repeating things can fix patterns of thought in our heads, so that when we're under pressure we find it easier to perform tasks and answer questions because we have that pattern available for instant recall.

✓ **Make connections.** Making connections between experiences and feelings can help people to remember significant events. So if you are writing out critical incident answers, add how you felt at the time. In an interview, by recalling the feeling, we will recall the example.

✓ **Do and review.** Have a process of practising, getting feedback and then deciding to make a change. Good practice is often iterative, where we circle round in a loop, getting ever better.

✓ **Smile more often when you greet people and make eye contact for a moment as you do so.** This is a classic way to reinforce good practice so that when you need to build rapport with an interviewer you're already doing it well. Developing good habits is a powerful way to improve job hunting skills. We can practise the way we meet, greet and talk to people all the time, so that we increase our confidence and can build rapport with ease.

PRACTISE ACTIVE LISTENING

Active listening is a key part of rapport building skills and the following exercise is a great way to have fun and improve our self-awareness of what happens when things go *wrong*. It only takes 15 minutes to complete and I've found that it makes a deep impression on people in workshops, as it did with me when I first encountered it as a delegate many years ago.

First, find a friend and then one of you decide to be the 'talker' and the other one the 'listener'. It doesn't matter which one you opt for because either way you'll learn something.

The talker's job is to talk continuously for four minutes and the way to do this is to go into minute detail. Pick a subject, such as a hobby or a holiday, that the listener won't know anything about and ramble on in gorgeously gruesome detail.

During these four minutes, the listener's job is to do four tasks, each one for a minute, whilst the talker carries on *regardless*. The tasks are:

- ✓ Minute 1: Ignore the talker and look away.
- ✓ Minute 2: Stare at them.
- ✓ Minute 3: Play with an object (perhaps fiddle with a pen, twirl your hair or push buttons on your mobile telephone).
- ✓ Minute 4: Just act naturally.

When the four minutes are over, the talker needs to stop talking and the listener has four minutes to try and repeat everything he's just heard.

When that's completed, discuss the following questions and see what you have learned:

✓ How did the talker feel during the exercise?

✓ What has the experience made you aware of?

This exercise is fun to do and it works because it sensitises people to how their actions can generate an *emotional impact* on others. If we manage to generate a reaction in a practice environment, imagine what happens in a real interview, where it's likely that emotional responses will be magnified by stress.

PRACTICE QUIZ

For fun, and to encourage us to start practising our job hunting skills *right now*, here is a quiz for you to complete. Have a go at answering all the questions and then check to see how well you did. There's one point available for each correct answer. Have fun:

1. What is the 90/90 rule all about?

2. Why do people wear dark-coloured suits in preference to lighter-coloured ones?

3. What does the ratio 100:4:2:1 mean?

4. What does STAR stand for?

5. What's the purpose of using numbers in our achievements?

6. What's the difference between a 'network' and 'networking'?

7. How much of our CV will people tend to read?

8. How would you grab people's attention with the title slide of a presentation?

9. What's one way to do well in a forced leadership exercise?

10. What is the purpose of a cover letter?

11. What does the blue demon say to us?

12. What can happen if we jump up and grab the marker pen?

13. What is the best guide to future performance?

14. Which part of a newspaper is more useful to read?

15. What is 'social gaze'?

16. Name one job hunting secret.

17. How can we make up for any gaps in our CV?

18. Name one way to build rapport with people.

19. Write down one closing question.

20. Write down one of your Aces.

SCORES

How well did you do? Have a look at the following table and smile:

✓ 1 – 5   Ahead of 10% of the competition

✓ 6 – 10   Ahead of 30% of the competition

✓ 11 – 15   Ahead of 60% of the competition

✓ 16 – 20   Ahead of 80% of the competition

Now add 5 points to your score as a *bonus* for having read any part of this book and check the table again. I've drawn up the figures, based on my sense of what most people actually know about how to get a job. In a recent workshop of 17 people (which contained a random cross section of the public) I asked who owned any books to do with job hunting? Seven people raised their hands. I then asked, who had completed a job hunting course of any description? Only three raised their hands. This is a shade under 18%, so whatever your score, you now know that in reality you're ahead of the majority of the competition if you've read this book and put the tips and tools, skills and secrets into effect, *because the chapters cover the whole job hunting process for the modern age from beginning to end.*

By reading this book you've just increased your selling skills and consequently you have increased your chances of securing a job: *Dramatically.*

Well done, you. You're a star. ☺

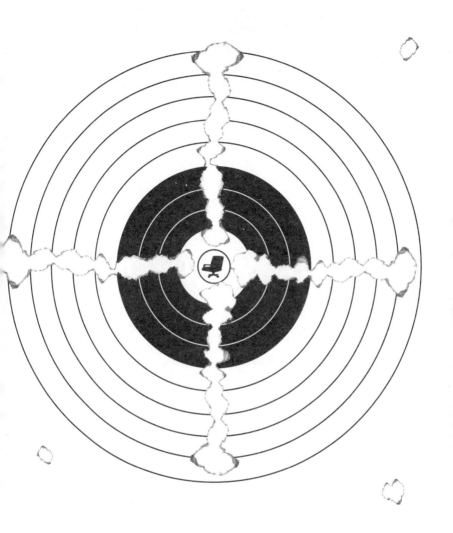

Section 9
CHECKLISTS

CHECKLIST A: BUILDING A NETWORK

HOW TO BUILD A NETWORK

This is easy to do. First grab a sheet of paper and scribble down the following categories, in any order across the page (to avoid getting stuck in fixed thinking patterns):

- ✓ Family.
- ✓ Friends.
- ✓ Neighbours.
- ✓ Leisure groups.
- ✓ Address book.
- ✓ Ex-colleagues.
- ✓ Your supporters group.
- ✓ Recruitment agencies.
- ✓ Directors/senior managers you know.
- ✓ People who already have the job you want.
- ✓ Your partner's address book.
- ✓ Contacts on Internet networking sites.
- ✓ Local networking clubs.

Then systematically write the names of everyone you know, under each category, and keep going until you've filled the piece of paper. When we're getting started it's not the size of our network that matters because we can easily grow it: It's being able to see it so that we can begin to *create networking opportunities* for ourselves.

CHECKLIST B: CV TIPS

CV TIPS

In order to get a sense of what makes for a good CV, here

are my favourite tips, culled from my experience of reading hundreds of CVs. Tick off each item after you have compiled your CV:

- ✓ Two pages maximum length.
- ✓ Tell the truth.
- ✓ Leave out interview-specific information.
- ✓ Give a clear summary of yourself.
- ✓ Put your name on both pages in the footer, in case the pages become separated.
- ✓ Avoid clichés.
- ✓ Don't have a section on key skills.
- ✓ Include achievements and state how you did them.
- ✓ Use numbers.
- ✓ Include a range of achievements.
- ✓ Avoid spelling mistakes at all costs.
- ✓ Tear the first page in half. (How much is it selling you?)
- ✓ Avoid silly fonts and crazy colours.
- ✓ Use a clear, readable font.
- ✓ Use white space to make your CV easier to read.
- ✓ Be selective about your interests.
- ✓ Ask three friends to check your CV.

CHECKLIST C: RAPPORT BUILDING TIPS

People buy people, which means that if we can build some rapport between us and make a little emotional connection then we are more likely to sell ourselves to them. The *90/90 rule* suggests that people form 90% of their opinion about us in the first 90 seconds of meeting us. In a large office this could be the time it takes for us to open the door, walk to the table and greet them. Rapport building is an essential skill and here are the top tips for success:

- ✓ Make eye contact.
- ✓ Shake hands readily.
- ✓ Smile.
- ✓ Show active listening.
- ✓ Ask questions.
- ✓ Vary the tone of your voice.
- ✓ Pause.
- ✓ Dress appropriately.
- ✓ Keep to time.
- ✓ Offer compliments.
- ✓ Say please and thank you.
- ✓ Use people's names.
- ✓ Follow the pace of the other person.
- ✓ Sit in a purposeful position.
- ✓ Notice areas of commonality.

CHECKLIST D: INTERVIEW CHECKLISTS

THE DAY BEFORE

Find something to put your interview kit in. The cheapest option is a smart folder from a stationery shop. A comprehensive interview kit includes:

- ✓ Copies of your CV.
- ✓ A copy of your CV for yourself.

✓ A copy of your STAR stories.

✓ A copy of the printouts of the client's website.

✓ A clean notebook.

✓ A pen.

✓ A spare pen.

✓ Business cards or calling cards.

✓ A banana.

✓ Your reading glasses (if you need them).

✓ Headache tablets.

✓ Essential computer equipment.

✓ Compatible computer file versions.

TWO HOURS BEFORE

Before you walk into the building (because that's when the interview really starts) read through this checklist to make sure everything is in order:

✓ Read through your CV to make sure you're familiar with key facts and dates.

✓ Read through your STAR stories so that you have them firmly in your head.

✓ Take three deep breaths, slowly and carefully.

✓ Make sure you have the names of the people interviewing you written at the top of your pad.

✓ Make sure you have eight keywords from your *Minute To Win It* in the margin of your pad so that you can look down and jog your memory if you need to. Say your first sentence out loud a couple of times.

✓ Remind yourself that you're *okay* and that you have a right to be here.

WHEN YOU MEET YOUR INTERVIEWER

Stand up, make eye contact and smile. Then reach out and give him or her a confident handshake.

During the Interview:

- ✓ Smile.
- ✓ Stop talking once you've answered the question.
- ✓ Use STAR answers to 'show' what you can do.
- ✓ Sip water to create thinking time.
- ✓ Use words like 'great', 'really like' and 'enjoy' to convey enthusiasm.

You're now better prepared than most people. *Go for it!*

CHECKLIST E: SAMPLE INTERVIEW QUESTIONS

There are five types of interview questions: Classic, critical incident, cutting, killer and closing. Here is a quick reference guide to interview questions:

Classic Questions

1. Tell me about yourself...
2. Why do you want to work here?
3. Give me three strengths and three weaknesses...
4. Why did you leave your last role?
5. What have you been doing whilst looking for a job?
6. Who else have you applied to?
7. What salary are you looking for?
8. What do you know about our organisation?
9. What skills or experience make you suitable for this role?

10. Describe your current working day.

11. How would you feel about relocating?

12. What was your previous salary?

13. Why did you choose to study for that qualification?

14. Which tasks do you find difficult to do?

15. Which tasks do you enjoy doing or you find boring?

16. Which achievement at work have you been most proud of?

17. What are your three best achievements to date?

18. What do you like most about this job?

19. What do you like least about this job?

20. Where do you want to be in two or five years' time?

21. What have you learned from your last role?

22. What do you think of your previous employer?

23. What sort of a person are you?

Critical Incident Questions *(Tell me about a time when...)*

24. You had to solve a complex problem.

25. You had to be really creative.

26. You had to improve a process.

27. You had to deal with a crisis.

28. You had to change course radically.

29. You had to overcome resistance.

30. You made a bad mistake.

31. You solved a very difficult problem.

32. You showed great perseverance.

33. You showed exceptional leadership.

34. You worked hard to get someone to adopt your idea.

35. You changed someone's mind.

Cutting Questions

36. What's your biggest mistake and what did you learn from it?

37. If I telephoned your former colleagues/team right now, what would they really say about you?

38. If your ex-boss was outside and was seeing me next what would he say about your past performance?

39. How can you convince me to take you on in this role?

40. Why do you have that gap in your career history?

41. Why did you leave your last role so quickly?

42. Why did you make that sudden career change?

43. What does 'passionate about change' on your CV really mean?

44. What really happened?

45. What other options did you consider? You said the 'team did the work' so does that mean you made no real contribution to the result?

46. How do you think that qualification will help you in this role?

47. How do you perform under stress?

48. You have talked about people being an organisation's primary resource, but none of your CV achievements are people-related. How do you explain that?

49. You said you were passionate about people. How can you justify that comment?

50. Here's a ball of wool (or pen, or mobile telephone, or rubber band). You have three minutes to try and sell it back to me, starting now.

51. Why should we take a risk on you?

Killer Questions

A killer question is one that kills off your chances and ends the interview; a sort of 'I'll get my coat' moment. Most people have *one question* which they dread, perhaps it's to do with a gap in their CV, a poor exam result, a sudden change of career, a business failure or several jobs in short succession. Whatever your killer question is you need to work with a friend to come up with a neatly polished and acceptable answer.

Don't be scared about your killer question: Be prepared for it.

Closing Questions

52. What would my challenges be in the first three months?

53. What would be my priorities on day one?

54. Are there any questions which I've not answered to your satisfaction?

55. Is there anything about my application which you are concerned about?

56. How would you describe the culture of the organisation?

57. How would you describe your style of leadership?

58. What's the next step from here? (Look for buying signals.)

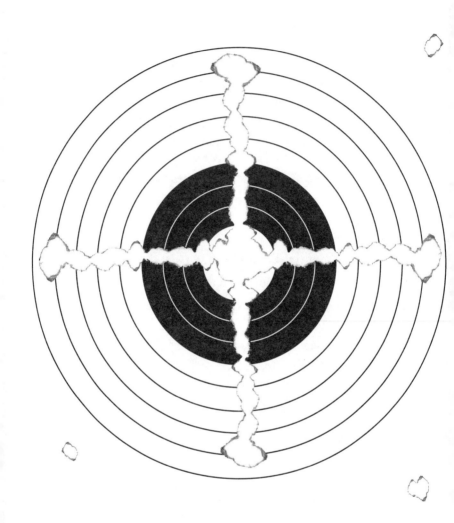

Section 10
POCKET GUIDE

POCKET GUIDE

This is a mini guide for people to cut out and keep. More details can be found in the relevant sections of this book. How do you choose what to distil out of a whole book? Well, this mini guide was compiled during a two-day job hunting skills workshop and shows the key points that the delegates were eager to learn about and put into practice:

PROCESS THINKING

✓ Job hunting is a process and we can work through each step.

✓ *Good processes lead to good outcomes.*

CAMPAIGN BUDGET

✓ Books.

✓ Business cards.

✓ Petrol / Rail fare.

✓ Coffees.

✓ Stationery.

SUPPORTERS

Write down the names and contact details of five people who will support you:

1.

2.

3.

4.

5.

CAMPAIGN

- ✓ *Thoroughbred*: This is what I would *really* like to do, e.g. a business coach. It relies on transferable skills.

- ✓ *Jumper*: This is what I would like to do, e.g. depot manager. It relies on some of my CV and some of my transferable skills.

- ✓ *Hack*: This is what I have done in the past and am happy to do again, e.g. postman.

ACHIEVEMENTS

- ✓ They are the building blocks of successful job hunting as they appear in CVs, networking conversations and at interviews.

- ✓ Every achievement can be valued, or measured in some way.

- ✓ If you haven't quantified an achievement, that only means you haven't quantified it *yet*.

- ✓ How to value it: What was the end result? Was it on time? On budget? How many people did it involve? How much time or money was saved? How can you measure the change between the start and the finish? What problem did it solve? How did it help the business to reduce costs or make more sales?

REASONS TO GO AND MEET PEOPLE

- ✓ Thinking of setting up in business and would like to hear your story…

- ✓ Learning about your experience of…

- ✓ Looking for tips to help me find a similar role in…

- ✓ Considering working as an intern and would like advice about…

BEING ASSERTIVE

✓ Don't say you're out of work; it sounds *passive*.

✓ Say you're looking for work; it sounds *active*.

INTERNET

✓ Social networking sites are here to stay, so make use of them.

✓ Google yourself and find out what a potential employer might see if they did the same thing.

TENACITY

✓ If you're cold calling someone, make *six attempts* to reach them before deleting them from your campaign.

NETWORKING PROCESS

✓ Create a list of people you know.

✓ Ask yourself: Who knows I'm looking for work?

✓ Tell people what you're looking for.

✓ Set targets to aim for when growing your network.

✓ Meet people.

✓ Hold lots of conversations.

✓ Keep going.

NETWORKING

✓ Do something to meet new people, e.g. join a social club.

✓ When talking to people, be *specific* as it's more memorable than being general.

✓ Networking works because people *warm up the referral* for you.

✓ Networking works because people *trust the judgement* of their contacts.

LOOKING GOOD

Do something else whilst looking for a job, such as voluntary work. Being busy gives us something to talk about at interview and makes us look *proactive*.

ACES

Write down your top three Aces:

1.

2.

3.

CV AND COVER LETTER

✓ It's okay to repeat things in them.

✓ Put your top achievement on your cover letter to whet their appetite.

✓ Don't waste space on your CV with key skills. Let the reader *infer* them from your stories, achievements and experience; it makes for a much stronger sell.

MINUTE TO WIN IT

Write down the eight keywords which you can use to tell people about yourself:

1.

2.

3.

4.

5.

6.

7.

8.

INTERVIEWS

In general:

- ✓ Have more stories than they have questions so they run out of bullets first.

- ✓ Interviewers tend to look for people who can demonstrate personal development, thinking ability, communication skills, determination and flexibility.

- ✓ If they ask about your three weaknesses, talk about what you have changed or learned to do better.

Look interested by asking purposeful closing questions:

- ✓ What do you see me doing in the first month?

- ✓ Can you tell me about continuous personal development opportunities?

- ✓ How would you describe the culture of the company?

- ✓ How would you describe your style of leadership?

Assert yourself by:

- ✓ Using *I* not we.

- ✓ Using words like *'great'*, *'good'*, *'really liked it'*, *'love it'*.

- ✓ Making eye contact.

- ✓ Smiling.

Negotiating:

- ✓ You have all the power until you sign.

- ✓ If you don't ask, the answer is always *no*.

- ✓ A great boss is worth more than a great salary.

SUPER TIP SECTION

THE ABSOLUTE BARE BONES FOR SUCCESS

SUPER TIP 1

Learn the answers to these critical incident questions: *Tell me about a time when you:*

- ✓ Showed exceptional leadership.
- ✓ Demonstrated great perseverance.
- ✓ Showed extreme flexibility.
- ✓ Solved a complex problem.
- ✓ Changed someone's mind.
- ✓ Handled a disagreement.

SUPER TIP 2

Go networking because people buy people.

SUPER TIP 3

Past behaviour is the best guide to future performance.

SUPER TIP 4

Be passionate, smile and make eye contact.

SUPER TIP 5

Practice creates flexibility and develops confidence.

SUPER TIP 6

Maintain your network by having friendly conversations with people.

SUPER TIP 7

Remind yourself that you're okay. You have skill and talent. You can do it.

ABOUT THE AUTHOR Richard Maun facilitates personal and organisational development through coaching, management consultancy and lively interactive workshops. He specialises in using Transactional Analysis in organisational settings and combines it with Lean thinking. He has worked with a wide variety of people in the public and private sector to help them act in awareness, improve team dynamics, increase leadership skills and refine business-related processes.

Richard now runs his own management development company and is a director of a training company as well as a visiting lecturer to a leading UK university. He also works as a freelance business writer and has published two books with Marshall Cavendish – *My Boss is a B@$T@*D* and *Leave The B@$T@*DS Behind* – that look at how to survive turmoil at work and how to set oneself up in business. Both are based on real-life experiences and contain practical tips and engaging stories.

For more information and free downloads, please visit Richard's blog site.

Richard Maun can be contacted via:
Blog site: www.richardmaun.com
LinkedIn: Richard Maun
Twitter: @RichardMaun